# ORIGINAL
# KIN

Also by Marian Sandmaier

*The Invisible Alcoholics*
*When Love Is Not Enough*

# ORIGINAL KIN

## The Search for Connection Among

## Adult Sisters and Brothers

# MARIAN SANDMAIER

A DUTTON BOOK

DUTTON
Published by the Penguin Group
Penguin Books USA Inc., 375 Hudson Street,
New York, New York 10014, U.S.A.
Penguin Books Ltd, 27 Wrights Lane,
London W8 5TZ, England
Penguin Books Australia Ltd, Ringwood,
Victoria, Australia
Penguin Books Canada Ltd, 10 Alcorn Avenue,
Toronto, Ontario, Canada M4V 3B2
Penguin Books (N.Z.) Ltd, 182–190 Wairau Road,
Auckland 10, New Zealand

Penguin Books Ltd, Registered Offices:
Harmondsworth, Middlesex, England

First published by Dutton, an imprint of Dutton Signet, a division of Penguin Books
USA Inc.
Distributed in Canada by McClelland & Stewart Inc.

First Printing, March, 1994
10  9  8  7  6  5  4  3  2  1

 REGISTERED TRADEMARK—MARCA REGISTRADA

LIBRARY OF CONGRESS CATALOGING-IN-PUBLICATION DATA
Sandmaier, Marian.
  Original kin : the search for connection among adult sisters and brothers.
    p.  cm.
  Includes bibliographical references and index.
  ISBN 0-525-93526-6
  1. Sibling rivalry.  2. Brothers and sisters.  3. Adulthood—Psychological
aspects.  I. Title.
BF723.S43S16  1994
155.6'4—dc20                                                                 93-25524
                                                                                  CIP

Printed in the United States of America
Set in Palatino
Designed by Leonard Telesca

*To Donna and Phil*
*and to the memory of Bob*

# Contents

# Acknowledgments

The idea for this book emerged from a series of conversations with Marilyn DuHamel, my friend of more than twenty years, who shared with me at a similar moment in our lives the need to understand more fully our relationships with our sisters and brothers. I thank her for giving me the chance to articulate thoughts and feelings I didn't know I had.

Once the book began to take shape, many people helped me in vital ways. I am grateful to my agent, Julian Bach, for his wholehearted enthusiasm for the topic from the moment I telephoned him with the idea, and for his continued support and interest throughout the project. I am deeply thankful as well to my editor, Alexia Dorszynski, for understanding from the beginning why and how I wanted to write this book, and also for helping me to hear what she called "the dog that wasn't barking" in several chapters, which led to a fuller investigation of certain key themes. I am grateful for her perceptivity, good ear, optimism, and faith in me throughout the long process of creating the manuscript.

In a very literal sense, this book would not have been possible without all of the women and men who so generously shared their sibling experiences with me. I thank each of them for the time and emotional energy they devoted to exploring the intricacies of their bonds with their sisters and brothers, and also for the genuine enthusiasm many expressed for this project. I greatly appreciate as well the pioneering researchers and thinkers on the adult sibling experience whose work helped both to inspire and to ground this book, especially Stephen Bank, Victoria Bedford, Victor Cicirelli, Judy Dunn, Deborah Gold, Michael Kahn, Monica McGoldrick, Joel Milgram and Helgola Ross. I also want to thank the Family Institute of Philadelphia for convening a conference on the still unorthodox subject of adult sibling relationships in early 1989, which helped me to develop further a number of ideas for this book, as well as my sense of urgency about writing it.

Many friends and colleagues contributed importantly to this effort. I can't think of adequate words to thank Carol Sipe, who read and reread every sentence of this manuscript despite a thousand other demands on her time, and whose astute (and always gently offered) suggestions I had the good sense to accept at least ninety percent of the time. Throughout this project I was also lucky enough to belong to two writers' groups, whose members celebrated with me as I finished each chapter and provided unfailing, saving support whenever I felt overwhelmed, stuck or temporarily demoralized by the necessity of producing still more words. For their helpful reviews of selected chapters, I am particularly indebted to Michael Davis, Rosemary Davis, Judy Ehrman, Cathy Gray, Ruth Greenberger, Joyce Howell, Kim Leiser, Sharon O'Brien and Michael O'Neill.

I wish also to thank the following people: Lee Vowels for her fast and accurate transcription of mountains of tapes, Scott Ailes and Phyllis Levy for providing helpful interview leads, and Jill Furst and Deborah Hillman for unearthing some obscure but critically important research sources. For many forms of support, including the gift of blocks of time and silence in which to write, I am grateful to Toni Sandmaier, Mary Ann Sheldon and Carolyn Sipe. Many others sustained me through this project by their friendship, encouragement and faith in my efforts, and I especially want to thank Paula Browning, Steve Davis, Barbara Dundon, Nina Hope, Scott

Huler, Janet Kaplan, Terry Long, Violette Phillips and Sue Madagan Sandmaier.

Very special appreciation is due the two people who lived with me through the long months of daily work on this book. My husband, Dan Sipe, believed in this project from the moment I began to talk about it, and he helped make it happen both by lightening my load in many practical ways and through scores of fruitful discussions about the book's major themes, perspectives and reasons to be. I also want my daughter, Darrah, to know that she has been patient and wonderful far beyond the call of seven-year-old duty—through a stretch of time that must have seemed like nearly forever. I thank her, too, for making so much of my "un-book" time a pleasure.

Finally, I want to tell my sister, Donna, and my brother Phil how much it has meant to me to write this book with such deep and unwavering support from each of them, even though neither of them ever knew—or asked to know—how they would be portrayed in the final rendering. I thank them for trusting me to re-create and interpret our experiences in a way that would be faithful to all of us, and for understanding, from the very first, why I needed to write this book. To both of you: I feel lucky to be your sister.

# Introduction

While I was working on this book, the question I was most frequently asked about it had nothing to do with the project's scope, viewpoint or principal findings. Instead, people seemed most eager to know *why* I was writing it. Often the question was posed as an assumption: I must have siblings myself, and my experiences with them, somehow or other, must have prompted insights that I now wanted to share with others— right? That I do have siblings, and that they provided the impetus for writing this book, are irrefutably true. But I undertook this book not because I was so savvy, perceptive and personally successful in my own sibling relationships, but precisely because I was *not*.

Until a few years ago, I gave little conscious thought to my bonds with my sister and two brothers. It wasn't that I didn't care about my siblings. And it certainly wasn't that these relationships were then so trouble-free that I couldn't have profited from thinking a bit more deeply about them. I was aware, for example, of a persistently unsettled quality about the bond between my older sister, Donna, and me. Born just sixteen months after her, I had played "bad sister" to her "good sister" from the very start, and I had always sensed in our relationship both genuine longings for friendship and reserves of deep, dimly understood anger. By our mid-thirties our bond had become more peaceable, yet our infrequent long-distance phone conversations remained unnaturally careful, each of us stepping over the dozens of subjects that would provoke in the other the flash of irritation, the tight-lipped rebuttal, then the retreating silence. But I was resigned to the fragile, tentative quality of our encounters, and so, it seemed, was she. We knew no other way to be.

Bob, meanwhile, four years younger than I, seemed simply unknowable. Archrival of my girlhood, he had been a tantrum-throwing wild child and family scapegoat who metamorphosed into a charming, vulnerable, maddeningly elusive grown-up brother who rarely answered his phone and who, under questioning, admitted to moving cross-country after college to escape the rest of us. Once we nearly talked about this. "Sometimes I don't even tell people my last name," he confided to me. "I just go by Bob." But we filled the silence that followed those words with our raucous laughter, and quickly turned to other subjects. Neither of us ever mentioned it again.

Phil, six years my junior, was the only sibling whom I could still see at a moment's notice. We lived just two towns apart, an easy fifteen-minute drive. I remembered him as a gentle, cheerful, affectionate child whom I had happily and outrageously pampered; in fact, on his birth, I announced to my parents that he was to be "my" particular baby. (Donna had already laid claim to Bob, and justice was a high-ranking value in our family.) In view of our history and our current proximity, I might have wondered why we now so seldom saw each other and why, when we did, we found it so hard to think of what to say.

But I rarely wondered, if at all. I didn't wonder because back then I believed I already knew the answer, which was simply this: *None of it really matters.* I knew that I loved Phil, just as I loved Bob and Donna, but my stance of distant cordiality toward all of them seemed both satisfactory and somehow inevitable. Even though I had long been deeply interested in family relationships, I had never read or heard any sustained discussion of bonds with adult brothers and sisters; in the surrounding silence, it never occurred to me that I was "missing" a critically important relationship. I honestly believed that my siblings were in no way central to my adult life, to my understanding of myself, or to my need for belonging and connection in this world.

Then, nearly seven years ago, something happened to explode that comfortable fiction. My brother Bob died suddenly. He was thirty-three, I was thirty-seven. By then we had lived a continent apart for nearly a decade, and our lifelong relationship had been, at best, a wary and volatile one. Yet his death flattened me. For the next three years I was immersed in a black, unrelenting depression that I could neither understand nor grope my way out of. I knew I had lost something primary to me, but *what*? I called organizations devoted to helping the bereaved, but my need matched no established category—was I seeking support after the death of my husband? Was Bob the name of my deceased child? I found no information, no supportive services of any kind, to help me face the loss of my adult brother.

Nor was I prepared for the domino effect set in motion by Bob's death. My ties with my surviving siblings, which I had thought were securely and forever fixed, now began to unravel with alarming speed. Suddenly, Donna and I began exchanging urgent marathon phone calls in which we struggled, with an almost reckless honesty, to piece together the jigsaw puzzle of our family. Where had Bob fit? Where did each of us fit? In what difficult, essential ways might the two of us fit together? I was exhilarated by our new level of connection and trust, but I also worried that I, the more "emotional one," was becoming too dependent on her. What if my sister suddenly backed away, disappearing once again into polite distance?

Meanwhile, my feelings toward Phil were shifting even more dramatically—and in a more troublesome direction. I became conscious of a rising fury toward my youngest brother, of a thousand character flaws in him that needed to be *fixed*. At the same time, inexplicably, I became acutely aware of wanting Phil to be more present in my life. I sensed that my anger and longing were somehow vitally linked, but just how they meshed—or why—I had no idea.

Yet I needed to know. I could no longer deny that my siblings were important to me, and I wanted to know how to proceed in my now more complicated, much less familiar relationships with Phil and Donna. I wanted, just as urgently, to comprehend Bob's meaning in my life. I needed to know, in short, how my sibling relationships *worked*. Did their dynamics mirror those of other kin relationships, or did this bond operate by an emotional logic and set of rules all its own? Did many sibling relationships change dramatically over the course of adulthood, or was my experience exceptional—even aberrant? What reasonable expectations might I now bring to my bonds with my sister and brother? On every count, I hadn't a clue.

My search for understanding was hampered by the absence of accessible information—and also by sheer embarrassment. I was so uncomfortable with my jumble of intense feelings for my siblings that with few exceptions, I even avoided comparing notes with friends. After all, the objects of my agitation were "just" my siblings—and adult ones at that. We had already been allotted an entire childhood and adolescence to resolve our issues with each other and hammer out satisfactory relationships. If I was still groping through "sibling stuff" at this late date, what did that suggest about me? Was I a case of arrested development? Neurotic dependence? By then, I understood on an intellectual level that bonds between adult sisters and brothers were significant and complex; emotionally, I felt like a jerk who should have gotten her sibling act together. By *now*.

It is a curiously common feeling. We accept without question that our parents are not merely critical players in our early lives, but continue to matter deeply to us through adulthood. There is nothing unusual about a grown woman discussing with a friend her continuing struggles to win her mother's approval, or a man trying, in middle age, finally to connect with his father. From Freud to Bradshaw and Bly, we have learned that parents are forever where the family action is: They are the ones who shaped our psyches in the first place; they are the ones we must come to terms with if we are to make our adult lives work.

And siblings? Few would contend that brothers and sisters are without importance to us. But curiously, siblings are believed to play only relatively small, supporting roles in an individual's life drama; rarely are they deemed central either as an influence or as a relationship. Granted, childhood ties between brothers and sisters are given some due, for the intensity of feeling between siblings who share blood, parents, home and possessions is simply too plain to ignore. But once "us kids" metamorphose into adults and leave the family home, it is as though the sibling license expires. Even though many of us continue to face unresolved issues and new challenges in our adult relationships with sisters and brothers, our culture's persistent equation of "sibling" with "child" grants us little permission to seriously address these continuing issues. The belief that sibling concerns are inherently juvenile was succinctly expressed by a man whom I called to request an interview for this book. When I told him about my project and asked whether I could talk with him about adult sibling relationships, he was silent for a moment. "Adult sibling relationships," he finally repeated, enunciating each word carefully as though trying to crack a code. "Sounds like a contradiction in terms."

This perception persists, even in the current age of family consciousness. In much of the popular and professional psychological literature—including works that focus explicitly on the family—adult sibling bonds are mentioned only in passing, if at all. Even the recent family-of-origin therapy movement, which encourages adults to reconnect with their original families, focuses almost entirely on deepening and healing one's bonds with one's parents. Meanwhile, because few graduate programs in clinical psychology or social work offer substantive training in adult sibling dynamics, many psychotherapists remain unprepared to help their clients cope with the complexities of their bonds with sisters and brothers. (Several people I interviewed reported that in all the months—or years—that they had been in therapy, the subject of their siblings had never been raised.) The message filters down: In our grown-up lives, our ties with brothers and sisters are not, and should not be, a major concern. They are supposed to matter, of course. But only up to a point. In moderation.

\* \* \*

Yet for many, that message doesn't quite take. We may accept it at some rational, I'm-busy-enough-anyway level. But for many of us, our culture's inattention to adult sibling ties collides with a quiet, intuitive knowledge—half-formed and tentative for some, strong and sure for others—that somehow, these are relationships that *do* matter deeply, bonds that provide something vital to our understanding of who we are, and some measure of connection, validation and belonging that no other relationship supplies in quite the same way. A sixty-one-year-old woman I interviewed tried to articulate the uniquely sustaining nature of her bond with her seventy-year-old sister: "There's a chemistry between us. It's chemical. It's spiritual. It's spooky-spiritual. It's so deep that you can't explain it to someone else. I'm happily married. I have lots of friends. But that's not the point. I can go only so long without a sister fix."

Certainly not every sibling relationship has the potential for a nourishing connection. As I conducted interviews for this book, I listened to people whose feelings of rage, fear or bitterness toward a sibling were so corrosive and encompassing that there was simply no room—or desire—for a positive bond to develop. I spoke with others who had barely known a brother or sister in childhood and now could feel for that individual only the faintest tug of family loyalty. At the opposite end of the continuum, several siblings I interviewed had been "best friends" from early childhood, remain necessary to each other, and could recall no significant tensions in the entire course of their relationships. Nobody needed to convince these brothers and sisters of the importance of the sibling bond: It was among the most vital and satisfying of their lives.

Relatively few individuals, however, could tuck their sibling relationships into such tidy categories. The vast majority of those I talked with described bonds of deeply rooted ambivalence, in which numerous intense feelings—positive and negative—coexisted rather than canceled each other out. Considering that sibling relationships usually emerge from intense, sustained interaction within the family during the most vulnerable years of one's life, such a potent mix of conflicting emotions is hardly surprising. Indeed, a growing body of research indicates that ambivalence toward brothers and sisters is both a typical and impressively durable phenomenon, observed in babies as young as fourteen months and still acknowledged by individuals in their seventies and eighties.[1]

Among those I interviewed, sibling "complaints" were remarkably diverse. For younger siblings, there was often a continuing struggle to be taken seriously, sometimes warring with a longing still to be taken care of. Older siblings frequently resented the lingering neediness of "kid" brothers or sisters now in their thirties and forties. There were sisters who wanted more intimacy with brothers; brothers who didn't understand what it was that their sisters wanted. There were brother pairs who couldn't stop one-upping each other; sister duos who were still trying to separate, to find the two individuals within the "we."

Yet such sticking points rarely defined these relationships. Often, painful conflicts coexisted with instant support in a crisis, belly laughs at private jokes, and a depth of empathy that brought some sisters and brothers to tears as they remembered an incident that had caused a sibling pain. Many could recount an emblematic story pointing to how smart, funny, generous or wonderfully outrageous a brother or sister was; some brought me photos so that I could glimpse a sibling's unique spirit. For most people, the continuing conflicts were upsetting primarily *because* the relationship was important to them; because they cared deeply about this sister or this brother and they didn't want to watch the bond loosen or fray. At the same time, because of the layers of silence and myth that envelop sibling bonds, many felt, just as I did, deeply unsure about how to proceed in their adult relationships with brothers and sisters.

This is a book about how and why our siblings matter to us—and we to them—not merely in our childhood pasts but in this present moment, and throughout the course of our adult lives. It is about how we can use that understanding to create more satisfying connections with our sisters and brothers, as well as to extend and deepen our knowledge of ourselves. Given the degree to which the adult sibling relationship has been marginalized in our society, the book begins with a deceptively simple question: *Why bother?* What makes the adult sibling bond distinctly different from any other relationship in our lives, and valuable in ways that no other bond, no matter how intimate or gratifying, can replicate? And if the sibling bond is in fact so critical to us, how and why has our culture managed so successfully to discount and distort it?

While this bond may indeed be vital to us, individuals tend to experience its significance in vastly dissimilar ways. I was struck, again and again, by the sheer range of responses to my question: How would you describe your current relationship with your sister/your brother? One woman responded a bit impatiently, "She's my *sister*. Having her is like having another self." Yet another woman ended our interview with these stark words: "I wish I'd never had a brother." Such striking contrasts prompt the question: What complex array of influences interact to create and maintain a particular sibling relationship? We tend to assume that these bonds are shaped by some nebulous force called "family background," yet even within the same family, individuals report dramatically dissimilar relationships with different sisters and brothers. This book will investigate why and how these variations so faithfully occur, and also how people experience very different kinds of sibling ties. What does it feel like to encounter one's sibling in adulthood as an intimate friend, as a semi-stranger, as a surrogate parent, or as an individual whom one has never trusted and still, at this moment, cannot imagine trusting?

Our siblings matter to us not only as relationships, but also as critical influences on our identity and personality development. This book is also about that shaping, yet largely unacknowledged, influence. It will suggest that for many of us, in certain developmental arenas, our siblings have played a role as great as or *even greater than* a parent's. It also will describe the ways in which early sibling imprints continue to make themselves felt in numerous realms of our adult lives: our expectations for friendship, our choice of intimate partners, our work aspirations and satisfactions, and our deepest convictions about the benevolence or harshness of the world we live in—and our own place in it.

This is *not* a book about birth order, which is merely one lens through which to view the sibling experience. Instead, we will investigate the full range of sources of sibling influence, including but by no means limited to the accident of birth chronology. Moreover, this book will bring to the forefront one critical factor that, inexplicably, has been little investigated in the research and theory to date on the sibling experience. That factor is gender. Gender refers not to the biological fact of one's femaleness or maleness, but rather to "the cultural definition of behavior defined as appropriate to the sexes in a given society at a given time," to borrow historian Gerda Lerner's definition.[2] I will argue that whether you have a sister or brother, in combination with whether you *are* a sister or brother, necessarily wields a profound influence on the meaning, impact, relationship style and current issues that define each of your sibling bonds.

This is also a book about possibilities. It is about how sibling bonds don't freeze into position at age six or age sixteen or even age forty-six, but in most cases continue to grow, shift course and change shape throughout our lifetimes, whether we plan for such evolution or not. It is about the particular turning points in our adult lives that provide the most powerful opportunities for strengthening—or fatally unraveling—the sibling bond. It is, finally, about clarifying what each of us wants from our own relationships with our brothers and sisters, and about the risks and rewards of trying to build more satisfying ties. The final chapter explicitly addresses those who would like to move their own sibling bonds in a different direction, and offers a variety of strategies and perspectives for beginning that process.

I gathered information for this book in two ways. The first was to survey the literature to date on adult sibling bonds, an exercise which in itself taught me much about the quasi-invisible status of this relationship in our culture. When I ordered a comprehensive computer search of sibling research over the past three decades, the vast majority of studies focused on childhood sibling bonds, with fewer than fifteen percent specifically addressing the experience and influence of adult sisters and brothers. Nearly as many studies examined the habits of siblings in the animal world, and in the course of my research I gleaned much information about the influence of siblings on the sexual preference of zebra finches, competitive behavior between acorn woodpecker sisters, nepotism among rhesus monkey brothers, and siblicide among blue-throated bee-eaters.

More encouragingly, I found that by the early 1980s, the output of adult sibling research had begun to accelerate appreciably, and that a core group of social scientists had begun to investigate aspects of the sibling bond that ranged far beyond the stock themes of birth order and rivalry. This recent and continuing growth of research interest has yielded a small but impressive body of scholarship on the adult sibling experience, one that attests to the relationship's complex and enduring impact. In order to present as full a picture as possible of what we know thus far about adult siblings, I have integrated current findings from a variety of fields, including psychology, sociology, demography, anthropology and gender studies.

Yet research, by its very nature, is measurement-oriented, and rarely reveals much about the content and texture of individual experience. To find out how people actually *felt* about their brothers and sisters, what issues burned for them, the palpable presence of this relationship in their lives, I consulted the obvious and ultimate authorities—siblings themselves. Altogether I interviewed eighty adult sisters and brothers from every region of the country, and from a range of class, ethnic and racial backgrounds. They included oldest, youngest and many varieties of "middle" siblings, spaced as closely as eleven months and as far apart as nine years. Most of those I spoke with grew up with one, two or three siblings, though several came from larger clans of up to eight brothers and sisters. The youngest person I interviewed was twenty-six; the oldest, seventy-nine.

I talked with most of these individuals in their homes and occasionally in mine, with each taped interview ranging from two to four hours. Nearly all those who spoke about their sisters and brothers for this book did so with extraordinary and compelling honesty, refusing to romanticize early family experiences and unflinchingly describing—often with deep emotion—the disappointments of their adult sibling relationships as well as their experiences of intimacy and solidarity. I have changed the names of all those I interviewed, and occasionally the identifying details, to protect their privacy.

As is the case in most families, in this book some siblings get more attention than others. At my request, individuals discussed only those sisters and brothers who were born of the same parents as they were. I chose this focus because a number of issues facing step-siblings and adopted siblings differ substantially from those of blood siblings, and the intricacies of these relationships require a far more detailed examination and analysis than is possible here. For the same reasons, I did not investigate in detail the numerous and complex issues unique to twins, or those facing individuals whose siblings have severe, chronic mental or physical disabilities.

Because I wanted to follow each person's sibling "career" in as much depth as possible, I asked interviewees to focus primarily on one particular sibling—the one who was, by their own definition, most emotionally significant to them. Most individuals chose to talk about the sister or brother who, they felt, had made the greatest impact on their personality development and life directions, and/or the one with whom they now shared a particularly meaningful bond—whether that bond was currently rewarding, troubling or some of each. Interestingly, while most individuals had more than one sibling to choose from, nearly all could readily name a brother or sister on whom to concentrate their thoughts. No particular birth order combination, gender mix, age spacing, childhood history or recent turning point dictated significance; for each person, the subtle interplay of these and other factors produced the sibling who was, at the time of our interview, "the one" whom an individual was most eager to think about and understand.

These interviews do not constitute a strictly representative sample of adult siblings, for my purpose was not to conduct a scientific study that would prove siblings to be definitively one way or another. My aim, rather, was to talk with a reasonably broad cross section of individuals who were willing to explore the meaning of their sisters and brothers in their lives. Yet while these interviews may not prove hypotheses, my hope is that they will generate some. For while I came to each interview with some prepared questions, their purpose was not to match a sibling to a particular type of relationship, but to elicit a unique story, to tell me what I didn't yet know. And as people began to talk about their sisters and brothers, I could all but see, in the words of novelist Rachel Hadas, "memory rising in their eyes like a tide," which led them to answer some of my questions at length and others not at all, frequently to put a different spin on this or that query, to plunge in directions I had barely even considered. My emphasis in these pages on gender, for example, appeared nowhere in the original outline for this book; it emerged only after I heard, again and again, how very differently people described the experience of being a brother and the experience of being a sister, and how different their connections *to* sisters felt from their connections to brothers. Frequently, the most illuminating moments of an interview occurred after I asked my last question: "Is there anything I *haven't* asked that you'd like to talk about?"

Very often, as I listened to others exploring the mysteries and challenges of their bonds with sisters and brothers, I thought of my own siblings. Each person's story is individual, of course, yet I found that when particular themes sounded— those of power, attachment, distance, loss, second chances—I couldn't help making connections with my own experience. Connections, and sometimes plans. My deepest hope for this book is that it may inspire readers to make similar linkages. I hope that some of what follows will resonate with your own experience, and that such points of identification—those sudden, deeply sensed moments of *yes, that's how it is*—may spark a different and helpful way of perceiving your own relationship with a sister or brother. Perhaps it will even lead to a conversation with a sibling that is not quite like any you've had before, one in which you discover a new bit of common ground, or find out something about your sibling or yourself that you never knew—yet needed to know.

And in the best of all worlds, that conversation will be the first of many.

# ORIGINAL
# KIN

# I

# A Common Knowledge

It is years ago again, the time when there were only the
two of them, before they noticed the rest of the world.
He looks at her for a moment with the eyes of then,
and she looks back. Neither wishes to return there;
both celebrate, in silence, what will never be lost.

Penelope Lively, *Moon Tiger*

When I answered the doorbell in the late afternoon of my
birthday four years ago, it didn't occur to me that my caller
might be my brother. Yet there was Phil, lean and tanned in
turquoise running shorts, grinning shyly as he juggled several
bulging bags of bulbs for the backyard garden that was my
passion. *Happy birthday.* There was a card, too, exquisitely
beautiful, which he had inscribed with a message of hope for
my happiness in the coming year. I was touched and I told
him so; we hugged. Had this been the opening scene of a
movie, this was the moment when he would have followed
me into the kitchen and we would have begun to talk about
all sorts of things—his feelings about his upcoming triathlon,
my excitement about a new book idea, why he was thinking
of leaving town—over steaming mugs of coffee. But this
wasn't a movie, and we didn't know what to say to each
other. *How's the writing? Good, good. How about you—in shape
for the race? Gettin' there. I've still got to train today, actually. I
should probably get started.* Ten minutes after the doorbell rang,
my younger brother was leaving. I had never asked him to sit
down.

I stared down at the freesia and gladiolus bulbs in my arms, conscious that I felt thoroughly rotten. Something about flowers and Nikes; promise followed by flight, a closing door. It seemed so much the story of our relationship. Phil and I lived only minutes apart, yet we saw each other, what—four, five times a year? When we did get together, it was almost always in the company of our mother, his woman friend, my husband or my daughter. In the ten years we had lived in neighboring towns, we had never seen a movie together, never had dinner one-on-one, never had so much as gone for a walk around the block as a twosome. Somehow, we needed the protective padding of others, though neither of us could have said exactly why.

Yet we cared for each other. It came out in expansive bursts: his volunteering to coach me when I decided, at age thirty-five, to learn how to swim. Several long phone conversations in the wake of a girlfriend crisis. My appearance at his first triathlon, held on the hottest day of summer, so that I could dump cups of water over his head as he ran and pedaled by. The bundle of bulbs for my birthday. There had been a time when such sporadic moments of connection were enough for me, or I had persuaded myself that they were. But lately I was noticing the gaps, the crowd scenes, the long silences. Sometimes I would look up at my six-foot-three-inch-tall brother and see, with a pang, a sweet-faced little boy who once watched me in the bathroom mirror, with perfect trust, as I peroxided his hair bright orange. The kid who fell out of bed with a loud *ka-klunk!* nearly every night of our childhood, and who stayed in a heap on the floor until I called to him from the other side of the wall, "You're okay, Phil. Back in bed." The bold explorer of desert canyons, racer of minibikes, catcher of giant catfish who once in a while, when nobody else was around, would ask if he could hold my hand.

On other occasions, this time-lapse process would happen in reverse. I would look at my little brother and notice, with a small shock, the man he had become. A seeker, thoughtful and honest and listening, chipping away at surfaces to see what lay beneath. A guy who tried, with guts and grace, to find something of worth in the most soul-bending situations, who didn't easily give up on himself or anyone who mattered to him. "You always learn *something*," he would chuckle as he finished recounting a story of derailed romance or misjudged friendship, some tale of betrayal or hidden agenda or plain bad luck that would have been worth a couple of months of depression for me. The truth was that my little brother, the family "baby" whom I had never expected to take seriously, had metamorphosed into the kind of man I liked and with whom I felt a genuine, though utterly silent, connection. I wanted to know him better. I wanted him to know me better.

Yet when we came face to face, there was something in the air between us that made us speak like strangers at a party, then duck out. That afternoon as I closed the door behind my brother, I felt sadder than usual about the distance between us. And angrier. Maybe because it was my birthday, maybe because the bulbs made me hopeful, maybe because I knew I wouldn't see him again for another three months, our familiar hi-goodbye act suddenly felt too false, exhausting and wasteful to put up with any longer. I wanted my brother back.

That moment marked the beginning of a conscious effort to reconnect with Phil, a bumpy, surprising, worthwhile quest that continues. In the movie version, of course, I would have instantly picked up the phone to dial my brother's number—or better yet chased him down in my car—to share my epiphany with him and launch a brief, triumphant journey to sibling intimacy. In real life, however, it was another year before I managed to ask Phil to have dinner with me—alone. In the meantime, I waged battles in my head. Some were irritated: Why should I do all the work? Why wasn't Phil making an effort to spend more time with *me?* Others were plain scared: What if I let him know I wanted the two of us to be closer, and he wasn't interested? I knew how much that would hurt. Why take the risk? I was also open to bad advice: A therapist acquaintance of mine opined that if Phil and I weren't close by now, I might as well hang it up. I remember nodding, relieved.

I wavered, too, because I could see that this was going to take work. There were reasons Phil and I always met in a crowd, conversed with such effort, bolted ten minutes after saying hello. At the time, I wasn't fully aware of the complex, interlocking patterns that had led to this disjuncture in our relationship—among them a family legacy of emotional independence, the very different lenses through which a male and a female sibling are apt to view each other, a shrinking family that magnified the value of each remaining member—but I knew that we *had* issues aplenty. If we were going to develop a bond worth having, we were going to have to work through a whole lot of that confusing and difficult stuff. I already had my husband, my daughter, dozens of other relatives and plenty of friends. Did I really need the complications of a connection with this grown-up brother of mine? Was it worth it?

When I decided, finally, that it was, I felt alone and a bit overwhelmed. I couldn't have known then, of course, how many other people were making similar decisions under far more challenging circumstances than mine. It was only later, as I interviewed people for this book, that I spoke with a man who had finally gathered the courage to tell his younger sister, a devout fundamentalist Christian, that he was gay, and who was now willing to "do what it takes" to try to resolve the resulting tensions between them. In another interview, a young woman told me that she had been very close to her older brother until her marriage, when her husband began to point out the brother's flaws to her and otherwise systematically discourage their sibling connection. Nonetheless, she recently had told her husband that despite his strenuous objections, she planned to go on regularly spending time with her brother.

I listened to many others who had invested similar effort or risk in trying to maintain connection, deactivate conflicts or balance lopsided bonds with their adult sisters and brothers. I talked with still others who were simply trying hard to accept what might never change. One forty-nine-year-old woman who had felt in competition with her younger sister all of their lives observed: "To this day she can drive me up the wall, but I still feel deeply drawn to her. She makes me angry, but I can't write her off." It seems that few of us can: Researchers estimate that fewer than six percent of siblings sever ties completely.[1]

For so many, what makes the sibling connection worth preserving, deepening and, in some cases, even fighting for? Consider, first, that a bond with a brother or sister is likely to be the most enduring of our lives. A sibling is there from the start, or nearly so, long before a spouse or a child joins us. Usually, brothers and sisters are still with us after parents die: Nearly eighty percent of elderly people still have at least one living sibling.[2] And while mere longevity doesn't guarantee intimacy, a sibling's presence in the world can provide a unique kind of emotional anchor, evidence that in a world of rapidly shifting and frequently temporary ties, somewhere and always, one belongs. Karen, a thirty-one-year-old high school teacher who is currently at odds with two of her three widely scattered siblings, nonetheless derives a profound sense of security from the permanence of the bond:

> There isn't the transient feeling that exists with almost every other relationship you have. There is always the possibility that you will divorce your spouse, maybe find a new spouse. Friends may or may not stick around. *But my sisters will always be my sisters. My brother will always be my brother.* [Punches her fist in her hand.] There's this clubhouse feeling we have, even long distance, and I don't think any fight or misunderstanding could ever sever it. We all know it. It gives us a lot of security. Outside of death there is nothing that will separate us.

Among older people, this sibling "thereness" factor may be particularly important: Numerous studies suggest that it is the perceived *availability* of a brother or sister, not the actual amount of interaction, that is linked to psychological well-being in later life.[3]

The tie of time mingles with the tie of blood. A brother or sister shares, on average, fully half of our genes. One looks at a sibling and sees shards of self: the shape of a nose, the way the body is held, a mania for music, a to-the-death stubbornness. To have a brother or a sister is to have someone who is, visibly and actually, part of oneself. Such deeply embedded likeness, issuing from and reinforced by shared parentage and a long, winding chain of ancestors, can spur a kind of primal connection—what Pat Conroy calls "this fierce interior music of blood and wildness and identity"—which transcends dramatic, sometimes difficult differences. It is the connection that allows one young woman to plan on financially supporting her schizophrenic sister after their parents die, explaining, "I wouldn't do this for anyone else in the world. But no one else in the world cares about her. I do."

But the genetic glue ensures only a primitive loyalty, the "hey, he's family" kind of response that may not encompass a real meeting of minds or hearts. The particular kind and depth of connection, validation and self-knowledge that adult siblings can offer each other issue from a different source—a shared history that is theirs and theirs alone. Tolstoy notwithstanding, families do not resemble one another, even the happy ones. Each lives by its own highly idiosyncratic set of rules, rituals and deeply held convictions about the world; each spins its own myths, keeps its own silences. As members of their own particular family, brothers and sisters share citizenship in an emotional country that no one else in the world can ever fully understand, no matter how precisely one may try to describe the culture or explain its customs. *You had to be there.* What was it truly like to spoon a steaming bowl of soup while one's mother softly read aloud stories of King Arthur and Robin Hood and Grimm's fairy tales, as one woman described to me the magical lunchtimes of her childhood? She tried hard to evoke the special wonder and comfort of those mealtimes, yet only her two sisters, who sat beside her at that same oaken lunch table long ago, listening to those same ancient tales from that same singularly expressive voice, can truly, thoroughly understand.

Siblings, of course, are not the lone inhabitants of family territory. Parents, too, share daily routines, rituals and crises. But mothers and fathers encounter family reality from an entirely different vantage point—one of power. They shape much of the reality that their children experience; indeed, many siblings connect in part from a sense of joint survivorship of parental folly.[4] Even within emotionally close families, developmental differences between children and adults are such that brothers and sisters inhabit a fundamentally different reality from their parents, one fueled by fantasy and magic and a brand of mutual silliness that often spurs the creation of secret worlds barred to "the grown-ups." Two sisters in their thirties recall, with conspiratorial glee, the scenario they regularly constructed as soon as their parents left the house:

TERRY: We played Miss America . . .

MARIE: We always played Miss America and we would go into my parents' bedroom and put on my mother's nightgowns and use her scarves for banners and put my father's pajama bottoms on our heads for long hair. I'd always be Miss Arkansas.

TERRY: We'd do the talent competition, you know, lip-sync to loud blaring records. Motown. We did this all the time . . .

MARIE: Remember how we took the lamp shades off all the lamps for spotlights?

TERRY: Our parents weren't home . . .

MARIE: No *way* were they home!

TERRY: And we'd stand up on the cedar chest, shine a lamp in the face of the other one and yell . . .

TOGETHER: *Now, Miss Arkansas!* [Both applaud.]

TERRY: It was fabulous.

In adulthood, such common experience becomes group memory, connecting us both to our origins and to those who shared them with us most intimately. Many siblings regularly cement this connection through a kind of "insider language," a repertoire of memory-packed words, phrases and shorthand descriptions that only a brother or sister can decode. Well into our thirties, when my brother Bob or I wanted to express an unusual feeling of any kind, he or I would say to the other, "I feel odd, terribly strange! My body vibrates with incredible energy!" These passwords, instantly recognizable to either of us as lines from a particular Superman comic book circa 1960, dependably hurled us back to the Formica-topped kitchen table of our childhood home in Chatham, New Jersey, where we would lounge for hours, Justice League of America comics spread out before us, cackling with delight as we quoted from Green Lantern and Aquaman and Wonder Woman, all the while munching endless stacks of white-bread-and-French's-mustard sandwiches. Such a shared and private vision always flooded me with the sure knowledge, in that chortling instant, that I *belonged*. To a particular history. To my brother.

Such "remembrance of things past" can also serve more urgent purposes. When adult siblings share memories of what happened in the family so long ago, they can begin to understand more fully how they came to be who they are. When memories mesh, they can powerfully validate experience: *They were there; I didn't just imagine it.* One woman I interviewed told me that at the age of thirty-five, she had finally allowed herself to remember that she had been sexually abused by her father. She intensely felt the truth of her memory; nonetheless, she was paralyzed by confusion and doubt. Why hadn't she remembered before? How could she believe this about her own father? Finally, with great trepidation, she told her sister about her retrieved memory. Did her sister think their father was capable of such an act? She said her sister was silent for a long moment, then spoke in a low, trembling voice: "He abused me, too." The two women then approached a third sister: She also had been a victim.

Traversing the past with a sibling can be a fundamentally healing process—one that can't be duplicated by friend, parent or therapist. I talked with David, a builder in his mid-fifties whose emotionally isolated childhood left him convinced that he simply wasn't smart or lovable enough to interest his parents—or, consequently, anyone else. Several years ago he began to reconnect with his older sister, whom he had long resented for being the "bright one" who had captured, he'd always imagined, the parental approval he was denied. First tentatively, then with a growing sense of urgency, this brother and sister began to talk about their early lives together. What had it really been like to grow up in that tiny Brooklyn row house, where he remembered once hurling his sister's entire prized collection of 78-rpm records into the closet, Frisbee style, to release his inarticulate rage? What David discovered profoundly altered his perception of his family, his sister and, most of all, himself:

The first thing I found out was that Beth—the family princess in my eyes—had been as miserable, as angry, as I was. It was a process of understanding that we were both going through the same war. We were both trying to survive. It was understanding that she wasn't the enemy.

And we practically re-created our whole childhood to process it all, to find out, how did we ever get from one end of the tunnel to the other? What really did happen? And we came to the conclusion that none of it—our mother's constant anger, our father's absences—was our fault, that we really hardly had any control over what went on. I was never stupid, but I had parents who didn't connect with the kind of intelligence I had. And I didn't deserve to be left alone so much. But we had parents who were probably too young and poor and miserable to want kids at all.

I couldn't have done this solo. Doing it solo would be like talking to a wall. Doing it with Beth, it wasn't a monologue: I had somebody to play it all off of. Somebody who went through it with me. [Urgently.] Somebody who understood what *it* really meant.

Genuine intimacy with a sibling, the only person who can truly comprehend the *it*, offers the potential for a rare depth of mutual sympathy. Here is a person with the capacity to know "where you're coming from" in the truest sense; to understand the very particular challenges of trying to tame or transcend your past; to fathom, at a visceral, remembered level, why your current dreams are as vitally important as they are. For David, the particular brand of solidarity offered by this bond is like no other:

It means that ultimately, I'm not alone. It's not just joint survivorship. It's having somebody in my life who went through the same building blocks in understanding what life is about. And I need to know that somebody *does* know. Having someone in league is very important. And there isn't anybody that you could have in league with you, other than a sibling, in just that way. It's very important for me to know that she's my sister.

Sibling versions of family reality don't always cozily converge. On the contrary, brothers and sisters frequently feel that "we grew up in different families" because of parental favoritism, different temperamental filters, or differences in family size, fortunes or stability at comparable points in each sibling's childhood. Yet even widely differing convictions of "the way it was" can enlarge one's understanding of family and self. Contrasting memories may uncover a useful new way to interpret an early, shaping experience, or provide a different lens through which to view another family member. What might it mean, for example, if you remember your father only as unapproachably distant, while your sister or brother can recall his vulnerability? Sometimes, a sibling's divergent view may prod one to become more fully conscious of one's own deeply felt version of reality. In *Brothers and Keepers*, John Edgar Wideman's moving exploration of his bond with his imprisoned brother, he reflects on the significance of this memory-trading process:

Strange thing is my recollections return through the door he opened. My memories needed his. Maybe the fact that we recall different things is crucial. Maybe they are foreground and background, propping each other up. He holds on to this or that scrap of the past and I listen to what he's saved and it's not mine, not what I saw or heard or felt. The pressure's on me then. If his version of the past is real, then what's mine? ... If I don't speak I have no past.[5]

The shared history between siblings also means that out there somewhere is a person who knows the child in you. For most of us, our siblings were our first peers: They were the ones we were down on the floor with, out in the woods with, the ones we conjured up bizarre games and stories with, the ones who witnessed both our most pitiful humiliations and our finest moments. In those early years, when home, neighborhood and school were often shared territory, and when we were still unskilled in the art of pretense, little could be concealed. It's all there, in a brother's or sister's memory bank: your once-painful shyness, your bravery, your capacity for nerdiness, your weird brand of humor, what thrills you, what makes you want to cry.

This stored knowledge has its hazards: In relationships fraught with resentment, awareness of an adult brother's or sister's vulnerabilities can be a weapon, brandished to threaten or wound. But a sibling's "file" on one's childhood self can also be a hidden source of strength. As we grow up, many of us bury pieces of our younger selves that we may have valued, but which don't jibe with our vision of a mature, full-fledged grown-up. As one presents a respectable but somewhat truncated adult self to the world, a sibling may be the sole keeper of one's core identity, the only person with the keys to one's unfettered, more fundamental self. A twenty-eight-year-old sculptor talks of her determination to reconnect with her older sister, with whom she once explored the woods on horseback and, in adolescence, secretly joined a spirituality group:

> Carol knows that part of me that is sort of a seeker, that is trying to find out more about life. That maybe more essential part of myself. My husband knows me better as I am as an adult, but she knows the parts of me that come from all those childhood roots. And because of that, there are things she understands about me that he won't ever understand. It's a big part of why I can't give up on her, even with things so crazy between us now.

A sibling can also help one retrieve parts of the self that have been altogether submerged. I know this from my own experience. While I'm not a timid person, neither do I consider myself particularly brave—especially in the realm of the physical. Whenever I hear of a friend doing something physically adventurous—scuba diving or mountain climbing or white-water rafting—I feel a rush of excitement and longing, followed instantly by the dampening conviction that, of course, such feats of daring are not for me, that I'm simply not equipped to take that class of risk. But not long ago, as my sister, Donna, and I were talking on the phone about the fun we used to have ice skating each winter on a neighbor's pond, she chuckled suddenly. "Remember, Marian, when you used to jump the hole?"

Jump the hole? What was she talking about? "You don't *remember* that?" she cried disbelievingly. "There was always that one corner of the pond that never iced over. Remember that hole?" Yeah. Well, sort of. My sister went on: "Nobody was supposed to go near it. So when there were no grown-ups around, you would skate straight for it. You always kept going until we could actually hear the ice breaking under your feet—and then you would leap across to the other side." As she spoke, that long-buried memory bubbled up: I saw the hole again, a black, enticing threat at the far end of the pond, banked by a crusty slab of earth where no trees grew. And I felt again those darkening late afternoons of winter, when we watched mothers and fathers unlace their skates—finally!—and disappear into warm dens and kitchens, ceding the pond to its rightful owners, the kids. All at once it came rushing back: the wind stinging my face, the joy of that headlong charge toward the hole, the heart-stopping crack of the ice, the thrill of the final, flying leap to safety. That was *me*. And however dormant or tamped down, it still is me. If I choose to, I can recover that daring twelve-year-old girl. A sister's gift.

Sibling as accomplice, as support, as validator, as coexplorer of one's most intimate history. These uniquely sustaining qualities of the adult sibling bond resonate with the experience of many of us, even as we may confront coexisting conflicts with our brothers and sisters. Strange, then, that these enlivening, nourishing qualities of the sibling bond have been so little acknowledged in our culture. On the contrary, we seem to have gone out of our way to deny them. We give lip service to notions of "sisterhood" and "brotherhood," yet our attention has remained firmly, almost exclusively fixed on the dark side of the bond. "Sibling" and "rivalry" are practically synonymous words in our society, bound as tightly as "mother" and "nurture," "child" and "innocence," "Satan" and "evil." Pundits throughout history have enjoyed trashing siblings: "Between brothers, two witnesses and a notary" is an old Spanish proverb. Likewise, George Bernard Shaw observed, "As a rule there is only one person an English girl hates more than she hates her mother; and that's her eldest sister."[6] Much later, the Smothers Brothers rode to fame on their "Mom loved you best" comedy routine, and today's tabloids, books and talk shows routinely spew tales of envy, resentment, revenge and one-upsmanship among celebrity sibs. I soon lost count of the number of people who, on hearing that I was writing a book about the sibling experience, replied unhesitatingly, "Oh, a book about rivalry."

No single individual did more to shape our culture's knee-jerk pessimism about the sibling bond than Sigmund Freud. Still our society's most influential explicator of human relationships, Freud conceived of the family as a kind of domestic boxing ring, with members perpetually engaged in numerous and fierce struggles over the scarce commodity of parental— particularly maternal—love. Siblings, therefore, were born to wrangle. There is no allowance for mixed feelings in Freud's sibling story, no room for affection alongside anger, envy mingled with love. There are only death wishes, "jealous hatred" and "murderous assaults."[7] It is difficult to exaggerate the blackness of Freud's sibling vision: In one essay on dream symbolism, he suggests that dreams about vermin—small, disgusting, destructive insects and rodents that prey on others— are really about one's brothers and sisters.[8]

The widespread public acceptance of Freud's relentlessly grim sibling portrait has partly to do with one man's enormous, enduring influence and partly to do with his theory's hard nugget of truth. Most of us feel that somewhere along the line, a brother or sister got "more" of something—looks, brains, talent, parental love or approval—than we did. Rivalry *is* a factor in many sibling relationships, even a dominant one for some sisters and brothers. Nonetheless, rivalry is clearly only one piece of the sibling mosaic, and for some brothers and sisters, it barely figures in the picture at all. We are now discovering that Freud's dismal sibling vision was far from unbiased: He derived his rivalry theory primarily from the dreams and declarations of patients whom he considered highly neurotic, and who struggled with deeply troubled relationships of all kinds. Still more telling, Freud's ties with his own seven sisters and brothers were fraught with bitter competition for the attention of his beautiful, adored young mother, to the extent that his biographer Peter Gay observes that Freud's theory of sibling jealousy "looks suspiciously like a self-portrait."[9]

Perhaps most significant, our deeply embedded concept of sibling-as-rival is highly culture-bound. We live in a society that is preoccupied—some would say obsessed—with achievement, competition and status. It is no coincidence that nearly all research on sibling relationships comes from the United States and other highly industrialized, individualistic Western cultures, in which affluence and mobility allow individual goals, by and large, to supersede group needs. This preponderance of Western-bred research makes the primacy of sibling rivalry appear normal, natural and universal, a bona fide fact of human nature.

This aspect of "human nature," however, applies to only a minority of human beings. Fully seventy percent of the world's population lives in collective cultures, in which economic need dictates the precedence of group cooperation over individual fulfillment. The self, therefore, is organized more closely around the "we" than the "I." In such cultures, the family is a powerfully interdependent unit within which siblings view each other as necessary, unquestioned, lifelong allies. "Your brother or your sister, you can deny them nothing" is the rule of the Ashanti of West Africa.[10]

While families in our culture train their children to soar as solo performers via Suzuki lessons and SAT scores, most cultures throughout the world teach their children to value a sibling's welfare as equal to—or more important than—their own. Sibling interdependence begins early: One comprehensive ethnographic survey shows that in the majority of 186 sampled societies, siblings and other children are the principal caretakers and companions of young children, thereby allowing parents to gather food and otherwise ensure family survival.[11] Anthropologist Thomas R. Williams, who has extensively observed child caretaking among the Dusun of Malaysia, reports: "It isn't unusual to see a three- or four-year-old running hard in play with his infant brother or sister on his back, head and limbs bobbing violently as the game proceeds."[12] Such early caretaking helps to prepare adult siblings for their lifelong role as each other's "keepers." In many cultures around the world, siblings arrange and finance one another's marriages; in others, men automatically "inherit" a deceased brother's spouse and children.[13] In polygamous cultures, sisters frequently marry the same man so as to be able to depend on each other for a lifetime.

This profound interdependence of siblings in many parts of the world frequently spurs a deep emotional attachment. Among the Kuma of New Guinea, a man values his sister over his wife, reasoning that he can always replace a spouse but never a sister, whom he considers an essential part of himself—an alter ego in the truest, deepest sense.[14] And in many cultures, lovers and spouses use sibling terms for each other to indicate the depth of their attachment. In Vietnam, for example, the terms of address for lovers and spouses are *anh* ("big brother") and *em* ("little sister").[15] Among the Karo Batak of North Sumatra, lovers often address the other as *turang*, which means "sibling of the opposite sex." When young Karo women and men flirt with each other, one way of finding out the other's true feelings is to ask, "How many siblings are in your family?" If the chemistry is potent, the other will answer with a number that is one more than the actual number of his or her siblings, and then add the phrase *ras kam*, which means "including you."[16] In such cultures, to feel "siblinghood" with another is the highest compliment, connoting the presence of, or potential for, a love bond that encompasses a sense of cherished, committed kinship.

In such cultures, the tightly woven sibling bond is firmly rooted in survival: Family members operate as a unit in order to fulfill basic material needs. In our own culture, by contrast, most of us can quite literally "live without" our siblings. The relatively greater affluence of the United States and other highly industrialized societies permits adult siblings to be far more independent of one another, in ways that pose real challenges to developing and maintaining strong bonds. Not only do few of us live in the same neighborhood as our adult brothers and sisters, but the perpetual motion machine that is our culture—nearly one in five Americans moves each year[17]—means that many of us are no longer even within a day's drive of a sibling. Long-distance phone calls help, but as one retired man with five widely scattered brothers and sisters and a battered budget noted, "You've got to have *money* these days to keep up with all your siblings." Indeed, when I asked interviewees, "What would you most like from your sibling that you don't now have?" the single most frequent answer was "more time together"—either to enjoy an already close bond or to help cement a more distant or problematic one.

But whether a brother or sister lives a street, a state, or a continent away, the bottom line is that in our society, the sibling bond is a quasi-voluntary one. While the familial roots of the sibling relationship imbue it with a fundamental permanence, the bond itself is what sociologists call "horizontal," one between peers in which responsibilities are limited and parameters for acceptable behavior wide. You can choose to talk daily, as does one sister pair I spoke with, or you can see each other only on holidays, when, admitted one man, "we seem to make a major effort to treat each other badly." You can support your brother or sister through continuous work, family or emotional challenges, or you can offer help only in dire emergencies—or not at all. You and your sibling can be best friends, or you can say, as did one woman of her younger brother, "I don't like him. I have never liked him. I have no *plans* to like him." One can expect little societal applause for trying to repair or deepen a bond with a brother or sister; similarly, little censure awaits those whose sibling ties unravel.

There is freedom here, and hazard. More than ties between other immediate family members, the adult sibling bond in our society is a bond of choice. Whether it functions as more than a formal kinship tie will depend, to an unsettlingly large degree, on how much two siblings value and need their particular relationship. Such emotional elbow room has clear advantages. If two siblings are too vastly different to enjoy each other, or if they share a past too contentious to overcome, they can limit contact, and guilt as well. Yet this semi-optional quality of the sibling bond also carries risk. It can be too easy to let a potentially satisfying tie fray from sheer busyness and neglect, from ancient wounds never healed, from that blowup over the holidays that still feels too messy or scary to try to patch up. The sibling relationship is an extraordinarily easy one to put off—perhaps forever.

Yet increasingly, there are compelling reasons to choose connection. We may not require our brothers and sisters for physical survival, but our needs for emotional linkages with them remain real and strong—and our society is changing in ways that are apt to intensify those needs. To put it simply, the ties that bind are fewer and looser than ever before. The very success of our culture's pursuit of individualism and self-reliance, combined with dramatic demographic shifts, has produced a nation of adults who spend large chunks of their lives unattached. Because Americans are postponing marriage, are divorcing at a high rate and are less likely to remarry than in the past, both men and women can now expect to spend more than half of their lives unmarried.[18] At any given moment in the United States, 82 million people are single.[19]

Even more to the point, many more single people are now living alone. We still like to envision our society as parceled into cozy pairs and family groupings, yet the number of Americans living by themselves has more than doubled since 1970, so that fully a quarter of the nation's households are now inhabited by just one person.[20] Even those who enjoy or prefer their single status may, at times, feel acutely the lack of family in their lives. There may be sneak attacks of loneliness, the question that rises out of three a.m. panic: *Who really cares?* Friends are important, yet a solid bond with a sibling—one who "knew you when" and who will forever be kin—may provide a comforting measure of deep-down belonging that is offered nowhere else. Not surprisingly, research indicates that single people are apt to spend more time with brothers and sisters, and to feel closer to them, than those living with a partner.[21] A sibling may also be the first one called in the crunch, as a twenty-nine-year-old Philadelphia woman well remembers:

> My sister is still the best listener I know, still the one I confide in when stuff really hits me. There's a lot of satisfaction in that. Once when I was living alone in the city, I had a horrible dream about nuclear war after seeing a TV

show about it, and at four in the morning, I knew there was nobody else I could possibly call. And it was no problem. She talked to me until I felt better, and that's exactly the kind of thing that has made our relationship stay together. There just aren't that many people in your life who know what to say to you at four in the morning—or who can even stand to hear your voice. [Laughs.] I feel blessed.

As we grow older, our siblings are likely to become still more important to our well-being—especially for members of the baby boom generation. In the past, older people on their own have typically relied on their children as their primary practical and emotional support system. When children were plentiful, this worked well: During the Depression, for example, three-quarters of all American families had three or more children, and nearly half of families had at least five.[22] But now, with most married couples opting for only one or two children and with many more women remaining childless, the future situation for today's young and middle-aged adults will be strikingly different. The emerging reality is this: Most baby boomers—the majority of whom have at least three siblings[23]—will face their elder years with more brothers and sisters than children.

The implications of this dramatic demographic shift are hard to predict. Today, nearly half of all elderly people are single, and that proportion is not expected to change over the next several decades.[24] Some demographers predict that after our spouses die, many of us will choose to live with our sisters and brothers in miniature mutual support societies—a scenario likely to intrigue some and horrify others. What does seem likely is that as other kin connections shrink, siblings will increasingly become the "family glue" for one another, the ones we will turn to not only for practical support but for emotional connection, an irreplaceable sense of belonging. Nora, a sixty-one-year-old woman with three siblings aged fifty-six, sixty-six and seventy, is acutely aware of the relentless attrition of family: Their parents have been dead twenty years; one sister is widowed; another sister lost a teenage child to cancer; other children are grown and scattered. Nora described her feelings of grateful kinship at a recent "siblings only" weekend organized by their brother:

> We went down to the beach on the first afternoon. We were all in sweatshirts because it was cool, and Bill took four low beach chairs, so we just sat at the crest, where the sand is up before it drops down. And we just sat and talked and looked out at the ocean. I just remember feeling so fortunate—just *feeling* it—it wasn't anything that anybody was saying, or anything special that anybody was doing. It's very hard to explain. What mattered was that we were all *there*. My family.

As we grow older, our siblings link us to our childhood family experience—and particularly to the parents who may no longer be with us. Purdue University psychologist Victor Cicirelli writes: "The family of origin gradually erodes over time as its members die and only fragments of the system remain. . . . but the whole endures in the parts as memories and symbolic representations within the remaining individuals."[25] This may help explain why many older siblings reminisce with such frequency and gusto. During their sibling weekend, Nora recalled the emphasis on "back-when" talk:

> It was so great. We didn't know where to start talking. And it was just nonstop. We laughed so hard that we ached. We really did. One night we tried to play cards, but we were hard put to play the cards, we had so many conversations going. Crazy and sad and funny stuff about when we were growing up. How difficult Dad was—and how we each tried to deal with him. The house in Cincinnati we grew up in, where Mother set up a pinball machine in the dining room. And I said to my sister Doris at one point: "I feel like I'm at a slumber party and it's going to last for a couple of days."

Ours is a society that makes much of independence, autonomy, go-it-alone "strength." Indeed, much well-accepted psychological theory defines maturity in terms of the ability to separate emotionally from important people in one's early life.

And certainly, healthy adulthood does include the ability to carve out an identity and a life that are distinctly, recognizably one's own. But few of us acknowledge enough, it seems to me, our concurrent need for attachment and belonging, the persistent longing throughout our lives to still be a "member of the club."

Some twenty years ago, John Bowlby, perhaps the world's foremost theoretician on psychological attachment, tried to make us understand: "For not only young children, it is now clear, but human beings of all ages are found to be at their happiest and to be able to deploy their talents to best advantage when they are confident that, standing behind them, there are one or more trusted persons."[26] Attachment, he wrote, is a lifelong phenomenon—and it should be. It is what keeps us healthy and life-embracing, not what defines us as weak.

"One or more trusted persons." I particularly like that phrase. It implies the possibility of a community of allies, a convoy of comrades with whom we might travel through life. So often, as we launch ourselves into a mobile and preoccupied adulthood, we narrow our vision of who counts, trimming our lists to partner, children, parents, perhaps a few close friends. None of these people, surely, is less necessary than a brother or a sister.

Not one of them, though, can give us just what a sister or a brother can.

# 2

# Roots of the Relationship

It isn't a matter of whether you *can* go home again. You
just do.

Patricia Hampl, *The Need to Say It*

How would you describe your feelings for your sibling?

When I asked that question of a pair of sisters, aged thirty-
two and thirty-six, their answers came in a jumble of anecdote
and emotion:

TERRY: Well, my birthday was Friday ...

MARIE: And I sent her about twelve cards. And a birthday
package to her office. I knew she'd had a crummy
week.

TERRY: I *knew* it was from you. Before I saw the card.

MARIE: And so she called from the office to say, "I didn't
open the package yet, but I really do love it." And she
said, "I love you." She said it like she was going to cry
if I didn't hang up.

TERRY: She's underlying. A given. No matter what else is
happening, no matter what else is going on, nothing

would get in the way of this. This relationship would always come first. If I was with Jack, if I was at my job and in the middle of something important, and she said, "I need you now . . ."

MARIE: She'd say, "I'm outta here."

TERRY: "I'm sorry. I have to go. My sister needs me now."

In answer to the same question, Julie, a forty-seven-year-old lawyer, reflected on her current tie with her older brother:

I really feel at the moment that if I didn't ever see him again, it would not be bad. I don't feel that I get anything out of the relationship. I don't get anything from Ed. He's very kind to me, he tries, but we have nothing in common. Okay, we went through the lunatic asylum together growing up. Victims together, survivors together. I'd be kidding myself if I didn't think we're bound in some very deep way. Like a war comradeship.

But we have nothing to talk about. There isn't a connection. The connection from somebody who knows what you're about. I'm bored. And then, when he gets talking about how we're so much alike, I'm angry. I have to restrain myself. Sometimes I think I might kill him. Not physically, but I think I might overwhelm him with so much anger.

Joe, a thirty-eight-year-old magazine editor, described his feelings toward his older brother, a nationally prominent cancer specialist, this way:

I look at him and I see a lot of things I disapprove of. Basically, Michael's a suburban Republican. *Unbelievably* conservative. I mean, when I was in college, conservatives were the people who voted for Hubert Humphrey. [Chuckles.] And he's a social climber. He likes to associate with the elite and he does. Also, he's tall and I'm short. Even worse, he's three years older than me, but I started going bald first. When he finally started going bald, I was delighted.

Yet if I can think of the people in the world whose death would leave the biggest hole, Michael would be right up there. Life would just be—how can you explain it? I don't see him a lot anymore, and I don't talk to him as much as I would like to. But when I need him—and I have, often—he's right there. It's so important to *know* that. He's the moorings, and I love the son of a bitch.

Three adult sibling bonds. Different from one another not merely in degree, but in kind. The two sisters had been intimates since childhood and were still best friends, happily involved in each other's daily lives and highly responsive to each other's emotional cues. Julie, by contrast, could discuss her brother in a two-and-a-half-hour interview without expressing a single positive emotion. Joe, for his part, took for granted that a big brother inspired a tangle of intense and conflicting feelings: jealousy, affection, exasperation, enduring need. What accounts for such vast diversity among adult sibling relationships? How is it that Virginia Woolf could declare in a letter to her sister, Vanessa Bell, "There is no doubt that I love you better than anyone in the world,"[1] while James Joyce could write to his wife, Nora, with equal certainty, "My brothers and sisters are nothing to me"?[2]

The influences that shape the tie between two siblings are not time-limited. On the contrary, the sibling bond has the capacity to grow and change throughout the life span, with no buzzer sounding at age eighteen or thirty or even sixty-five to signal its developmental end point. Nonetheless, most researchers concur that the foundation of the adult bond is usually constructed in childhood, during the years when brothers and sisters encounter each other most continuously in the acutely emotional arena of the family. If no positive attachment at all develops during those early years, research indicates that it is unlikely to emerge in adulthood.[3] The encouraging news is that when some genuine connection *does* take root in childhood—even amid considerable conflict—it doesn't wither easily. My own interviews reflected the hardiness of such early bonds: Many who could claim some meaningful childhood attachment to a sibling were impressively able to work through later struggles and silences, even some that had escalated almost to the point of estrangement.

What happens, then, in each of our childhoods to allow that essential connection to grow and thrive—or prevent it from taking root at all? The answers, of course, are enormously complex, encompassing a radically untidy mix of familial, sociocultural, and individual forces that can be only introduced in the space of this chapter. No single influence is enough to "cause" a particular type of sibling bond, nor does any of them operate independently to simply add up, one by one, to a satisfying or troubled tie. Instead, each influence interacts with all of the others rather as chemical substances do, combining to collectively heat up, cool down, fuse or explode a particular sibling connection. Some influences are more universally shaping than others: One of these, gender, is so critical and has remained so long unacknowledged that I have chosen to explore it separately and in depth in subsequent chapters. Still, no sibling blueprint exists. For every pair of siblings, the exact weight of each factor will differ, as will their precise paths of intersection, with each element cutting through or wrapping around the others in ways that uniquely pattern each relationship.

The birthplace of the sibling bond is, of course, the family. There, before one ever meets a sister or brother, much groundwork has been laid for how one will perceive and respond to that individual. Family theorists conceive of the family as a living "system," a delicately balanced structure composed of intricately interrelated parts. A shift in one part of the system, therefore, reverberates throughout. Since a major change in one member's behavior may throw the system precariously out of balance, or even topple it, each family tends to develop its own distinctive, self-preserving set of values and rules that guide interactions among members. Rarely are we sat down and taught our family's rules; instead, much is transmitted through the code of example, reward, punishment and oft-told "family legends" that extol or deride the behavior of one member or another. As we grow up steeped in this potent brew of family truth and tenet—much of it handed down from generation to generation—we tend to soak it up unconsciously and uncritically; we know no other way to be.

From our own family we absorb, first of all, key messages about the nature and importance of family itself. Is it presented as a haven, a burden, a fortress? Are members supposed to form a tight, inviolable unit, or a loose federation of individuals? What messages are conveyed about the obligations of kin, the acceptable styles of interaction? One sister-brother pair I interviewed linked their current closeness, in part, to the sense of family solidarity they learned—and lived—early on:

JOHN: Even today, I think of us as The Six. My parents, brother, two sisters and me. We had a strong family identity; we traveled as a group; we presented ourselves as a group. We always had a sense of something very special about our family. There was a warmth about it; we felt very connected. [To Kate.] Remember the meets? Remember those? [They giggle.] She was a gymnast in high school—just an incredible athlete— and she had meets all over the region. Dozens of 'em. And we'd hit the road as a family, darn near every time.

KATE: The support was incredible. I would be warming up in some strange gym or other, and the family would file in. In comes Mom, in comes Dad, and here comes Gary, with his hands stuffed in his pockets, and there's John and here's Bonnie, pulling up the rear. An immediate cheering section.

JOHN: You didn't think about it. You were expected to support one another. It was expected, it was made extremely clear, it was not subtle. [Laughs.] But I very much wanted to be there. I remember feeling nervous for her.

The ideal of solidarity, however, doesn't automatically spur closeness between brothers and sisters. If family unity is fostered within an "open" family—one that encourages members to form attachments outside the family circle as well as within it—siblings are apt to view each other as freely chosen friends. But when the rule of closeness is born of a distrust of outsiders and a consequent reliance on family members for the fulfillment of all needs, it can stifle rather than support, transforming younger siblings into unwanted burdens and older ones into premature parents. Joe, the editor quoted at the beginning of this chapter, is aware that at age thirty-eight, he is still highly dependent on his older brother—"I want him when I want him"—and that Michael has recently begun to withdraw from his younger sibling's perpetual neediness. As Joe grapples to understand how the brothers have come to this pass, he remembers his mother's family dictum:

> The family should be tight. The family should be primary. My mother was tribal. Actually pretribal; tribes represent an agglomeration of clans. For her, it never got beyond a clan. The clan is the primary unit. Those outside the family are absolutely suspect, from my mother's point of view. As far as the five of us were concerned, my mother's favorite catch phrase was "Charity begins at home." Don't use it up on friends. She had a very instinctive sense that it really was the family versus the world.

Each family also has it own emotional code of conduct governing the range and intensity of feelings that members are permitted to express toward one another. This code is generally written in accordance with a particular family's needs for emotional connection and separateness among its members.[4] Generally, the more extreme a family's need for either closeness *or* distance, the shorter and more explicit the list of sanctioned emotions. For example, if "closeness" within a particular family requires that members deny their differences, the expression of angry or rivalrous feelings may be forbidden. Conversely, if a family highly prizes independence, expressions of warmth or need may be too threatening to permit. A family's emotional code cannot but deeply influence sibling ties. If rage toward a brother or sister is routinely corked, it only builds up power until it may finally explode into violence—or harden into bitterness. Similarly, if vulnerability is outlawed, brothers and sisters may grow up as semi-strangers, bound by blood but essentially alien to each other.

Depending on how the rules are written, one's family emotional code may also support—or interfere with—efforts to repair or strengthen a tie with an adult brother or sister. In *Brothers and Keepers,* John Edgar Wideman's book about his own journey toward sibling reconnection, Wideman describes the challenge he and his brother Robby faced as they tried, at ages forty-three and thirty-three, finally to get to know each other.

> We were both rookies. Neither of us had learned very much about sharing our feelings with other family members.... Privacy in our family was a birthright, a union card granted with family membership. The card said you're one of us but also certified your separateness, your obligation to keep much of what defined your separateness to yourself....
>
> So Robby and I faced each other in the prison visiting lounge as familiar strangers, linked by blood and time. But how do you begin talking about blood, about time? ... His privacy and mine had been exclusive, sanctioned by family traditions. Don't get too close. Don't ask too many questions or give too many answers. Don't pry. Don't let what's inside slop out on the people around you.[5]

The family "rule book," of course, does not develop in a vacuum, but is deeply influenced by the larger social and cultural context in which a family lives. Just as highly industrialized and developing societies each hold radically different notions of the meaning of family, so different ethnic and racial groups *within* our own society hold widely divergent views of family importance, obligations and acceptable styles of interaction. These values, in turn, powerfully influence the development of sibling bonds. Monica McGoldrick, a family therapist who has extensively studied the influence of ethnicity on families, writes:

> Ethnicity patterns our thinking, feeling and behavior in both obvious and subtle ways, although generally operat-

ing outside of our awareness. It plays a major role in de-
termining what we eat, how we work, how we relate, how
we celebrate holidays and rituals, and how we feel about
life, death and illness. We see the world through our own
cultural filters and we often persist in our established
views in spite of clear evidence to the contrary.[6]

The influence of ethnicity, which McGoldrick defines as a
group's "peoplehood," based on a combination of race, reli-
gion and cultural history, varies dramatically from family to
family. Such factors as class, geographic mobility, intermar-
riage patterns, and number of generations removed from the
original culture affect the depth of the ethnic imprint. Nonetheless, evidence is accumulating that few Americans remain
wholly immune to the family values and styles of relating in-
herited from their culture of origin.[7] For example, those who
grow up in families of WASP and other northern European
heritages are likely to view themselves, their siblings and their
parents as a related collection of individuals. "Give me space"
might be their rallying cry. In many such families, children
learn that self-reliance and individual achievement are prized,
obligations to siblings are limited, and the ideal kinship bond
is what anthropologist Colleen Leahy Johnson calls "intimacy
at a distance."[8] A show of strong feeling, even of the affectionate variety, may be seen as invading others' territory. For one
woman I interviewed, the product of a long, uninterrupted
WASP lineage, such vigilant boundary-keeping was reflected
in the way her family kissed: "You would stick out your face,
but never let anybody feel your body. There was no hug involved. And it would always be the cheek that was offered.
*Never* the lips."

In my own family—my siblings and I are third-generation
German American on both sides—I can see how the stoic lid
we learned to keep on our emotions even now influences our
adult relationships. "Stiff upper lip!" was a favorite exhorta-
tion of our father, and to this day, when I become aware of
any strong feeling toward my brother or my sister—love, hurt,
anger, fierce pride—my first impulse is to squelch it rather
than share it. Since my siblings learned similar lessons about
the hazards of emotional display, our "natural" drift has been

toward a kind of cordial distance, one we battle, even now, with conscious, concerted effort. It is as though our feelings are jointly poised at some invisible boundary line of taste and rectitude; to let them cross over feels sloppily intrusive, a violation of our mutual "sibling rights."

To many Italian Americans, such tiptoeing around the edges of sibling boundaries is apt to seem ludicrous, if not utterly incomprehensible. In many Italian American families, connection supersedes autonomy, and freely voiced feelings are a sign of caring, not a regrettable lapse of control. Siblings, especially those of the same sex, are frequently lifelong intimates. When Colleen Leahy Johnson studied sibling relationships in Syracuse, New York, she found that a stunning sixty-three percent of middle-aged Italian American women saw a sibling *every day*, compared to just twelve percent of their WASP counterparts.[9]

Among African Americans, the value placed on siblings is reflected in the use of "sister" and "brother" to describe not only blood relatives, but anyone to whom one feels a strong connection. Provision of mutual aid is at the core of the black family value system, as a sixty-three-year-old black household worker, the oldest of nine supportive siblings, remembers learning from her mother: "She always used to say to us to stick together, and help each other. And we do. You should share things with your brothers and sisters. Maybe somebody out of a job, need money. If you have it, you give it. That's what it is all about." While this readiness to "be there" for one another is partly a response to poverty and oppression, it is also heavily influenced by traditional African culture, which values collectivity above individualism. A recent study of sibling relationships among eighty middle-class, college-educated older Americans found that themes of loyalty, solidarity and enduring affection emerged in interviews with black siblings nearly three times as frequently as they did in interviews with whites. Even more striking, whites were *five times* more likely than blacks to feel hostility toward their siblings.[10]

In other cultures, mixed messages may strain sibling ties. While Jewish families tend genuinely to prize family cohesion and loyalty, a concurrent emphasis on children's achievement may spark rivalry among brothers and sisters—even as they are urged to stick together. Similarly, Irish American families typically expect brothers and sisters to be friends, and they usually try hard to comply. Irish Americans visit their adult siblings as frequently as they do their parents, and may feel extremely guilty when they fail to feel close to a brother or sister.[11] Yet competing cultural tendencies—the swallowing of emotions, a tolerance of ridicule between family members, parents' frequent designation of a "good" and a "bad" child— often undercut this comradely sibling ideal, and adult bonds may be badly frayed beneath public shows of solidarity.[12]

Such culturally influenced family ideals, convictions and rules for behavior set the stage for the development of sibling bonds. But it is the action on that stage, a highly charged mix of ad-libbed and scripted behaviors and roles played out by each family actor, that shapes the unique character of each sibling connection. That family relationships are enormously complicated is hardly news, but I never realized just how complicated until I came across a little-known "family portrait" sketched by numbers-crunching sociologist Paul Mott. Mott calculated that in a family of 4, no fewer than 11 potential relationship combinations exist among members. The more brothers and sisters one has, the more unwieldy things become: In a family of 5, there are 26 possible connections; a family of 6 has 57 potential relationships; in a 7-member family, there are a staggering 120.[13] While readers may be relieved to know that this mountain of possible combinations will not be analyzed here for their sibling relevance, it is nonetheless useful to envision each family relationship as operating in the context of several others, perhaps scores of others, each one pushing, pulling, straining against or bouncing off the others in intricate patterns of mutual influence.

Few of us, however, need a primer on family theory to be convinced that our parents had something to do with our feelings for a brother or a sister. Many have still-painful memories of how it worked: *She* got more attention from Dad; Mom thought *he* was smarter; *they loved her more than me.* Parental favoritism—or its absence—is a powerful shaper of the sibling bond in our culture. In a retrospective study of sibling relationships among seventy-five middle-class Americans aged twenty-two to ninety-three, University of Cincinnati psychologists Helgola Ross and Joel Milgram asked respondents how they felt toward their adult siblings—and more important, how they believed those particular feelings had developed. Breaking up into small groups, participants talked with one another for more than two hours, sifting through memory, perception and emotion to explore both the nature and roots of their sibling connections.

When Ross and Milgram transcribed and analyzed these conversations, they found a striking pattern. Those who felt close to their brothers and sisters remembered not only an emphasis on family unity in childhood, but also a notable *absence* of parental favoritism coupled with a clear recognition of each child's individual talents and accomplishments. Conversely, when participants explored sibling rivalry in their lives—both its childhood origins and the forces that kept it alive in adulthood—the number one theme that emerged was parental favoritism.[14]

While one might question the reliability of memory as a data collection tool, similar results have emerged in observational studies that allow researchers to watch family relationships in action. In one such study, Pennsylvania State University psychologists Clare Stocker, Judy Dunn and Robert Plomin visited the homes of ninety-six families to watch and videotape daily interactions among mothers and pairs of siblings aged three to ten. They observed that when mothers in fact lavished more attention or affection on one child than the other, the behavior between the siblings themselves was more competitive and conflict-ridden, especially when the younger sibling was the recipient of more maternal "goodies." [15] And surprisingly enough, parents admit to playing favorites: Two-thirds of mothers acknowledged feeling more intense affection for one child than another, while eighty-eight percent said they disciplined one child more frequently than another.[16]

In my own interviews, parental favoritism was a shaping theme. Many felt a sibling-parent-sibling triangle to be more apparent, painful and enduring than the more notorious Oedipal one. Some described a particular, almost magical closeness between a parent and a sibling, some nameless mutual identification that felt impenetrable to the excluded child and sometimes remained, twenty or thirty years later, a source of rage or bitterness toward the "chosen one." Favored siblings, by contrast, who usually had been lured from the sibling camp to the parental one at an early age, tended to feel emotionally distant from brothers and sisters and, in extreme cases, wholly indifferent. It is no coincidence that James Joyce, who wrote off his brothers and sisters as "nothing to me," was the hands-down favorite child of *both* of his parents, an outrageously coddled firstborn son who, according to his sister Eileen, was showered with money and books for his education "whether or not his family had enough to eat."[17]

Parental partiality also may take the form of overprotection of a child who is ill or otherwise labeled "fragile," with the "well" child left to fend for himself or herself—or expected to cater to the pampered one. Forty-five-year-old Matt, a childhood asthmatic who is now trying to understand his older brother Stuart's long-standing avoidance of him, remembers with horror how his brother was forced to defer to the "sick one":

> Now I can see how he must have resented the fact that I got so much more attention than he did. I was always on the couch. Always sick. Camille. I was always allowed to take a day off from school. I got a lot more stroking than he did. I used to have to drink this wretched stuff for some malady I claimed to have, and it just tasted horrible. And I can remember saying, "I'm not going to drink this stuff unless Stuart does." And he would have to drink it.
>
> I also had my pick of food. We would all be sitting around the dinner table, and I would look at what Stuart had on his plate and I would announce, "I want that. I *want* that. *He* has a better piece of meat." And my mother would pick up her fork and stab the piece of meat on Stuart's plate, and give it to me.

Others described the high regard of one sibling in the family as particularly talented or accomplished—the "brain," the "athlete" or the "artist"—with the biggest share of parental attention, sacrifice and reward flowing to the designated "successful" child. This child may be chosen not because he or she is actually the most gifted, but because his or her particular abilities mesh with the family's most highly prized values— ones that are often generations in the making. My father, for example, was a hardworking, highly successful businessman whose father before him was a hardworking, highly successful businessman. Dozens of times, my siblings and I heard the story of how my grandfather quit school at age fourteen to help his widowed mother support a family of eight, and how, by dint of brains and hard work, he rose from furnace-stoker's helper to the top management of a major steel company. My father, while boosted by a college education, essentially followed his father's brains-and-sweat road to success; it was the unquestioned "Sandmaier way," the blueprint for an admirable human being.

So when I began to get good grades in school—better than those of my siblings, who were plenty smart but less zealous in piling up proof of it—my father began to pay attention to me in a way he never had before. I am sure that he did not mean to single me out, nor was he probably even aware of it. But the moment my A's started to flow, the family legacy kicked in. My schoolwork was exclaimed over; I was bragged about to my grandfather; I was described as "Our Student" to office colleagues, neighbors, school principals, restaurant waiters. I inhaled my father's approval like a drug, and to guarantee the supply I scrambled for still better grades, piled up more achievements and awards. Donna, my elder by sixteen months, responded by withdrawing from the competition entirely, and silently resenting me. Bob, four years younger, retaliated by besting me at every game in the universe—poker, pool, Monopoly, myriad varieties of verbal karate—and regularly, triumphantly calling my father's attention to it.

And what of my own feelings toward my siblings? They were revealed to me, unbidden, in a single, stomach-turning moment when I was fourteen. It was "report card day," and after dinner my father called me into his study and asked me to close the door. "This is for your good grades," he said, holding out a five-dollar bill. I felt a little jolt of excitement: Approval *and* cash made a heady combination. But there was more. "Don't mention this to the others," my father continued in a lowered voice. "They didn't do as well as you. You're the only one I'm rewarding this way."

My pleasure vanished; I felt suddenly caught, exposed. *Five bucks, no big deal,* I told myself, but I knew in that moment that to take the money was to betray my sister and brothers, to agree with my father that on the school front I was, after all, "the best," and that they were, in some way that mattered, lesser. I felt suddenly their vulnerability, how all of us were at the mercy of his appraisals. *They did their best. They could be me.* But if I didn't take the money, my father would not understand. Not in a million years. I saw then and there that if I did not betray my siblings I would have to betray my father, and in so doing sever my bond with him as a "real Sandmaier," the sole source of my power to make his eyes light up, to make them stay focused on me. It was no contest. I walked out, the five-dollar bill locked in my fist.

The depth of our hunger for parental love gives fathers and mothers enormous power to influence the sibling bond—for good as well as for ill. A parent's ability to communicate that "there's enough love to go around," as well as genuinely to appreciate each child's distinctive personality and talents, can provide a secure base of self-esteem from which to regard a sibling benevolently, even one who is widely deemed by the world "more successful." In a small study of the adult siblings of famous Americans—prominent politicians, corporate executives, actors, best-selling authors—most of the "nonfamous" brothers and sisters expressed unambivalent pride in their sibling's celebrity. More than any other factor, they linked their lack of resentment to growing up in families that actively supported each child. "All of us always got our parents' love" and "We are all equal, there are no jealousies" were typical comments, and when asked if they had particular talents of their own, all could readily name them.[18] While these notably congenial ties may not be representative—those racked by rivalry toward a celebrity sib might be less likely to volunteer for such a study—such findings nonetheless suggest the power of parental evenhandedness to promote positive sibling ties, even when tested by vastly unequal wealth, public recognition and other proof of having "made it" in our culture.

Parents also wield influence by their absence. When a parent dies, walks out on the family, withdraws into alcoholism or mental illness or otherwise abandons children, brothers and sisters may turn to each other for emotional—and sometimes physical—survival. Psychologists Stephen Bank and Michael Kahn, authors of *The Sibling Bond,* write that "these siblings' relationships and identities are intertwined, sometimes for life, because they have jointly faced traumatic psychological losses at crucial stages of their development."[19] A brother or sister, moreover, may be one's sole remaining source of love and nurture. Bank and Kahn observe that siblings in such straits may develop a "Hansel and Gretel" bond of intensely committed, mutual caregiving that is not to be confused with the merely friendly and companionable ties many siblings develop.

Such a bond of primal loyalty developed between writer Richard Rhodes and his brother, Stan, whose mother committed suicide when they were toddlers, creating "a hole in the world" that widened and deepened terrifyingly when their father remarried a monstrously abusive woman. For emotional sustenance, the boys clung to each other; for physical survival, they mapped out elaborate plans of high-risk cooperation to escape punishment by beating or starvation. In Richard Rhodes's eloquent book on their early lives, *A Hole in the World,* the adult Stan helps his brother remember one such boyhood survival plan, and Richard reflects on its lasting impact on their relationship:

"You had to pee at night," Stan reminds me. "You got spanked for it a whole bunch of times. We had double bunk beds. You slept on top and I slept down below. So we developed a technique where you would do it up there and hand it down to me. . . . and then when I got up in the morning—I was usually the first one to get up—I'd grab that bottle, and since, you know, it was time to get up anyway, I would tiptoe into the bathroom and urinate, and then pour your urine out of there, rinse it and everything all in one shot and then tiptoe back and hide the bottle for the next time. . . ."

From morning to morning my brother risked a severe beating to dump my urine for me. "That was horrible," he says, meaning denying a child the toilet. "Gee, that was really horrible. That was something you can never forgive her for." I haven't, and I won't, but suffering is never meaningless. The memory of the woman's malice will always return to me now with its complement, knowledge of my brother's courage in risking himself to help me, and gratitude for it and love.[20]

While Stan, the older of the two brothers, frequently acted as Richard's protector, a fundamental equality permeated their relationship, as each boy understood the other to be both a fellow victim and the only caring force in his life. In other cases of parental deprivation, however, one sibling dons the cloak of "mother" or "father" and the other that of "child," setting the stage for an unbalanced bond of profound, sometimes lifelong dependency. When Virginia Stephens—the future Virginia Woolf—was only thirteen, her mother died suddenly. Only two years afterward, her much older half sister, Stella, who had become a beloved surrogate mother, also died. In the wake of such devastating loss, Virginia turned the full force of her neediness on her steady, nurturing older sister, Vanessa, cleaving to her with a single-minded, desperate intensity that never abated throughout the sisters' lives. Virginia turned to her sister to nurse her through numerous bouts of mental illness, and throughout her life resented competing claims on Vanessa's energies and affections—including those of husband and children. Never able to separate emotionally from her sister, Virginia experienced any absence as a terrifying shriveling of self, "a kind of drought caused by the lack of Nessa,"[21] with her return magically restoring Virginia to life: "Mercifully, Nessa is back. My earth is watered again."[22] At age fifty-five, Virginia could still write to her fifty-eight-year-old sister:

You can't think how I depend upon you, and when you're not there the colour goes out of my life, as water from a sponge; and I merely exist, dry and dusty. This is the exact truth: but not a very beautiful illustration of my complete adoration of you; and longing to sit, even saying nothing, and look at you.[23]

What must it have been like for Vanessa to be the lifelong target of her sister's bottomless, worshipful need for maternal care? Virginia, never one to flinch from reality, guessed at her sister's feelings in a letter to her: "I often wake in the night and cry aloud Nessa! Nessa! Doesn't that comfort you? Well, not much, you say."[24] In fact, Vanessa periodically defended herself through distance or silence, which only spurred Virginia's anxious efforts to draw her sister close again. Yet overall, Vanessa was remarkably tolerant of her younger sister's relentless need for her. In fact, the pleasures and comforts of this extraordinary sisterly bond seemed ultimately to outweigh its complex burdens, and by all accounts was a deeply necessary relationship to both.

The much celebrated bond between these notable sisters, in fact, clearly exemplifies the multiply determined, intertwined nature of influences on any sibling relationship. Here was a bond that might easily have been strained or even severed by Virginia's boundless hunger for her sister; indeed, many siblings who find themselves a "brother's keeper" because of a parent's death or abdication respond with resentful rage toward the sibling who is now their charge; not uncommonly, such involuntary servitude results in lifelong bitterness toward one's early sibling burden. For the Stephens sisters, however, other, solidarity-promoting forces were more compelling, softening the impact of Virginia's unflagging neediness. Among these influences is one so basic, so necessary to a satisfying sibling bond that it is often forgotten: The sisters liked each other.

Not all siblings do. Many respect each other, appreciate each other, even love each other deeply. But genuine liking is something else: It's the jolt of pleasure one feels at hearing a brother's or sister's voice on the other end of the phone line; it's the source of uncontrollable joint chortling over a very good, very old joke; it's the ineffable attraction that allows some individuals to say, "If she wasn't my sister, I'd still want her for my friend." For some, the feelings run deeper still, issuing from a powerful mutual identification that a fifty-four-year-old man tried to articulate as he described his special affinity with his older sister:

> There's a communion. It's body language, it's brain waves; it's not just a power, it's a *force*. Whatever it is, it means that when she and I get together, we need very few words to get a sense of where the other is. And there are times when I'll try to tell her something but my words are clumsy and don't say what I really want to get at. And she'll say, "Oh, you mean such and such." And she'll be right. That's really what I *did* mean. It's very gratifying, it's such a thing to be prized. You can't buy it. There is an understanding beyond words.

Such elemental rapport between two siblings cannot be explained entirely as the product of "close family values": Many individuals from warm, cohesive families could name one brother or sister with whom they shared a uniquely powerful affinity, one markedly stronger than their ties with other siblings. Some who experienced this sense of communion with a brother or sister had felt it since childhood; others didn't "discover" a sibling until adolescence or early adulthood. Research is largely silent on the sources of such sibling rapport, perhaps because human attraction doesn't easily lend itself to precise analysis. In my interviews, however, this emotional sympathy between siblings seemed to be largely about the fortunate "fit" of two personalities, a delicate balance between likeness and difference that allowed two siblings to feel deeply at home in each other's presence, yet also fascinated or inspired by what was admirably unique in the other. Often common interests both reflected and cemented such psychic kinship: a passion for the outdoors, a mania for B-movies, a common need to figure out the family, a shared vision of a just world.

The foregoing, of course, assumes mutual sibling attraction. Not uncommonly, however, one sibling plays frustrated suitor to a hard-to-get brother or sister. Age is a critical factor here: Research indicates that the younger of two siblings tends to place more importance on the relationship,[25] and my interviews strongly bore this out. A common theme was the intense, one-way admiration—verging on hero worship—of a younger sibling toward an older one. This lopsided bond was nearly always forged in childhood, when an age gap of only two or three years could easily render an older brother or sister a worldly, larger-than-life luminary and a younger one a pesky, uninteresting "baby." While some older siblings treated their younger brothers and sisters with notable kindness throughout childhood, a more common dynamic was graphically sketched by a twenty-nine-year-old woman, the self-described childhood "shadow" of a sister two years her senior:

> It was a little bit like, you know, those cartoons where there's the big bulldog and he's stomping along by himself and there's the little dog that keeps jumping around him saying, "Look at me, what d'you think?" And the big bulldog goes *whack* and the little dog skulks away for about two seconds, and then he's right back in there again, trying to get the big guy's attention. It was a little bit like that.

Age gaps between siblings clearly lose some of their power as one advances through adulthood, and some brothers and sisters I talked with had little trouble renegotiating a bond of equality with a former "hero" or "baby." For others, however, such early imbalances remained a source of struggle, with many younger siblings still angling for an older one's approval or respect, or trying to wrest free of their need of it. Many older siblings, by contrast, expressed a wish to be allowed to be more vulnerable and "real" with a younger brother or sister who still idealized them; others recognized that, to some degree, they still treated a younger sibling like a not-too-bright child—or worse, a vassal.

Large age gaps can hinder what psychologists call "sibling access"—the chance for brothers and sisters to get to know each other in the first place. Several of those I interviewed were still in grade school when a sibling left for college; one man described his much older brother as "always out the door, disappearing from sight." When sisters and brothers are no more than three or four years apart, by contrast, they are more likely to share large chunks of time, space and experience. They may attend the same schools, play sports together, share friends, and face family crises at a similar developmental stage. Compared to more widely spaced siblings, they are more apt to "have a history," that deep well of shared experience and understanding that gives the sibling bond its distinctive power. Not surprisingly, such a history influences the intensity of adult bonds: Numerous studies indicate that both intimacy *and* rivalry in adulthood are more likely between closely spaced siblings.[26]

Such sibling access intersects with what might be called "world access," that is, opportunities to develop strong peer bonds outside the family. Among my interviewees, several grew up in rural areas where they were miles from the nearest neighbor, spurring many to make best friends of their only regular companions—brothers and sisters. Frequent moves also tended to boost solidarity, for siblings often entered strange new worlds as each other's sole bulwark against loneliness and found themselves able to identify, perhaps for the first time, with a sibling's pain.

My sister, Donna, and I agree that a major turning point in our own bond occurred when our family moved from the small northern New Jersey town of our childhood—a place where we had lived for a decade, knew everyone and had minimal need of a sister—to the vast, grassless suburbs of San Diego, where we were launched into adolescence without a single friend. We began making forays to the beach together, absorbing California-speak and the finer points of surfer culture, and once in a while talking about what it felt like to be outsiders in our new Catholic high school, the "girls from New Joisey" who didn't know the true meaning of tennis, tan lines or hydrogen peroxide.

But misery-trading turned out to be only a minor factor in our growing solidarity. More important, this was the first period since our toddler days when Donna and I had actually spent substantial time together—enough to begin to get to know the sister behind the stereotype. I had long ago dismissed Donna as a terminally virtuous elder with whom I had nothing in common, but during those sidekick years I discovered that we both loved Motown and sick humor, we both viewed nuns as thinly disguised psychological terrorists, and that my sister—the identified "good girl" of our family—was born for conspiracy. I still smile when I think of an afternoon more than twenty years ago when the two of us were home alone and a fuming, grudge-carrying ex-boyfriend of mine gunned up to our house in his flame-red TR-4 and began to hammer on our front door, bellowing my name. Before I could even wring my hands Donna was motioning me to follow her into the bathroom, where she efficiently directed my escape through a window and up onto the flat roof of our ranch house. From my perch, I heard her open the door and calmly explain to my pursuer that he could look wherever he wished, but "believe me, my sister's not home."

Of such small moments—both those remembered and those submerged—is the foundation of the sibling bond constructed. Not long ago, I read *Cat's Eye*, Margaret Atwood's chilling novel about the cruelties of childhood, and I was stopped by her conception of time and memory: "You don't look back along time but down through it, like water. Sometimes this comes to the surface, sometimes that, sometimes nothing. Nothing goes away."[27] Everything that happened between ourselves and our siblings in those early years is stored in some deep yet accessible burrow within, influencing the way we now feel when a brother or sister enters a room, wins a promotion, calls our name, doesn't show up. There is an imprint, whether we choose to look at it or not.

For those who choose to look, however, unexpected possibilities may emerge. As we look down through time to watch sibling memories float upward, their shapes and weight may shift as we notice the forces that jointly forged those early moments of need, pain, rivalry and love. So little, really, was under our control. What child has any say about a family's fortunes and fissures; about a parent's choice of one child over another; about matchings or mismatchings of temperament; about family members' permission to say to each other, "I love you"—or "Stop"? This is not to suggest that brothers and sisters bear no responsibility for what transpired between them in childhood; only that when ancient pain or guilt still blocks connection between adult siblings, a widened perspective may help to make a path. To understand that "we were in this together," once upon a time, is not enough to bridge all silences, heal all wounds or forge genuine intimacy between brothers and sisters. Still, more than likely, it is a vital first step.

# 3

# Sources of Self

---

A life is not the mere growth of the original seed. It runs the continual danger of being halted, broken, damaged or turned aside. Yet a happy beginning does encourage the subject to get the best that can be got from his circumstances.... I believe I should count the fact of having had a sister, younger than myself but close to me in age, as one of my pieces of good luck.

Simone de Beauvoir, *All Said and Done*

It is suppertime at our house, circa 1962. We gather around the dining room table, the six of us, and for the first minute or two we behave like any hungry family, passing food, yelling for the salt, scrambling for the extra Pepperidge Farm roll. Then my father, a partner in a large certified public accounting firm, clears his throat. Abruptly, we quiet ourselves. "Mind if I get technical on you?" he inquires of my mother on this particular evening. She does not. "I'd like to talk about billing procedures," he begins, and it is understood that no one else will speak until he is finished explaining the intricacies of invoice preparation, which we further know will not occur until the very last forkful of dinner has been swallowed. This means that our own assortment of stories—the small discoveries, triumphs and scraps of weirdness that each of us kids has collected in the course of the day—will once again go unshared and unheard. We know this is unjust, and we also know the futility of saying so. So what can we do?

We do what we always do; it is a choreographed response honed by years of nightly practice. I watch Donna go stoic:

She stares down at her plate and eats methodically, her face a mask. I watch Phil, the youngest, look attentively at our father, nod in response to a lengthy description of bill collection techniques, and chuckle at the joke about credits and debits. My brother Bob and I, meanwhile, begin a slow, deliberate dance of sabotage. He scrapes his chair; I shift noisily in my seat. He burps; I have a coughing fit.

My father's soliloquy continues. We escalate. Now we are mouthing a silent counterconversation. It might be dialogue from a comic book ("You're all washed up, Superman! I'm hanging you out to dry!"), it might be code words to an inside joke, it might be lyrics from a song we consider particularly moronic; it doesn't matter what we choose, as long as it has the power to make us both dissolve, finally, in helpless, diversionary laughter. My father stops in midsentence. He stares hard at each of us. We stare back. "Until I was so rudely interrupted," he says, pausing for the expected apology. Now we are silent. Donna and Phil shift uncomfortably in their seats. My father explodes: We are bad-mannered, disrespectful *oddballs*, Bob and I. We have succeeded in ruining dinner for everyone. *Are we happy?* He waits again. More silence. More staring. Bob and I lock eyes for an instant. We do not crack. We will never crack.

For years I thought that this piece of family dinner theater, re-enacted literally hundreds of times during my childhood and adolescence, was only about my father and me. About feeling profoundly unseen and unheard by him much of the time, and about my enraged attempts to repay him in kind. I was dimly aware that this recurring drama was also about Bob and my father, though I spent little time reflecting on their particular issues. What I missed entirely were the powerful, unspoken mutual influences that were bouncing back and forth among the four kids at that table. I saw my siblings as bit players, I heard them as background noise. I hadn't a clue that my daily interactions with them—at the dinner table and everywhere else—were eliciting a stream of silent identifications, comparisons and cues for behavior that were subtly shaping the person I am today.

Even back then, I knew that Bob and I were implicitly the "bad ones" in our family, while Donna and Phil got to be the "good ones." Yet while I had mixed feelings about these role assignments, I accepted that they merely reflected our innate personalities: Bob and I were born for rebellion, while Donna and Phil were natural people-pleasers. Everybody said it; everybody knew it. What I never noticed, back in those days of supper-table sabotage, was how heavily each of us depended on the cooperation of our siblings to allow us to "be ourselves." If, for instance, my older sister had not habitually withdrawn from confrontation as far back as I can remember—her dinner-table compliance being only one example—would I have had the opportunity to develop my proclivity for dissent, a lifelong role that has both served me well and often gotten me into trouble? Similarly, if Bob had not joined me in that nightly ritual of rebellion and in countless other family showdowns, would I have had the confidence to develop the part of me that still, today, doesn't easily back down? Or, lacking any ally, would I have doubted the legitimacy of my anger and come to believe that I was simply a rude, ungrateful troublemaker—and quickly learned to suppress my less sanguine feelings? I know that my siblings are not the only influences on that particular aspect of my identity and personality; the revelation for me is that they are very significant ones.

Only recently have siblings been acknowledged as key players in identity and personality development. Parents, and most especially mothers, have long been given both full credit and full blame for children who turn out to be self-confident or self-doubting, independent or dependent, basically happy or basically miserable. And there is no denying that in most cases, parents *are* the most critical influences on an individual's psychological development. For most of us, parents are our primary attachment figures, the people we most depended on for nurture in our earliest years and who thereby provided the grounding for our adult belief that we are—or are not—fundamentally lovable, capable people.

But siblings count, too. It is widely accepted that the foundation of identity and personality is laid during the emotionally vulnerable childhood years—the very years in which most people interact most continuously and intensely with their brothers and sisters. An observational study of 140 siblings under the age of seven found that even when mothers were available, brothers and sisters interacted with each other an average of *eighty-five times* per hour. Moreover, these siblings subjected each other to an enormous range of behaviors likely to influence personality and self-concept, including praise, physical violence, consolation, threats, orders, hugs and insults.[1] Largely because of such concentrated, continuous and often passionate interaction, John Bowlby observed, brothers and sisters are frequently "subsidiary attachment figures," members of a small cadre of emotionally significant people in one's childhood who, along with parents, contribute importantly to the development of personality and self-esteem.[2]

Among those I interviewed, sibling influence was widely viewed as self-evident. Nearly every individual I spoke with believed that a brother or sister had a major, enduring impact on some aspect of his or her personality development. Most felt, moreover, that "sibling footprints" could be felt in one or more critical realms of their adult lives: the choice of an intimate partner, expectations for friendship, a career path followed or bypassed, a readiness to take risks. As one woman described her older sister's unique and enduring impact:

> Katherine touches the part of me that knows there's something better in me, that believes I can reach whatever it is that I'm after. I used to hate it when she would say to me, "Rise to the occasion." But the truth is, there isn't anyone else in my life who believes that I *can* rise to the occasion the way she does. She's seen me do it, she has markers all along the way of our childhood. And because of that, she almost only needs to say that—to say "Try"—for me to try whatever it is. And I try because both of us believe that I can.

When we reflect on the psychological impact of siblings, most of us think immediately of birth order. This is not surprising: Over the past several decades, a vast number of studies have linked one's chronological place in the family to a daunting list of personal characteristics, from achievement and intelligence to political leanings, sexual preference, fear of bodily harm, chronic back pain, height, alcoholism and even the likelihood of getting traffic tickets. But several years ago, Swiss social scientists Cecile Ernst and Jules Angst reviewed 1,500 birth order studies published since 1946 and found their results consistently, sometimes dramatically, contradictory. (One example: While numerous highly publicized studies indicate that firstborns dominate among groups of prominent scientists and businessmen, Ernst and Angst came across other studies—far less publicized—showing that firstborns are equally overrepresented among less conventionally achieving groups, including stripteasers and unwed mothers.) They concluded that "this kind of research is a sheer waste of time and money" because nearly all studies looked at birth order in isolation, without considering what *else* might be going on in a particular family. The frequently cited high achievement of firstborns, for example, tended to disappear when such factors as educational level and socioeconomic circumstances were taken into account.[3]

It is not that birth order necessarily explains *nothing* about personality, only that people are far more complex than their sibling chronology. Most researchers concur that both the nature and degree of sibling impact on personality are linked to a wide range of interlocking factors, which may include birth order as well as the emotional and physical health of all family members, each parent's treatment of each child, individual temperaments and whether one is the older or the younger of a sibling pair, apart from specific order of birth. Gender also makes a critical contribution. As will be discussed fully in the next chapters, being a member of a pair of brothers, a pair of sisters, or a sister-brother duo uniquely influences the kind of impact siblings have on each other.

Sibling influence begins with the development of identity— the life-shaping answer to the question "Who am I?" Noted family theoretician Salvador Minuchin writes that "in all cultures, the family imprints its members with selfhood. Human experience of identity has two elements: a sense of belonging and a sense of being separate. The laboratory in which these ingredients are mixed and dispensed is the family, the matrix of 'identity.'"[4] In other words, one develops a sense of self partly from the affirming *connections* one makes with family members, a secure sense of "we" that supports feelings of belonging and self-worth. At the same time, one carves out a unique identity partly from the *distinctions* one makes between oneself and family members, creating a defining sense of "me" that allows one to feel irreplaceably individual.

As we fashion our identities through this intricate, continual dance of connection and separation, the influence of brothers and sisters is apt to be significant. As individuals who share our generation, roughly half of our genes, both of our parents and a unique history, siblings are family members with whom we are apt to sense deep commonalities—and, at the same time, from whom we urgently need to differentiate ourselves. As models and allies, and as warnings and foils, sisters and brothers do nothing less than help us create ourselves.

The precise ratio of "I'm like you–I'm not like you" convictions that individuals develop vis-à-vis their siblings varies enormously among brothers and sisters. The most satisfying bonds tend to encompass a balanced mix of intimacy-promoting likeness and independence-promoting individuality, allowing for relationships "balanced on the fulcrum of equality," write psychologists Stephen Bank and Michael Kahn in *The Sibling Bond*.[5] Yet relatively few siblings strike this ideal balance between affinity and autonomy. More often, the "sibling scale" is tipped—modestly or dramatically—either toward identification ("I'm like you") or toward differentiation ("I'm *not* like you").

On the continuum of identification, some individuals so admire qualities in a brother or sister that he or she becomes a critical role model. For some, a respected sibling may be the source of very particular values or interests; for others, a brother or sister may offer nothing less than life-shaping direction. Karen, a thirty-one-year-old artist, remembers how her older sister Amy, whom she deeply admired and who "played a starring role" in her adolescence, steered her from a seductive, self-destructive path:

> She kept me on an even keel. One area particularly. My oldest sister, Nancy, and my brother, Don, were pretty

heavily into drugs in their teen years and continued right through their twenties being involved in different kinds of drugs—hallucinogenic ones, mostly, and pot. Everybody started pretty early. Nancy was sixteen when she started and she got my brother into it when he was fourteen or so and it just trickled down. And they eventually got Amy to try it, too, and she had a very bad experience with it. She came to me and said, "Don't do it." She told me about her experience and she also saw it as incredibly stupid. And I absolutely made up my mind not to do any drugs at all.

And it's really pretty amazing that I never did. Considering it was in the house. It was all around. My brother was growing pot plants out in the yard and I hung out some with him and his friends 'cause that's how I got to meet my boyfriends. They all did drugs. I could have been drawn into it and when you're artistic, you always want to see things in a new way. But Amy was on the other side of the fence, and her approval was worth a lot in my mind. The two of us were always a unit, just like Nancy and Don were a unit.

I wouldn't say I worshiped her, but I did want to be like her, and for a long time I thought she had the answers. She really, really saw drugs as a dead end.

When a sibling role model is nurturing, mature, and doesn't seek to "clone" an admiring brother or sister, his or her imprint can be clearly positive. But less constructive scenarios may be played out. While Karen was fortunate enough to identify with a sister who steered her away from drugs, numerous studies document that adolescents are more likely to begin using drugs, alcohol and cigarettes if an older sibling already does—particularly if the younger sibling admiringly identifies with the "user" sibling.[6] Drug use, of course, is only one example. Not uncommonly, adolescents are deeply attracted to the maverick qualities in an older, rebellious sibling, particularly if they view that sister or brother as their only escape from an otherwise oppressively conventional family. In *Blue River*, Ethan Canin's lyrical novel about the hidden underside of a brother bond, Edward, the "good" brother, secretly admires and yearns to be like his violent, womanizing "bad" brother, Lawrence. While their mother and her friend, Mrs. Silver, try to coax Edward toward a life of God and propriety, Lawrence is silently luring him toward another world entirely:

> But I wanted nothing of religion. I wanted what you came home with, Lawrence: I wanted the smell of smoke and liquor and cologne, and of a certain acrid sweat, like sweetgrass, that meant you'd been in battle. Mrs. Silver, more than anyone, tried to bring me to the church, but I would not come. Instead, I waited for you upstairs, while on the porch they prayed for you to change your ways. Their voices dropped in earnestness. If you'd been in a scrape, they prayed harder, and on those afternoons I would hear your name, their quiet verses, then your name again, and a flush would rise in me.[7]

Sibling hero worship usually wanes by early adulthood, when most individuals have made sufficient progress toward autonomy to begin to view a once-idealized brother or sister as a fallible human being. Yet frequently a sibling's impact lingers—in a personality trait emulated; a particular career, intellectual or athletic interest pursued; a set of attitudes toward the opposite sex; a characteristic style of relating to colleagues or friends. One thirty-four-year-old woman, who viewed her oldest sister as my "number one adviser" throughout her childhood and adolescence, still battles a knee-jerk tendency to attach herself to mentors:

> For a long time I tended to look for anybody who wanted to be my big sister. Desperately seeking sisters. In one job I tried to form a kind of partnership with an older woman who turned out to be just a competitor, who used everything I shared with her to promote herself, to undermine me. I was devastated because I figured she had looked at me the way I'd looked at her—as a sister.
> But it wasn't just about trust. It was also a confidence thing. I think having an older sister I looked up to so much was a good thing in the sense of having someone to

go to, but a handicap in the sense that I never relied on myself to figure out what was best for me. I had always looked for answers outside myself, and so I was still searching for that one who knew. You know, before I really start whatever it is, let me run it past *somebody.*

A "hero" sibling is rarely untouched by a brother's or sister's reverent identification. Admiration confers power, and the way one handles that power vis-à-vis siblings may help to set enduring goals and relationship patterns. For some, an adoring sibling provides a peerless training ground for manipulation: Lyndon Johnson habitually ordered his worshipful little brother and sisters to do all of his farm chores for him, and it wasn't lost on him that they usually complied.[8] But the experience of power also may be channeled in more constructive directions. As a trusted model, support or pioneer to a sibling "disciple," many individuals develop a strong sense of their capacities to teach, nurture or inspire.[9] For the young Simone de Beauvoir, the teacher-pupil bond she forged with her adoring younger sister, Poupette, helped her discover her gift for—and deep pleasure in—making an impact on the minds of others:

> Teaching my sister to read, write, and count gave me, from the age of six onwards, a sense of pride in my own efficiency. . . . When I started to change ignorance into knowledge, when I started to impress truths upon a virgin mind, I felt I was at last creating something real. I was not just imitating grown-ups: I was on their level, and my success had nothing to do with their good pleasure. . . . for the first time, I, too, was being of service to someone. I was breaking away from the passivity of childhood and entering the great human circle in which everyone is useful to everyone else.[10]

The long-term impact of identifying with a brother or sister is also affected by the degree of mutual attachment between the two siblings. Sadly, feelings are frequently *not* mutual. In a series of studies analyzed by Penn State psychologists Judy Dunn and Robert Plomin, both children and young adults were asked to judge the balance of power in their sibling bond through such questions as: Who has liked spending time with the other more? Who has been more supportive of the other? Who has started fights more often? In every study, siblings consistently reported striking disparities in affection, control, trust, supportiveness and anger. More important, researchers found that such imbalances were strongly linked to personality development: The greater the "sibling gap" in affection and in hostility, the more apt the less-loved sibling was to suffer low self-esteem, depression and a wide range of behavioral problems.[11]

In my own interviews, the deep yearning in childhood for a sibling's love and approval—and the failure to win it—was a remarkably oft-cited experience, one that most individuals felt had a searing impact on their self-concept and later relationships. As a child, one woman so adored her cold, distant older brother—"he seemed so bright, so quiet, so mysterious and wise"—that she literally tried to buy his love by turning over her allowance to him each week. When she tried to walk to school with him, he would silently cross the street and walk off; in her memory, "I was always trying to be a sister; he was always trying to be alone." She entered adolescence viewing men as foreign countries to be conquered, yet she became instantly contemptuous of any man who showed genuine affection for her. She was waiting for the "right one" to come along. Finally, he did: "When I was still in college, I met a man who was very quiet, very smart. He was a real loner. Distant in that slightly bored, 'I've got better things to do' sort of way. He looked like my brother, too. I married him."

If unrequited sibling affection can contribute to an enduring sense of unworthiness, consistent caring from an admired brother or sister may help to instill the happier quality of self-confidence—especially among one's peers. While a parent's love may communicate the fundamental message that "you're good," affection from a respected sibling is a more specialized stamp of approval, one that conveys "you're fun, you're cool, you're worth spending time with" as a comrade and an equal, not only as a family member. The impact of such sibling acceptance may be particularly critical for those whose other peer relationships are troubled in childhood or adolescence,[12] as a thirty-eight-year-old woman well remembers:

> The hardest time for me in school was from when I was eleven till I was about fourteen. There was no question that I was one of the kids that got picked on the most and it was definitely horrible. My old sense that I was okay was from spending time with Susan.
>
> She basically got me through that period in my life. I knew I had one ally, and because she was at the same school, I would hang out with her to avoid having to face the girls in my class. She provided me with that unquestioning "I care about you. I think you're okay." She didn't always have to say it; just being with her made me feel that way. I could count on her when I couldn't count on anybody.
>
> I think I got from her a very basic feeling that I'm an okay person. Somebody has always thought that and has reflected back to me that I'm somebody special. I don't know where else I would've gotten it in my family. My mother always made me feel that she cared, but it was like "You're my little baby." But it was Susan who gave me confidence in the world, out in public. I was very proud of the fact that I had an older sister who was so close to me and who liked me. By the time I got to college, I really did feel that I was worth being friends with.

Sometimes, sibling identification can go too far. Some brothers and sisters actually experience each other as a mirror image or "double," a phenomenon that is usually associated with identical twins but can also occur between nontwins who have never had the chance to develop a sense of their own distinctiveness. This may occur when parents consistently treat children as an undifferentiated mass, a fate most likely to befall closely spaced siblings of the same gender—"the girls" or "the boys." More often, however, siblings become psychologically "stuck together" because of extreme mutual dependence from an early age, usually arising out of a vacuum of parental care. Since any degree of separation is experienced as a profound abandonment, many such siblings enter adulthood still emotionally fused.

While from an outsider's perspective such "tight" sibling bonds may appear enviably intimate, genuine intimacy requires a sharing of the self. In fused relationships, by contrast, Carol Gilligan observes, "There is no self to share with another; instead, the other is required to bring the self into being."[13] The stunting and painful impact of such fusion was movingly described by Marianne, a forty-three-year-old teacher who is still extricating herself from a lifelong "emotional twinship" with her thirty-nine-year-old brother, Tim. The children of an abusive, alcoholic father and a chronically depressed mother, the two siblings grew up as each other's only reliable source of affection. Even when they left home for college and other friends and interests should have beckoned, Marianne and Tim couldn't break free of each other:

> He was like my lover. He was my love. I was at Temple and he was at Georgetown, and we'd be on the phone all the time, tons of times, back and forth, Philly to Washington, Washington to Philly. I would go down to visit him; he would come up to visit me. We talked on the phone three or four times a week, no big deal. At the time, it seemed okay. If somebody had said to me, "Your relationship with your brother is very enmeshed and extreme," I'd have said, "Don't be ridiculous, this is love." Sibling love. But this is not.
>
> It was much weirder than that. Much, much freakier. He would talk about my experiences like they were his experiences. He would go into great detail about some big revelation he'd had and I would say, "Wait a minute, that was *my* epiphany!" And I did the same thing with him. We also looked a lot alike then, both tall and thin with real curly hair. Sometimes we would look at each other in the mirror and he'd put his arm around me and say, "Which twin has the Toni?"

As long as the emotional twinship remained mutual, Marianne existed in a kind of emotional bubble, isolated from the rest of the world, yet safe and "real" in the knowledge of her brother's adoration. The shattering crisis came three years ago, when Tim, who is gay, fell in love for the first time:

> He met Jack and I didn't know it. He wasn't telling me. What I noticed was that what used to be four, five times a week on the phone turned into one, two times a week, and then less. When I finally met Jack I saw clearly that he had chosen somebody over me and I was absolutely enraged. I hated him. I hated what was happening to us. There was nothing he could say to make me feel better. It was true. He was replacing me.
>
> I was no longer Number Only. I was now just a sister and he had a life.

The crisis pushed Marianne into therapy, where she recognized for the first time how emotionally welded she was to her brother, to the point that she felt herself "falling apart" without his constant presence. Part of her separation struggle involves discovering now, at age forty-three, the ways in which she is distinctly different from her brother, with strengths and quirks and passions that are authentically hers—and hers alone. For Marianne, this process is sometimes exhilarating and just as often frightening; in any case, she acknowledges, "There's no going back. This is the only way you get to be you."

Most of us embark on this sibling differentiation process less painfully, and much earlier in our lives. In fact, the majority of individuals I talked with emphasized how "opposite" they had always felt from a sibling in certain domains of personality, even as they strongly identified in other areas. Research backs up this common perception of sibling contrasts: In one study of 383 college students by Columbia University psychologist Frances Fuchs Schachter, well over half of the sample reported feeling fundamentally different from their siblings in personality, based on their ratings of self and sibling on such items as good-bad, cheerful-depressed, active-passive, rugged-delicate, tense-relaxed, introverted-extroverted, conventional-unconventional and achieving-nonachieving.[14] While these contrasts are often explained as the result of "having nothing in common" or being "born opposites," in fact, the experience of growing up with brothers and sisters is apt to profoundly influence the development of those differences—as well as the way one feels about the "self" that emerges in relation to a sibling.

One way this happens is through parental assignment of roles to each child in the family. Many of us are given several roles along different dimensions, including achievement (the scholar, the artist, the jock); behavior (the devil, the angel, the loner, the clown); and family function (the caretaker, the peacemaker, the scapegoat). While a child's observable trait is often the basis for a particular role, the two are not synonymous: A trait becomes a role when a set of specific expectations is attached to it. Very often, children's roles fulfill unspoken, often unconscious parental needs. A child who enjoys drawing may be labeled "the artist" because her mother is—or always wanted to be—an artist. Similarly, a child may be assigned a negative role, such as "the wild one," that signifies a quality that a parent fears or cannot accept in himself or herself. Bank and Kahn write, "Each child ultimately absorbs a unique blend of what the parents hate and love about themselves. . . . the advantage of having siblings is that no one child has to be the sole bearer of the family projection process."[15]

Nonetheless, no child escapes notice of his or her own roles and those of his or her siblings—and such roles are rarely value-free. Arising as they often do from parental identifications and fears, most roles are clearly stamped by parents as "good," "tolerable" or "unacceptable." Such ratings may well invoke insidious, identity-shaping comparisons: If your brother or sister is the "smart one" and intellectual prowess is what is most valued in your family, what does that mean about you? Does it make you, by comparison, the "dumb one," even if no one says it outright? That is precisely what David, a fifty-four-year-old builder who grew up in the shadow of a brilliant, favored older sister, concluded about himself:

> Beth was—is—a very bright person. Very good at school, very questioning, always able to put things to-

gether very quickly. For both of my parents, learning and knowing is what it's all about. Both of them are enormous readers, have an insatiable drive to learn. And I couldn't read. I don't think I read a book until I was in the tenth grade. I could do mechanical things very well, which nobody else in my family could do or cared about. I was busy taking apart things and putting them back together, and everybody else was busy reading their brains out.

I remember being at the dinner table, where my sister and father would have endless conversations about politics and world affairs and art. Their lives, when they were together, were very full. They'd be talking about some theater thing: Who are the actors? What have they done before? What were the reviews like? Beth was still in *grade school* when she was doing this. I think she could read before she was born. [Chuckles.] And I just couldn't participate at all. I felt very lonely and not very smart.

And I wasn't considered smart. My attention span wasn't too long. I couldn't do school things, and my parents would get very angry: "Why can't you learn?" They didn't say "like Beth," but the comparison felt very explicit to me. There was a lot of anxiety: What's going to become of him? What's he going to *do*? Nobody cared that, for example, when I was only eleven I got an electric train and I set the whole thing up myself. I put the wiring together, I put the track together, I built bridges, I fixed anything that broke. Or that out in the backyard, I made entire, complicated towns and road systems out of the hedges. By the time I was in high school, I had become very quiet, very uncommunicative. I didn't know it then, but I was seriously depressed. I really felt I wasn't good at anything, except building things, and that didn't count.

David remained depressed for several years. It was only in his late twenties that he began—with Beth's support—to unravel the family sources of his "dumb me" conviction, and finally to stop using his sister as the gold standard of intelligence and competence. The parental favoritism that so negatively influenced his identity is not uncommon: In one study of families of children who participated in "gifted" school programs, parents reported feeling closer to, and prouder of, their "gifted" child, and consistently gave more recognition to that child than to his or her siblings. The study's author, psychologist Dewey Cornell, concluded, "The positive labeling of one child in the family as 'gifted' may indirectly label the sibling as 'nongifted.' To the extent that giftedness is a prized attribute in the family, the nongifted sibling of the gifted child is at a disadvantage."[16] The study's findings strongly supported this assertion: Children with a "gifted" brother or sister were found to be far less well adjusted—more anxious, tense, frustrated, shy and easily upset—than children who were not raised alongside a celebrated sibling.

In many families, one brother or sister is the designated "sick one" or, when behavior is the issue, the "bad one." While such labels often serve the purpose of masking a family's more pervasive problems—i.e., *you're* the problem, *we're* not—nonetheless, the presence of such a child in the family can be a chronically exhausting and demoralizing experience. To help keep the family from flying apart, another sibling is frequently designated the "well-adjusted one" or the "good one," assigned to keep the peace or be the solid citizen in whom parents can take pride. In *The Prince of Tides*, Tom Wingo reflects on the way his sister, Savannah, was "nominated to be the lunatic" in the family, while he was to contribute a countervailing steadiness:

> My designation in the family was normality. I was the balanced child, drafted into the ranks for leadership, for coolness under fire, stability. "Solid as a rock," my mother would describe me to her friends, and I thought the description was perfect. I was courteous, bright, popular, and religious. I was the neutral country, the family Switzerland.[17]

As Tom Wingo did, many siblings of disturbed or disabled children embrace their "good kid" role. Not only does it boost their status in the family, but it jibes with their own developing vision of themselves. In contrast to a sister who is mentally retarded or a brother who chronically makes trouble at home or school, one may develop a powerful, valued sense of oneself as competent, strong, helpful and mature. In other cases, one sibling's "problem" label may save another from having to wear it. In my own family, I was known as a rebel and a heretic, but I never felt stigmatized by those designations; on the contrary, I felt that they defined much of what made me interesting and worthwhile. I am only now recognizing how much my brother Bob contributed to my capacity to feel good about this outspoken, nonconforming aspect of my personality.

Bob, four years younger than I, was the quintessential "bad child," a genuine wild thing who, as a small baby, stiffened and screamed at the gentlest touch. Quite likely he was born with an immature nervous system, but in the 1950s—the pre–infant psychology, pre–family systems era—he was viewed by everyone in our family and a long list of pediatricians, teachers and neighbors as simply "destructive." Certain recurring scenes stand out: Bob's daily tantrum on our living room rug, where he would shriek for hours and scratch his cheeks until they bled; whole rooms in our house dismantled after some argument that my brother felt he had lost; my extraordinarily patient mother suddenly retreating to her bedroom so that, I only now realize, she could prevent herself from striking him. The impact of Bob on our family was enormous and multifaceted, but one by-product was that next to my brother, *I always looked good*. I could sass my teachers, I could flunk conduct, I could run away from home for long enough to spur a small search party—and get off with a mere talking-to from my parents. No matter what I did or refused to do, I could never be "badder" than Bob. At great cost to him, my brother was my permanent buffer against a problem-child identity.

Because I was similar enough to Bob to avoid being labeled as his opposite, I never was pressed into service as the "good child." In this I was very lucky. For while the role of family angel may confer certain benefits, it is also apt to exact a price. Angels, after all, are invisible beings. Parents are frequently so overwhelmed with the demands of a disturbed or disabled child that they may subtly or explicitly encourage their "good" child to be excessively self-reliant, "the one we never have to worry about." Carolyn, a forty-four-year-old social services administrator who grew up as the "well sister" of a severely asthmatic younger brother, traces her experience of being profoundly unheard and unseen:

From the time I was four, I had this little brother who was sickly and needed all this attention. He would have an attack and everybody would rush to the hospital. Then he would come home and live in an oxygen tent for months. He'd get a little bit better, and then it would start all over again. My parents were always hovering over him. He was close to death many times.

I felt like an unnecessary being. My mom was always fretting over him. She just wasn't there. And so when I was eight or nine, I began to feign illness. I have it in my childhood diary: *Got sick today, but Mother wouldn't let me stay home.* My diary is filled with my attempts to be sick, my stomachaches, my headaches, my earaches, my this or that. Once in a while it worked. And I got dry tea and toast, but that was about it.

My feeling was that I had to be an instant grown-up. I remember very vividly how solicitous my mother always was with Gary, saying, "Don't do this, honey, you might get sick." But with me it was always, "Come now, Carolyn, you can handle it." To the point where my brother says now that I had a business suit on since I was four. I took care of business. I had to be quiet. I couldn't make noise. I didn't invite friends over. I didn't cry.

Carolyn entered adulthood with her suit still on, a perpetual big sister who took care of everybody's business but her own:

I went through my twenties and thirties not knowing how to ask for attention or love, or how to get it. In my earlier relationships, the crummy ones, I thought I had to make dinner for them, sew buttons on their clothes, wait up for them if they were late. I did expect a little something back from female friends, but men were definitely needy. They had to be taken care of. Until I would finally come apart and they would leave.

At work, it was the same thing. Strong caretaker. I will take care of business *for* you. I've always been able to do that well. Give it to me, *I'll* handle it. For years I quietly worked my petunias off with no recognition and I wondered, What's wrong here? I didn't get it. That I could ask for credit, praise, help, whatever it was I needed. No. I couldn't do that. I had to get sick to do that. Sicker, even, than my brother.

When I turned forty, I got a brain tumor. It's the crowning irony, isn't it? To get my mother's attention, everybody's attention—to be worth that—I had to get a brain tumor. I can't prove that, of course, but I really feel it. My body did that for me. And it was enough. I did get the message.

While the impact of Carolyn's identity as the self-sufficient "well sister" is more dramatic than most, her story underscores the life-shaping legacy of roles developed in relation to siblings. In many such cases, parents are key "identity brokers," assigning the valued or devalued roles that in turn influence the way siblings view each other—and themselves. But brothers and sisters don't always passively await such role assignments. Frequently, siblings are highly motivated to become different from a brother or a sister, and carve out a contrasting identity largely on their own.[18]

The motivation to become "not like you" often stems from a basic conflict: the need to shine in the family as a winner, and the simultaneous wish to avoid destructive sibling rivalry. Many siblings solve this dilemma through a process known in psychological parlance as "deidentification." By this process, one sibling surveys the territory to which another has already staked a claim—artistic talent, toe-the-line dependability, social skill—and develops a distinctly different, equally valued realm of personality or achievement in which he or she can reign supreme. If an older sister is "the jock" of the family, for example, her younger sister may steer clear of tennis and basketball courts and instead concentrate on developing her musical abilities. Even when siblings choose the same career, they often carve out noncompeting subterritories within it. One lawyer I interviewed, whose sister and brother are also attorneys, noted, "I'm the politically correct public defender; my sister's the academic, law review one; my brother is the corporate hotshot—we call him 'The Briefcase.' "

This turf-building process is not a question of creating an identity out of nothing, but rather of honing and highlighting particular qualities or skills one already possesses, and of *not* developing others that a sibling has already claimed. While this "niche-picking" process may not entirely eliminate rivalrous feelings, it does allow siblings to play them out more covertly, in ways that are less threatening to the relationship. Frances Fuchs Schachter, the Columbia University psychologist who developed the theory of sibling deidentification, observes, "by polarizing, the 'unconventional' sibling can feel superior to the other in originality or spontaneity, secretly viewing the other as banal or rigid, whereas the 'conventional' sibling can feel superior in responsibility or dependability, secretly viewing the other as wild or explosive."[19]

Not surprisingly, Schachter has found that deidentification is most common among siblings who are prime candidates for rivalry: first pairs, whose early competition is not diluted by the presence of other siblings; and same-sex siblings, who are apt to share a common set of socially valued goals and attributes. When I first came across these data I thought immediately of Donna and me. As a same-sex, closely spaced first pair who were often mistaken for twins, we had pressing reasons to find ways to tell ourselves apart. While our task was made easier by our very real temperamental differences— from babyhood I was notably noisier and less compliant than Donna—looking back, I can see that we probably exaggerated our differences and that each of us, moreover, imbued her own identity with special, superior virtue. As the "good" sister, Donna could easily cast herself as my moral better; as the "bad" one, I viewed myself as the queen of daring, the ultimate iconoclast. The faces we presented to the world were reflected back to us, reinforcing our polarized identities: Was it only a coincidence that my sister landed the Madonna role in our high school Christmas pageant, while I played the outspoken, malcontent Leonard in *The Man Who Married a Dumb Wife*?

That we played out these roles in such close and constant

proximity within our family probably only sharpened our contrasts, and may have had a constricting effect, too. I see now that Donna was so dependably thoughtful and helpful—the one who always tried to give our perpetually busy mother a break, the one who was always careful not to hurt our father's feelings—that I may not have developed those qualities to the degree I would have otherwise. My sister took care of it; the job got done without me. It seems equally likely that Donna may not have developed the part of her that is genuinely rebellious and resistant, in part because I played out that side of her *for* her. I remember how surprised I was when she told me, several years ago, how furious she, too, had been in the wake of our father's dinner-table monologues. Yet as long as I agitated on her behalf, she could remain safely silent. In recent years we have begun to talk about the artificial division of psychological labor that required each of us to live with a part of herself submerged, and we've begun to compare notes on our recent, conscious efforts to reclaim traits—my capacity for gentleness, her capacity to say *no*—that we once thought were the exclusive property of a sister.

Sibling influence resists easy, stay-put categories. With any one brother or sister, realms of identification and deidentification are apt to coexist: One might admiringly identify with an older sister's political ideals, for example, yet distance oneself from her confrontational mode of expressing them. Over time, too, this precise mix of "like me" and "not like me" influence may shift: the hipper-than-thou big brother whom one desperately imitated as a teenager may, by one's twenties or thirties, have lost his appeal as a model. To complicate matters still further, sibling influence is not always a one-on-one proposition. The more sisters and brothers one has, the more picking and choosing takes place, with each sibling offering different, critical pieces of information about who to be—or not to be.

No one, of course, is merely a collection of responses to a brother or a sister. Siblings are but one piece of the puzzle of self. Yet in our efforts to make sense of who we are and how we got that way, we frequently bypass our brothers and sisters, or pause too briefly to consider their imprint. "Oh, my *sister,"* we may groan or laugh or sigh at an encroaching memory, then hurriedly move on, change the subject, ponder the "real" forces that have shaped our lives. We forget that our siblings were our earliest comrades and competitors, heroes and antiheroes, mirrors and counterpoints—just as we, without a doubt, were once theirs.

# 4

# Male and Female: How Gender
# Shapes the Sibling Bond

In the beginning is the question: Is it a boy or a girl? . . .
There is no existence in our culture prior to and
separate from gender.

Ellyn Kaschak, *Engendered Lives*

Once upon a time, Marilyn's three siblings were the center of
her world. The youngest member of a close-knit, middle-class
African American family, she remembers her bonds with her
sisters and brother as warm, necessary and slightly magical,
"like we had this little team that nobody outside could ever
touch." Oldest sister Katherine was her most profound role
model, a scholar and seeker who "was always taking me
places, opening me up to something brand new." Next was
Terry, whom Marilyn laughingly calls her "worldly" sister, the
one who taught her how to dance, do her hair, figure out the
mystery of men. Finally and with just a trace of wistfulness,
she speaks of big brother Charlie, the hero of her youth, "the
one who took me through the woods on bikes with the dog,
and it would be kind of dangerous and kind of exciting and
nothing would ever happen to me because he was with me."

Much has changed since those early, leisurely days of bicy-
cle journeys and basement disco lessons. The four siblings are
scattered across two states, and Marilyn, now thirty-three, has
a husband, three children and a demanding job as advertising
manager of a small magazine. "So what are your relationships

like now with your sisters and brother?" I ask her. She laughs, only a shade embarrassed, as she admits that she and Katherine talk on the phone every single day. "She's in New York, I'm down here in Virginia, but we do it anyway," she says. "Early in the morning when the rates are still low, while we're getting ready for work and the kids off to school. Just to touch base." Marilyn is on the phone less often with her other sister, Terry—but only because they live a town apart and can visit frequently. "Sometimes I'll go over there for a whole day on the weekend, with my kids. We'll sit with each other all day long," she says, smiling with obvious pleasure.

There is a small silence. "Charlie is in New York, too," she says finally. "We speak less than once a month. Sometimes several months will go by." This clearly hurts her, bewilders her. She wonders aloud how the silences can stretch so long between her and the brother whom she loves so deeply—and who, she knows, loves her. "It's not his style," she ventures. "He's not as verbal." Yet Marilyn senses that there is more to it than that. When they do talk, she says, she is conscious that the conversations are very different from the ones she has with her sisters. "We mostly talk about what he's doing on his job," she says. "The next adventure, the next mission he's going on in his career. He's in sales, too, and he'll tell me about the pitch he's going to make next week and how much money it might make for him. But we don't talk much about how he really feels about any of it. Or about what's happening with him as a *person*. His marriage, his future—all the things I know about my sisters.

"With my sisters, we'll talk about *anything*," she says, smiling broadly again. "All the little intricacies of what you're going through and where you're headed. I know their loves and their hates and the things that make them suffer, their crying, their children, their friends and their friends' children; I know how they feel about all of these things. Maybe we're *too* much in each other's business sometimes," she admits with a laugh. "But whatever it is, very little of it goes on with my brother. With Charlie, it's just sort of 'how ya doin', just checkin' in.' "

Indifference, however, is not the issue. "All the *feelings* are there between us," Marilyn emphasizes. "The times we do visit and then have to say our goodbyes, my brother hugs me, real tight, you know, real solid, like he wants to take me with him. Or like he wants to hug me forever. He wants to really make it last. He wants me to know how he feels about me." She is silent for a moment as she tries to puzzle it out: How can there be such warmth and caring between the two of them, yet such unbridgeable distance?

Marilyn's sense of missed connections with her brother, as well as her deeply intimate bonds with each of her sisters, is very much her own particular story—but it also sounds the themes of a larger one. It is the story of sisters and brothers as women and men, and of the way growing up female or male in our culture profoundly shapes the needs, expectations, strengths and vulnerabilities that each of us brings to our sibling relationships. It is about the ways in which sisters experience and build the bond differently from brothers, and the ways in which those differences influence attachment to one's siblings, responses to rivalry, and the ways in which conflict is confronted and resolved—or is not. It is about, therefore, the way the particular "gender mix" of each sibling bond—sister pair, brother pair, or sister-brother duo—uniquely and necessarily imprints itself on a number of key realms of the relationship.

It is also a largely untold story. Gender, which refers to culturally defined femininity and masculinity rather than one's biological sex, is not generally understood to influence critically either the sibling bond or the kind of psychological impact brothers and sisters have on each other. In part, this is because mass-media coverage of sibling issues has focused almost exclusively on birth order research, which has fed a widespread public assumption that chronology alone—Who's on first? Who's the squeezed-out middle kid? Who's the coddled baby?—is the key to understanding oneself vis-à-vis one's siblings.

Yet in fairness to the media, it is only recently that sibling researchers themselves have begun to pay attention to gender. In my survey of the psychological research on siblings over the past decade, I counted 98 birth order studies, 185 studies on the impact of a handicapped or chronically ill sibling, 65 studies on the impact of childhood sibling bereavement—and a total of 34 studies that made gender a major subject of inquiry. Significantly, however, sibling gender differences *do* frequently emerge in studies that are primarily interested in some other aspect of the bond, such as rivalry or ethnicity or interactions among elderly siblings. Yet these illuminating findings have gone largely unnoticed: Of the scholarly and professional books published on the sibling bond over the past decade, the majority treat gender as a peripheral issue to be quickly noted, then dismissed, and a few do not even list "sister," "brother," "sex roles" or "gender" in their indexes.[1]

Such silence is both baffling and wholly unjustifiable. Gender is fundamental to the nature and course of every relationship we have, including those with our brothers and sisters. Across race, class and culture, conceptions of masculinity and femininity are among the most powerful organizers of identity and behavior; indeed psychologist Kenneth Keniston observes, "Gender is the first, most unchanging and deepest of all the meanings attached to human beings."[2] That this meaning deeply influences nonblood relationships is already apparent: When we ponder our ties with intimate partners, for example, many of us readily consider the influence of societal norms for masculinity and femininity on everything from conversational styles to attitudes toward "commitment" to divisions of labor within the relationship. We may celebrate, rail against, or work to diminish these differences, but few of us deny them.

Yet when we seek to understand our bonds with brothers and sisters, rarely does gender come to mind. Ensconced as we are in a culture that idealizes the family, we tend to assume that blood bonds are somehow beyond the reach of hard-edged masculine and feminine categories, with all of the divisions, polarizations and inequities that they embody. Yet the very opposite is true. For it is *within* our childhood families that we learn, first and most deeply, the meaning of being female and being male in our culture, and our bonds with sisters and brothers both reflect and help to shape that primary education. This is not to discount other critical influences on ties among brothers and sisters, for family background, ethnicity, class, older-younger issues, personality "meshing" and a host of other factors remain enormously significant. Nonetheless, we still need to ask: What does it mean that a sister is a woman, that a brother is a man? For to continue to dismiss or marginalize the impact of gender is to leave huge holes in our understanding of why siblings form the kinds of bonds they do, leave the kinds of legacies they do, and, as adults, experience their continuing connections and conflicts the way they do.

When people speak of their sibling relationships, they often begin by talking about "closeness." They want to be closer, they never were close, they wonder why they do—or do not—feel emotionally connected to a brother or a sister. While sibling intimacy has been linked to numerous factors, one consistent finding that is often overlooked is that sister pairs tend to share the closest bond, followed by brother-sister duos, with brother pairs the most loosely connected of the three combinations. These gender differences in intimacy are often dramatic, occur across social classes, ethnic groups and birth order compositions, and persist throughout the life span.[3] In my own interviews, I found an interesting pattern: Sisters of sisters *and* brothers of brothers were equally likely to define their bond as "really close" or their sibling as "my best friend," but women and men seemed to mean something quite different by these descriptions of their same-sex tie. Women with a "close" sister relationship spoke of lengthy conversations full of mutual self-revelation and emotional support as well as the pure pleasure of "just talk"; they described an empathy rooted in a fierce mutual identification; they conveyed, moreover, a sense of *necessity* about the relationship, a centrality that pushed them to maintain a continuous, regular connection. Natalie, a sixty-year-old legal secretary, tries to articulate what it means to be close to her sixty-four-year-old sister, Claire, who lives at the opposite end of the state from her:

> When we get together we just *glom.* We talk intensely to each other. When my son was small, he described our relationship wonderfully: "When Aunt Claire comes to visit, it's like you take her and you put her in the playpen, and you jump in with her, and nobody else can get in!"

Isn't that vivid? He said it all. It was the whole thing. I wanted her all to myself.

We have this ongoing need for closeness that isn't really transferable. There are things you just don't discuss with your husband or children the way you do with your sister. When one of us is in pain the other aches; I don't know how you get that, but we have it. And I suspect that the deeper you've ever gone with anybody, the higher you can also feel. We can get insane together; there is a joy that nobody understands. If we stopped talking, if we got mad at each other, I could last a couple of days at most.

By contrast, closely connected brothers are more apt to view their relationship as "outward bound," a comradeship expressed through the sharing of activities and interests rather than intimacies, and bolstered by the provision of practical support rather than emotional nurturance. Compared with sisters, brothers also tend to be comfortable with longer stretches of absence and silence. One thirty-four-year-old photographer described his "very close" bond with his thirty-six-year-old brother, who is creative director of an ad agency, this way:

When Pete last visited, he wanted to play a lot of tennis, so I said, "Okay, well, let's take the tennis court tour of southeastern Ohio." So we got in the car and spent the whole day stopping at six or seven different public tennis courts, playing a few games at each one. Another day we hiked all around Lake Erie. We had a wonderful time. It's funny, but I already imagine these are things we'll do when we're retired. [Chuckles.] We'll probably go hiking as old men together.

We like to talk, too, and a lot of it revolves around the creative interests we share. We really, really enjoy getting together and discussing advertising. We'll look at a television or magazine ad and we'll analyze it together, and Pete will frequently ask my opinion about a campaign he's doing. We'll rip it apart; we'll put it back together. It's one of the major avenues for us to express our affection for each other.

I only get to see him once or twice a year, so in between we use the phone. We're both busy, so lots of times it's leaving messages on each other's machines, back and forth. But we do try to talk at least every couple of months.

The sister-brother bond ranks squarely in the middle of the sibling "intimacy hierarchy," yet it may be the most challenging to negotiate to the satisfaction of both parties. Even when a sister and brother love each other deeply—as Marilyn and Charlie, described at the beginning of this chapter, obviously do—their bond often suffers from a frustrating mismatch of needs and goals. There is frequently a sense of chronic push-pull, with a sister straining for a particular style of relating that her brother is not prepared to return. Marilyn muses:

It's like we define things differently. What I think of as exploring an issue—you know, looking at all the many dimensions—Charlie sees as whining, wasting time muddling around. A couple of times I called him with a problem—once with my job, another time with my husband. What I really wanted him to do was help me kind of play with it, help me to try on things. You know, "What if you did this, how would that feel?"

But Charlie's response is to want to kill my boss, punch out my husband. When I had the job problem, he told me to just quit, get on a plane and come to New York, and he would help me get situated and start a new life. [Sighs.] He's gotta *do* something, save me, gotta make it happen *now.*

Marilyn's and Charlie's mutually misread signals reflect Deborah Tannen's observation of "the difference in what women and men think talk is for: To him, talk is for information. . . . But to her, talk is for interaction."[4] Brothers and sisters frequently disagree not only on conversational goals, but also its permissible content. Topics that a sister may be eager to explore—the progress of relationships, the intricacies of family emotional history, personal doubts or fears—are issues that her brother may be reluctant to discuss. This clash of needs can result in persistent, unspoken tension between a sister and brother: If she pushes for "deep talk," he may feel his privacy invaded and find reasons to avoid her, yet if she adjusts herself to his conversational comfort zone, she may feel squelched. When I interviewed one brother-sister pair in their late twenties who agreed that they were "best friends," I asked them what kinds of things they talked about when they got together.

"We're not the kind of brother and sister that's gonna go out and sit at a diner with a cuppa coffee for three hours," the young man responded firmly. "We're just not. We don't play Freuds with each other, let's explore this and that. We're not really that way—and in a way I think it's good. You don't want to get too sappy." While he was saying this, his younger sister, sitting next to him, was quiet. When he finished talking, she simply said, "Besides, I'd hate to bother him."

Of course, not all sibling duos fit neatly into the gender-typed categories described above. I spoke with men who actively sought and valued emotional intimacy with their brothers, as well as with members of brother-sister duos who reported that they could discuss "just about anything" and felt no significant clash of relationship styles or needs. Among sister pairs, several were emotionally distant, either because of unresolved tensions or, less often, because one sister simply disliked the other and had no interest in pursuing the bond. (Interestingly, however, every woman who reported a "close" sister bond described the degree of intimacy that characterized Natalie's bond with her sister, Claire.)

Clearly, gender alone neither causes nor blocks sibling intimacy, and many other factors help to nudge the bond in one direction or another. Gender does, however, powerfully *predispose* brothers and sisters toward differing degrees of connectedness and separateness. Among those I interviewed, many more women than men experienced high levels of emotional sharing and support in their sibling relationships. Moreover, among those who specifically reported a "close" sibling tie, sisters tended to describe a bond that included more self-disclosure and that was more emotionally central to their lives than the bonds described by brothers.

The powerful influence of gender on sibling relationships is mirrored in research findings on another important peer bond—friendship. There psychologists have found strikingly similar gender patterns: Ties between women tend to be most intimate and confiding, followed by those between opposite-sex friends, with male friendships least likely to include emotional sharing.[5] In *Just Friends*, Lillian Rubin's classic study of American friendship, she states that "women's friendships with each other rest on shared intimacies, self-revelation, nurturance and emotional support. . . . In contrast, men's relationships are marked by shared activities. What they do may differ by age and class, but that they tend to *do* rather than *be* together is undeniable."[6] A 1991 survey of fifty-seven studies on the subject of self-disclosure suggests the sheer size of the gender gap in intimacy: More than half of the studies found that women shared more information about themselves than did men, while only four percent—a total of two studies— found men to be more self-disclosing than women.[7]

What accounts for such persistent differences in male and female modes of relating? Such contrasts were once viewed as merely "natural" and therefore immutable, based entirely on inborn sex differences that automatically caused men to strive for autonomy and women to seek affiliation. But while research suggests that some biologically based sex differences affecting behavior may exist, they are too few and too small to explain the significant contrasts in women's and men's behaviors on so many fronts, including those influencing relationships.[8] As Robert Stoller has noted, the efforts of "biological systems, organized prenatally in a masculine or feminine direction, are almost always . . . too gentle in humans to withstand the more powerful forces of environment in human development."[9] Among the most potent of these environmental forces, numerous researchers and theorists concur, are cultural mandates that slot boys and girls into different, mutually exclusive roles and modes of behavior. Through this process of gender-role socialization, human capacities are artificially split into the camps of "masculinity" and "femininity," which, even today, permit only limited spillover or cross-fertilization.

As most readers are well acquainted with the concept of gender roles, the briefest account will make clear the way they operate to curtail men's human potential for intimacy. Psychologist Robert Brannon concisely summarized the behavioral components of the masculine role as (1) "No Sissy Stuff" (avoid behaviors even remotely perceived as feminine); (2) "Be a Big Wheel" (achieve success and status); (3) "Be a Sturdy Oak" (suppress emotion, cultivate self-reliance); and (4) "Give 'em Hell" (be aggressive).[10] The injunctions to steer clear of "feminine" behaviors and to keep a lid on emotions explicitly forbid the free expression of feelings, particularly the "sissy" feelings of fear, sadness or loneliness that expose emotional vulnerability and thereby threaten a man's oaklike posture. Meanwhile, the remaining injunctions to "be a big wheel" and "give 'em hell" exhort men to prove their manhood by establishing themselves as better—stronger, smarter, richer, more powerful—than other people. Taken together, these mandates for masculinity systematically teach men to separate themselves from others—by simultaneously "besting" them and hiding from them.

While boys are learning to stand alone and win, girls are busy practicing the arts of caring and connection. A cross-cultural survey of child-rearing practices in 110 societies documents that from early childhood, girls are more likely than boys to be assigned nurturant tasks such as caring for younger siblings and helping older relatives.[11] And while many women now pursue careers and other activities that reflect a shift toward acknowledgment of their own needs, the injunction to "give" does not soften. Jean Baker Miller notes that in her psychiatry practice, women of all backgrounds continue to struggle to pass this acid test of femininity:

Women constantly confront themselves with questions about giving. Am I giving enough? Can I give enough? Why don't I give enough? They frequently have deep fears about what this must mean about them. They are upset if they feel they are not givers. They wonder what would happen if they were to stop giving, to even consider not giving? The idea is frightening and the consequences too dire to consider.[12]

While many women profoundly and rightly resent the societal *requirement* to take care of others, most find genuine satisfaction in the emotional connections that tend to flow from an orientation toward others. More than men do, women actively pursue intimate relationships. A number of theorists believe that gender-role socialization, all by itself, can't entirely explain this more committed bond-building behavior. One must look as well, they believe, to critical differences in the early psychological development of boys and girls. According to this theory, first articulated by Nancy Chodorow,[13] because women are the primary caretakers of infants, nearly all men and women experience a woman as their first emotional attachment—the person with whom they identify so deeply and completely as to feel "one" with her. But as a young child emerges from babyhood to begin the work of forming a distinct gender identity and sense of self, a girl goes about these tasks differently than a boy does.

A female child is able psychologically to "become" a girl while continuing to identify closely with her mother, because they share the same gender. A girl's developing sense of herself as female, then, occurs in the context of continuing emotional attachment to her mother. Consequently, she grows up tending to experience herself as fundamentally connected to other people rather than as basically separate from them, and deriving both deep comfort and a sense of self-worth from the maintenance of intimate connections. A little boy's passage to masculinity, by contrast, requires him to *break* his first and most profound attachment and source of identity. Since his mother now represents the tabooed feminine—the opposite of what he is mandated to become—he must detach from her and begin to identify with his designated model of manhood, his father. To protect himself from the pain of this first, wrenching separation, a boy constructs a barrier wall against feeling and attachment that does not readily crumble. Psychologist Lillian Rubin writes of this "man-making" process, "This is the beginning of the development of the kind of ego boundaries so characteristic of men—boundaries that are fixed and firm, that rigidly separate self from other, that circumscribe not only his relationships with others but his connection to his inner emotional life as well."[14]

An appreciation of the impact of this early psychological drama does not negate the shaping power of gender-role socialization. Rather, the two influences tend to work in tandem, mutually forming and reinforcing men's and women's contrasting postures toward intimacy and separateness. For example, the young boy's need to excise the feminine in himself—his identification with his mother—*in order* to become masculine may set up a man to feel easily and deeply threatened by any felt trace of "femininity" in himself. But the culture powerfully reinforces this fearful vigilance by defining masculinity, to a significant degree, as an absence of femininity ("No Sissy Stuff") and by monitoring boys with particular zeal for any signs of gender-role transgression.[15] Similarly, girls may be primed for empathetic connections by their close, unbroken identification with their mothers, yet cultural mandates to "think of others" and to "stop being selfish!" make it difficult for many women, even today, *not* to consider the needs and feelings of others first without a massive attack of guilt. In short, psyche and society work hand in hand to shape "masculine" men and "feminine" women, a task that involves, as much as anything, separating both sexes from large pieces of themselves.

I do not mean to suggest, however, that women's and men's customary modes of relating are immutable. While it seems likely that fundamental stances toward intimacy—female trust and male wariness—that emerge from the construction of gender identity will continue as long as women are the primary caregivers for young children, it is equally true that individuals are not cast in stone by kindergarten age. Throughout our lives, we continue to be molded by experiences, relationships, ideas and crises that are significant to us; to deny the possibility for change flies in the face of the steady progress that many women and men have made during the last few decades in expanding their behavioral repertoires. In my own sibling interviews, I was impressed by the evolution toward mutuality that took place in a number of relationships because of a brother's successful efforts to become more emotionally available, or a sister's refusal to continue doing all of the "feeling work" in the relationship.

* * *

Nonetheless, the impact of gender-shaping processes on the sibling bond is undeniable, and is felt from the earliest years of the relationship. Even as young children, sisters spend much more time than brothers do caring for, playing and talking with, and giving support to their siblings.[16] In my interviews, younger siblings tended to have intense, detailed memories of the way an older sister or brother responded—or failed to respond—to their bids for nurturance, and to link such early experiences to the tenor of their current tie with that sibling. With a few notable exceptions, older sisters were remembered as providing some measure of sustenance and companionship, as a thirty-seven-year-old woman remembers:

There was a sense of comfort. Part of it was that Sarah was always interested in her sisters. So if she was dating somebody, right from the beginning the guys who dated her had to accept us. She would take us places with them—to the zoo, to the movies. Mom made her do some of this and I'm sure it annoyed her sometimes, but I don't think she thought of me as a pest. There was just a sense that she'd try to include me.

She also gave me information. Sarah didn't get into as much trouble with my mother as I did, so obviously she was doing something right that I needed to know. She would help me get some perspective. Just to tell me that, you know, it wasn't as bad as I thought it was and sort of try to help me stay out of trouble a little bit. She took care of me that way.

By contrast, themes of distance and longing permeated siblings' memories of their older brothers. This was not a universal recollection: Some individuals from close families, in particular, recalled a big brother's protectiveness or generous willingness to include them in his adventures. But many more remembered feeling summarily shut out of an older brother's world, especially during his adolescence. Exclusion was enforced by physical means—locked bedroom doors and frequent absences from the house—and also by emotional ones, particularly a brother's frustrating silences. Only a few siblings recalled relying on an older brother for emotional nurturance, and one thirty-year-old man still vividly remembers the incident that taught him *not* to do so:

> When I was in junior high school I read this Ann Landers column about how older brothers should help their younger brothers out by spending fifteen minutes a day of quality time with them. I remember thinking, "How hilarious," since my brother was never around—but at the same time I liked knowing that he *should*. Well, later that year my girlfriend announced that she was moving away, out of state. She was my first girlfriend and I was hysterical, just really upset. So I came home and my eyes were all bloodshot and my face was red and I could hardly talk. And Mark was sitting there in the den with a friend, and I went over and I said [whispering], "Could I just have fifteen minutes with you?" And he laughed. Not nasty, just like, "You gotta be *kidding*."

At every stage of life, brothers tend to put less energy and sheer elbow grease into the relationship than sisters do. In her study of sibling relationships in young adulthood, psychologist Joan Pulakos found that compared to brothers, sisters spent more time pursuing activities with siblings, and were more apt to "just talk" with a sister or brother as well as to discuss important relationships and decisions; overall, they valued the relationship more.[17] A recent Gallup Poll on family ties found that more than three times as many American women as men are in daily contact with their siblings, and that men are more likely to "never talk with" a brother or sister.[18] In later life, moreover, both men and women are much more apt to choose to live with a sister than with a brother.[19] One gets a sense of sisters as the linchpins of many sibling bonds, operating at or close to the center of many individuals' lives and meeting the major share of people's needs for continuing sibling connection.

The Pulakos study also found that sisters were more apt to talk *about* their siblings than were brothers, a pattern I encountered repeatedly in my interviewing process. On hearing that I was writing a book about the adult sibling bond, many women volunteered to talk with me about their own relationships, and nearly all I approached greeted the prospect of an interview enthusiastically, as an opportunity to further clarify issues they were already thinking about or trying to resolve with a brother or a sister. While some men were equally eager to be interviewed, many more insisted that talking with them would be "a waste of time," since they hadn't thought much about the relationship and therefore didn't believe that they had anything interesting to say about it; others simply told me that the issue was too private to discuss. Overall, approximately half of the men I approached for an interview "about a sibling relationship that is significant to you" refused my request; not a single woman did.

Given the more consistent attention and nurturing that sisters bring to the relationship, it is not surprising that siblings of both sexes tend to value and need the sister bond more—and to be more influenced by it. Both women and men tend to name a sister as the sibling whom they are most emotionally attached to, feel most acceptance and approval from, and can confide in most readily.[20] In later life, sisterhood may grow still more powerful: In a study of sibling bonds among the elderly that paid careful attention to gender differences, Purdue University psychologist Victor Cicirelli found that the closer a man or woman felt to a sister, the *less* likely he or she was to be depressed. Feeling close to a brother, meanwhile, had no such protective effect for either sex.[21]

These findings, which held across varying educational levels, birth orders and family sizes, suggest not only a deeper attachment to sisters, but also the particularly potent effects of sisterly nurturing on older individuals, whose parents and spouses may no longer be alive to provide critical "I care about you" functions. Sisters are simply more apt than brothers to take on the dozens of small and large "kinkeeping" chores—the just-to-say-hi notes, the checkup calls during an illness, the invitations to dinner—that are performed in the service of relationship maintenance and that for some recipients may make the difference between feeling connected and feeling utterly alone.

While the differential effects of brotherly and sisterly nurturing have begun to be documented in the sibling literature, most such studies limit their focus to the impact of *having* a sister or a brother—not what it feels like to *be* one. My own interviews suggest that in several key realms, sisters do experience the sibling bond differently than brothers do. Sisters, by and large, are more emotionally bonded to their siblings than brothers are; in several instances, women described to me a level of sibling attachment that closely seconded the depth of connection and need they felt for parents. In fact, in one of the few studies that has directly addressed this issue, college-age women reported feeling as close to their "closest sibling" as they did to their mothers—and significantly closer than they felt to their fathers.[22] Indeed, to have her sister and brother in her life, one woman told me, was

> to know that I can be loved very, very deeply and very greatly beyond a parental love. And that I can be really, really important to someone, and give that back. . . . These are things that I think you usually think about in terms of a child and a parent. But this is in addition *to*—a very great and very powerful and very deep and everlasting love that one person can give another. That I can *have* this.

While such depth of feeling may initially sound extravagant to some, it becomes more comprehensible when one considers the interaction of female development with the unique features of the sibling bond. Because young girls forge their identities *through* attachment to their mothers, they tend to approach other important relationships unencumbered—as well as unprotected—by the barriers against intimacy that boys have constructed. The staying power of this developmental difference has been documented in recent research on psychological boundaries by Tufts University psychiatrist Ernest Hartmann. Among adults of all ages, Hartmann has found that women tend to maintain much "thinner" interpersonal boundaries than men do—that is, they feel much less emotional distance from, and more active empathy and identification with, other people.[23]

Certain "other people," however, count more than others. A woman's basic sense of relatedness is apt to be felt with special intensity for a sibling, who is *in fact* a part of her, a blood relative with whom she shares both genes and generation, and whom she has encountered repeatedly from the earliest, most emotionally vulnerable days and years of her childhood. The interaction of these potent bond-building factors may create in a sister an especially fierce and thoroughgoing sense of sibling connection, particularly in the absence of other divisive influences such as parental favoritism or a family rule of distance. Such a predisposition for sibling attachment, however, also makes sisters particularly vulnerable to an all but inevitable facet of the sibling experience—separation. Marilyn, who began this chapter with her description of "magical closeness" with her three older siblings, vividly remembers the pain she felt as an adolescent when, slowly and inexorably, they all began to recede from her life:

I always felt like I couldn't get enough of them. So when they started to leave home—I think all along the way it was like slow death for me. I really felt abandoned. I still have pictures in my mind: getting ready to grocery shop, and Terry not being there. Coming home from school and not seeing Charlie at the dining room table, doing his homework. I really *felt* that. They were real, real important to me. Their presence. The interaction. They were gone. I was alone. It took me a long, long time to stop feeling sad, and to stop looking everywhere for substitutes. It took years.

A man's attachment to his siblings tends to be a more deeply ambivalent business than it is for a woman. On the one hand, a brother's different developmental history has led him to establish thicker walls against emotional connection than a sister has, so that the prospect of genuine intimacy with a sibling may fill him with considerable anxiety. Then, too, concerns of pride and image may interfere. A "real man" is supposed to be capable and confident, easily and entirely in command of himself and his world. Yet a sibling knows too well the little boy behind the fragile mask of manhood—the former crybaby, the monster-phobic kid, the stringy, girl-shy adolescent—and may have little patience with certain adult male poses and postures. As one man laughingly said of his younger brother, who had just bought a Jaguar to solidify his newly minted executive image: "Who does he think he's kidding? He used to put macaroni in his ears at the dinner table!" It is not merely that a sibling may unmask a man to others, but that a sibling may unmask him to *himself*, by reminding him of the disowned pieces of himself that fail to jibe with his retouched masculine self-image.

But if there are reasons to keep one's distance, there are also urgent reasons to connect. Men are by no means immune to the attractions of belonging and mutual understanding uniquely offered by the sibling bond. Who else but a sister or brother so thoroughly knows the pain and comedy of one's history? And the risks of exposure notwithstanding, who else can so acutely sympathize with the vulnerable kid behind the "everything's cool" male persona? Many men deeply want this opportunity for connection, and those who achieve it may be rewarded beyond their expectations.

In a carefully designed study of 173 men who were scrutinized at regular intervals after they graduated from Harvard in the 1940s, researchers George Vaillant and Caroline Vaillant found that emotional health in late midlife was strongly linked to "a close, enjoyable relationship with at least one sibling" in one's younger years. Remarkably, neither job nor marital success predicted well-being as strongly as did sibling closeness.[24] While the researchers offered no clarification of this striking finding, one might speculate that since sibling closeness was measured at only one point—early adulthood—those men who reported a strong sibling tie at that time continued to enjoy a close bond throughout their lives, affording them an enduring source of support and belonging.

Among the men I spoke with, the majority did articulate a wish for a closer sibling bond. But while for many, "more closeness" simply meant the opportunity to share more activities, others expressed a wish to know a brother or sister more intimately, and to be known in return. Among those who had already begun this quest, catalysts for change varied. In some cases, a brother's active bid for sibling intimacy occurred in the wake of a life change powerful enough to shatter the layers of social taboo and emotional defense against vulnerability, thereby allowing him to feel his submerged need for human connection—in particular, a sibling connection. For a number of men, it was a clear-cut "hitting bottom" experience—a divorce, a parent's death, a job loss, facing up to an alcohol problem—that spurred their recognition of the need for sisterly or brotherly closeness. Some expressed a kind of wondering gratitude that after years of sporadic connection, a sibling was still "there for me."

For others, however, progress toward deeper sibling connectedness emerged from slower, subtler shifts of consciousness. Some men reported becoming increasingly disenchanted with their designated gender role, one that had promised them the satisfactions of creaming the competition but instead had consigned them to a depth of loneliness they had never bargained for and were less and less willing to tolerate. Several acknowledged that their emerging recognition of a sibling's emotional importance had been influenced by the growing movement among men to consciously question their roles and to seek more intimacy in their lives. To the degree that this new consciousness continues to resonate with men and reaches beyond its current middle-class, highly educated base, it seems likely that men increasingly will be encouraged to re-evaluate and deepen their connections with their sisters and brothers. For a sibling is a special kind of intimate, offering not only the potential for supportive companionship, but also invaluable aid in efforts toward self-understanding. A forty-four-year-old woodworker who described his earlier relationship with his sister as "two atoms inhabiting the same family, living in their own spheres," described the change that occurred after he sought a therapist's help in working out—for the first time—some "old, old stuff":

I began to wonder what Connie thought about all of this—all the family sadness and terrors. I realized that she was the only other person who could understand the infrastructure. Understand very deeply what both of us had gone through. Yet when you're locked away like that for so many years, it's not the easiest thing to do. To talk. To trust.

But we did begin to talk. Not dark secrets, but some pretty deep thoughts about what it was like to be in that kind of family at that kind of time. I got to understand how it worked for her, too. And it wasn't until later that I realized that Connie had been trying to extend herself to me for a lotta years. But I was still on my own planet. Yeah, the brother from another planet.

Now, once in a while, we'll say to each other, "I love you." There aren't too many people who say that to me; I don't move in circles where people say that so much. But I can say that it's very, very important to me to hear that. To feel that. I'm damn lucky.

The sibling relationship, of course, is not only about love and intimacy. It is also about rivalry, anger and conflict, and brothers and sisters face these challenges to the bond in distinctive ways. For men, competition is a cornerstone of their gender role, a major channel for proving their competence and establishing their status in relation to others—including their grown-up brothers and sisters. And adult siblings *do* compete: One study found that nearly half of subjects aged twenty-two to ninety-three still felt rivalrous with their brothers and sisters, primarily over continued parental favoritism but also over the "prizes" of achievement, intelligence, physical attractiveness and fitness.[25] Brothers perceive themselves—and are perceived by their siblings—as initiating these contests more often than sisters do,[26] and if a ruthless, winner-takes-all attitude prevails, the sibling bond may not survive the struggle. When rivalry is kept within bounds, however, a brother's relative comfort with his need to win may help to keep the competition "clean." One man recalled telling his brother as they contemplated a partnership in the family business: " 'Look, I want to run things as much as you want to run things.' And he said to me, 'Well, that's a problem.' So we had these long discussions about sharing power. It didn't solve all the problems, but we know that we both want the same role in the company—king. We'll either work that out or one of us will bail out."

For sisters, by contrast, openly acknowledged sibling rivalry is apt to be frightening. Carol Gilligan writes that while men tend to be motivated by "the wish to be alone at the top and the consequent fear that others will get too close," women tend to be guided by "the wish to be at the center of connection and the consequent fear of being too far out on the edge."[27] Because competition is about establishing a hierarchy of differences through the exercise of power, it *necessarily* disrupts the connectedness that women tend to prize highly. This fundamental incompatibility between rivalry and intimacy puts many sisters in a special bind, because the sibling experience readily spurs just the kinds of competitive feelings that could endanger the tie. Many sisters react by withdrawing from all sibling contests early on, or by letting long-held grievances simmer into adulthood until they erupt, finally, over something "minor." Laura, a fifty-two-year-old teacher who had always felt that her mother had outrageously favored and spoiled her younger sister, Nan, recalls the day that she and her sister—both in their mid-forties at the time—tried to divvy up the belongings of their childhood home:

> We had tons of stuff to divide and I thought this was really going to be fun. I mean, Mother had lovely stuff. So when I won the coin-flip to start the choosing, I said fine, I'll take the grandfather clock. And Nan burst into tears and left the room.
>
> When she came back, all red-eyed, she told me that I should give her the grandfather clock. Why? Well, because she was the *baby*. I was the one who was always and forever giving in, keeping the peace. Well, she started to hound me about this clock—which she knew very well I loved—and something happened. I exploded! I turned around and left the house, and I drove home thinking [whispers], *I never want to see my sister again.* I was that angry with her. I just hated her because I thought, She has always gotten everything and I'm never supposed to mind. And we're just working that through now, the feeling on my part that Nan is always trying to get whatever it is.

Two themes emerge from this passage. One is the sheer intensity of Laura's long-repressed fury. The other, more quietly expressed, is her ultimate need and subsequent efforts to preserve her tie with Nan. Women, by and large, are committed to maintaining their bonds with their sisters or brothers, and they tend to make more concrete efforts to heal and strengthen a faltering relationship than men do. One researcher found that adult sibling pairs were more apt to report positive change in their bond when at least one member of the duo was female.[28] In another study, the majority of sister pairs reported a gradual movement toward greater closeness over the course of adulthood, while the proportion of brother pairs who did so was much smaller.[29] One gets a sense of sisters talking through their issues, digging for sources of anger, pushing through tensions, making amends as needed, in order to preserve their sibling connection. One also senses the hazardous silence of brothers.

Within relationships generally, men seem more reluctant to face down sources of conflict. When psychologist Paul Wright asked nearly 500 young men and women how they would respond if one of their close same-sex friendships had become tense and strained, about equal numbers of men and women said that they could imagine ultimately severing such a frayed bond. Before taking such a drastic step, however, more than eighty percent of the women said they would first try to talk with their friend about the sources of strain—while fewer than half of the men said they would try to talk things out before giving up on the relationship.[30]

Certainly, to some extent, women's greater willingness to do relationship repair work stems from their greater felt need for connections—including those with their sisters and brothers. Psychiatrist Jean Baker Miller observes that because many women's identities are so tightly tied to their ability to form and maintain relationships, "for many women the threat of disruption of connections is perceived not as just a loss of relationship but as something closer to a total loss of self."[31] Laura, as furious as she was with her sister, felt both anxiety and a pervasive sadness after the blowup. After several weeks of tense silence, she visited Nan to try to get to the root of their rupture:

> I realized that she really didn't understand how she'd come across. So I went over there and I sat down with her

and I said [whispers], "You know, Nan, after that fight at the house, I felt like I never wanted to see you again." And she started to cry. And I told her that I was so upset because I felt she was manipulating me—and that she had always done that and our roles from way back had set us both up for it. And I told her that the *reason* it hurt so much was because it made me feel that she didn't care about me. That was the bottom line. And I think it hit her for the first time. She'd never understood. And I said, "Look, Nan, I love you." And I told her that I really hoped that we could be close.

The brothers I talked with who were having "sibling problems," by contrast, seemed more tolerant of the emotional distance that inevitably accompanied tensions, and therefore felt less urgency to initiate repair work. But very likely, male silence in the face of sibling conflict also is rooted in a fundamental lack of confidence in the domain of emotions. Even today, relatively few men are well practiced in articulating their feelings or in carefully attending to the feelings of others. Most learned early on that such emotional discourse belonged in the waste bin of "sissy stuff," and that to risk "mucking around" in the realm of feelings was to invite pity at best, ridicule at worst. The same male gender role that prohibits personal sharing, however, also insists that men be highly competent at whatever they do—to know the answers, to master the subject at hand. But how can a man feel competent at something he has rarely been permitted to practice? Moreover, even the most experienced "emotion workers" know that the business of resolving personal conflict tends to be a slow, muddy, imprecise process, ultimately highly worthwhile but unlikely to produce the kinds of ready or measurable results that permit many men to feel successful.

Pride and status concerns also may keep many brothers from readily trying to resolve sibling conflict. As Deborah Tannen explains so well in her best-selling book, *You Just Don't Understand*, men tend to approach conversation as a vehicle for preserving status, and are therefore exquisitely sensitive to interactions that might make them feel or appear at a disadvantage. To approach a sibling with an emotional need—"I

want a better relationship with you"—or to take some responsibility for a conflict—"I'm sorry about what I said over the
holidays"—may feel too much like losing for many men to
initiate such an exchange. Many of the brothers I talked to un-
mistakably felt pain about a fractured bond with a sibling, yet
most of them hoped that their sister or brother would initiate
the rapprochement, and could think of little else to do but
wait for that to happen. The few men who did make the first,
risky move, however, were usually gratified by the response.
One man who had been angrily arguing with his younger
brother for weeks over the brother's handling of a family
business deal finally decided "not to yell back anymore" and
instead to acknowledge his own part in their conflict:

> I said to him, "Look, I realize that whenever I say any-
> thing that you perceive to be critical, you blow up. You
> think, here's Dave criticizing me again. Here's Dave not
> respecting all the good things I've done. And if I've come
> across that way, I'm sorry." And then I told him that I had
> my insecurities, too, and part of my blowing up at him
> was about my fears about making the company go, being
> successful, all that. And I told him I thought he really *was*
> doing a good job.
>
> And as I was saying all this he got a big smile on his
> face. And I thought to myself, God, why can't we just *do*
> this? You know, deal with the psychodynamics, instead of
> always getting red in the face and yelling.

The differences between brothers' and sisters' experiences
of key sibling issues—those of conflict and rivalry as well as
those of attachment and intimacy—mean, inevitably, that
brother pairs, sister pairs, and brother-sister duos will approach and resolve these issues in highly distinctive ways. Yet
the "gender imprint" goes still deeper. One's particular sibling
gender mix also profoundly influences the nature of the psychological *impact* that siblings have on each other: the roles we
are assigned or are barred from, patterns of identification and
deidentification, and the specific legacies of parental favoritism. Critically important as well, the kind of relationship we
develop early on with a brother or with a sister—close or dis-

tant, one-down or equal, supportive or ridiculing—is apt to make a deep imprint on our sense of adequacy as a woman or as a man, and on our enduring expectations for both same-sex and opposite-sex relationships.

Just how do these influential processes occur for sisters of sisters, for brothers of brothers, and for brother-sister pairs? What does it feel like to *be* a partner in each of these duos? Finally, how do gender issues interact with the many other critical influences that create, maintain and permit change in the sibling bond? These questions are addressed in the next three chapters, and they are answered primarily—and most eloquently—by sisters and brothers themselves.

# 5

# Sisters: Braided Lives

Sometimes I feel like a sisterless child.

Louise Bernikow, *Among Women*

Two sisters dominate Steven Soderbergh's edgy and disturbing film *sex, lies and videotape*. Ann, a married homemaker, is prim, gentle and sexually repressed; Cynthia, a bartender, is single, hard-edged, and conspicuously sexual. Each sister's persona seems an affront—even a threat—to the other's, and throughout the film they irritate each other, insult each other, miss each other's points. "She's loud," complains Ann to a visitor, wrinkling her nose. Cynthia sums up her sister no more charitably: "She is *hung up*."

But beneath the sneers and the divisions, another reality bubbles. The sisters can't leave each other alone: They call and visit each other compulsively, if only to argue about whose life makes more sense. Yet these lives aren't quite as polarized as they seem. Both sisters are involved with the same man, and their shared lack of feeling for him is merely expressed differently—Ann's through avoidance and Cynthia's through loveless sex. As the story unfolds, we catch glimpses of Ann's sensuality, of Cynthia's pain. Eventually, each leaves the man. At the close of the film, Ann ventures into Cynthia's territory—the low-life bar where she works—bearing a birthday gift for her sister. Cynthia tentatively asks for Ann's new phone number, and when Ann responds, "Gotta pen?" Cynthia flashes her sister a sudden, newly vulnerable smile.

When I first saw this film I remember feeling its disorienting strangeness, but also that the sister bond it depicted was real, recognizable, utterly convincing. In Ann and Cynthia I saw Donna and myself; I saw, too, the scores of sisters I had interviewed for this book. What I recognized was not Ann's and Cynthia's particular issues but rather how deeply felt were the differences between them, differences that so often divide sisters and spur them to fight about nonissues, to steam in hurt silence, to nearly give up on each other. Nearly—yet rarely entirely. For I recognized, too, in Ann's and Cynthia's relationship the fundamental connectedness that imbues so many sister bonds, a tie of mutual attachment and subterranean identification that may frequently be strained by tensions and resentments but that is rarely severed—because sisters, by and large, will not let that happen.

Sisters rarely let go of each other because their sibling bond tends to be supported by a common emotional agenda—the maintenance of critical relationships—and a corollary willingness to share the kind of "nurture work" that sustains connections. This rarely means, however, that sisters tend their bond with equal energy at every stage of life. Even among the very close sisters I talked with, many reported intervals of little communication—the early years of marriage and hectic young motherhood were frequently cited sisterly "down times"— followed by reconnection, or the forging of a deeper connection, during less demanding life stages. Other sisters reported an early bond fraught with tensions, followed by efforts to develop a genuinely positive connection for the first time in their thirties, their forties, or even their sixties.

Throughout their lives, many sisters have at their disposal a potent tool for the cultivation of their sibling bond— conversation. For most members of sister pairs whom I interviewed, talk was not just the most effective means of preserving and deepening their relationship, but their hands-down *favorite* way to do so. For sisters who were already close, talk was celebrated as fun and therapy, at once a path to deepened intimacy and a critical aid to self-exploration. A close sister, in fact, was viewed as a kind of ultimate conversationalist, someone who was not merely willing to explore one's emotional history but who actually had *been there,* as both validating witness and supporting player, and who therefore brought to any conversation a very particular knowledge of her sister's issues and sensibility. Among the sisters I spoke with, talk tended to be both cause and consequence of intimacy: Sisters talked in order to dissolve geographic or emotional distance, and the closer they drew, the more they talked to enjoy and take sustenance from their connection.

The greatest strength of sisters—their energy for intimacy—is linked to the greatest challenge they face: an acceptance of the limits of their bond. Many of us still have an idealized sister floating about our minds and hearts, one forged from some combination of our genuine longings for closeness and the cultural myths we have absorbed about the unstinting quality of female nurturance. Moreover, our belief in the possibility of such an "angel sister" was powerfully reinforced by a book that millions of us read in our girlhoods, reread, fantasized about and never quite got over—*Little Women.* Louise Bernikow speaks for many women when she writes that this novel

> presented me, in my childhood, an image of what I did not have. I never forgot it. . . . The presence of sisters seemed to me a wonderful thing, standing for companionship, physical intimacy, all varieties of warmth and some vague sense of a circle of female protection. . . . I bought the myth of devotion.[1]

Devotion may be a part of the sister story—but it leaves out a lot. It makes no room for thoughtless or petty remarks, for forgetting to phone, for hot disagreements about how women should behave in the family and in the world, for the hundreds of ways in which female siblings disappoint each other by not being "perfect." Partly, we want our sister to take better care of us than she does, to be the sisterly counterpart of the all-giving, all-forgiving fantasy mother. I know that I hold a double standard of sibling behavior in this regard. In time of crisis I expect—unfairly and unfailingly—a quicker phone call from Donna, a stronger dose of empathy, a closer reading of my state of mind, than I expect from Phil or ever expected from Bob.

I also recognize that I want Donna to *be* more like me than she is, and nearly every sister I spoke with acknowledged similar wishes and accompanying frustrations. One's sister may be experienced as so much a part of oneself that it is difficult to accept her as essentially *other*—someone who may possess a whole set of values, habits, tastes in men, child-rearing philosophies and dreams for the future that one simply does not share, cannot imagine sharing. When Donna expresses a political conviction that is very different from mine, or when she seems to lack sufficient enthusiasm for a topic that I find wholly absorbing, I can still feel suddenly lonely—even betrayed. When our deep "togetherness" emerges, by contrast, I can feel almost unreasonably happy.

I am remembering a recent evening when I was brewing a pot of coffee in preparation for calling her, and the phone rang; it was Donna. As we settled into our customary trading of "what's happening" stories, it emerged that we both had recently experienced a nearly identical epiphany about the poisonous effects of perfectionism on our work lives, one which had been precipitated by an eerily similar crisis, and which was now having similar liberating effects on each of us. We cheered our shared breakthrough and we talked about its link to our particular stage of life; at the close of our hourlong conversation, we vowed to help each other through any "relapses." I hung up the phone, jubilant. My sister and I understood each other. Life was good.

Where do jealousy and rivalry fit into the sister story? Few sisters I spoke with—even those who were "best friends"— had not wrestled with these feelings at some stage of their relationship. The arenas of competition were diverse, ranging from career success to the quality of their mothering to the accomplishments of husbands and children. Two struggles, however, seemed to inflict particularly painful and lasting wounds. One was rivalry over attributes that society still promotes as essential to feminine adequacy—physical beauty, thinness and the ability to attract men. The other, still more fundamental struggle was over mother love.

Several women still grieved over a mother's apparently greater affection for and approval of a sister, who was nearly always the designated "good daughter." In such cases, the unchosen daughter often felt that her mother identified with her sister in some deep, unspoken way that she was powerless to dilute, and which relegated her to the status of perpetual outsider. Fathers appeared in such emotionally charged triangles far less frequently, perhaps because of gender differences in parent-child identification patterns, and also because fathers were more often described as simply "away"— physically or emotionally—from the center of family life.

Sisters may feel rivalrous toward each other, but few can express their competitive urges comfortably, or even fully acknowledge such feelings to themselves. It's little wonder. For even as we were schooled in the rewards of sisterly devotion by *Little Women*, we absorbed lessons about sisterly envy from another kind of "hearth" classic, the Cinderella story. From this emotionally resonant folktale, we learned that rivalry between female relatives is nothing less than catastrophic, wiping out love, fueling hatred and cruelty, and, before the spruced-up Disney version, punishable by torture. (As originally written down by the brothers Grimm, the story ends with birds plucking out the eyes of the stepsisters.) While the Cinderella story is obviously not the source of women's fear of sisterly rivalry, it both reflects and reinforces the entire education most women receive about the costs of competition to relationships. Rivalry is a dangerous business, we learn; it cannot be worked through or integrated with caring. Yet among sisters growing up together, neither can it be easily avoided. Therefore, it must somehow be safely contained.

Deidentification, described in an earlier chapter as a process by which siblings divide up available roles and realms of achievement, seems to be a particularly common strategy for taming sisterly competition. Virginia Woolf's haunting reminder to her sister, Vanessa—"as you have the children, the fame by rights belongs to me"[2]—was echoed in the sisterly pacts struck by a number of women I interviewed. If one sister had already appropriated the role of "the pretty one" or "the popular one," the other was apt to turn to a different realm—often academic or creative—and thereby become the designated "smart one" or "artistic one." Similarly, if one sister had already cornered the market on "goodness," the other was apt to hone her talents for rebellion. Such sole proprietorship of particular attributes, often reinforced by family role assignments, often did contain sisterly competition—but nearly always at a cost. Several women I met with who were undeniably attractive still struggled with deep feelings of physical inadequacy because a sister had long ago claimed the "beauty" turf. Likewise, a number whose sisters had been academic superstars still felt not quite bright, regardless of their actual intellectual abilities or accomplishments. Many adult sisters I talked with were finally beginning to reclaim traits and talents once monopolized by a sister, in the process discovering the pleasures of having, after all, "a lot in common."

Sisters also show sisters how to be women. This is widely understood to be the task of mothers, yet many women I spoke with felt that a sister had an enormous, enduring impact on their female self-concept, their expectations for relationships with men, and their acceptance or rejection of traditional norms of femininity. Particularly during adolescence, when the process of "gender intensification"[3] converges with enormous physical and emotional changes, mothers were often remembered as too removed from the scene of battle, or unable to sufficiently understand a daughter's jumble of new feelings about her body, sex, boys and her future, to be of much practical help. But a sister, especially an older one, was frequently remembered as a far more accessible model. She was *living* it, developing physically, steeped in the rituals of primping and dating, moving toward or away from a career beyond the home, knowing herself to be any boy's equal—or not. Women with older sisters talked of closely watching this process of growing up female, copying this, editing out that, seeking information through questions or snooping or both, in the process piecing together a personal vision of womanhood.

Long after they grow up and leave their childhood home, sisters continue to watch each other. Openly or covertly, each observes how the other navigates her intimate relationships, mothers her children, develops a career, confronts aging, copes with success and with loss. Sisters may compare notes and actively help each other through these passages; always, they observe "how things work out" for a sister, compare their own progress, glean useful information. Throughout this life-long process of mutual awareness and influence, sisters continue to work through the fundamental issues of their relationship—issues of intimacy and separateness, of support and rivalry, of sameness and difference. With effort and luck, they are able to discover room in their relationship for all of them.

## Ellen: Trading Places

Ellen, a vibrant, elegantly attractive woman of thirty-eight, has mostly wonderful memories of her forty-four-year-old sister, Julia. During their growing-up years in a middle-class suburb of Chicago, Julia played a kind of fairy godsister role to Ellen, taking her downtown to plays and museums, sewing her exquisite clothes and giving Ellen a starry-eyed, hopeful glimpse of the world of dating and boys. Because Julia shared so much with her, Ellen tried not to resent her older sister for the one thing she possessed that Ellen could never get—the approval of their mother. In fact, for many years Julia was an essential substitute mother, the one person Ellen could depend on to make her feel that "in the end, it will all work out." Then everything changed.

From the time I was eleven, there were all these guys around. I remember thinking, where are these guys *coming* from? They were all really handsome, they were all bringing flowers to my sister, taking her out somewhere. Julia was always dating. I remember watching her go out on dates to the Pub Tiki. Which was to *die*. Gardner McKay, right? [Laughs.] She would go out the door looking beautiful, really glamorous—this was back in the days when you really dressed up for dates. And she would bring home stuff to me, like a glass shaped like a coconut or some kind of monkey thing from the table. I remember how I couldn't wait to go.

And I just figured I *would*. I had the sense that she dated, so I would date. That this was what was going to happen to me. A lot of it was because Julia tried to share it with me—well, as much as you could with a kid. When she had her sweet sixteen party, I got to go, and she let me invite a friend. It was *wonderful*. That was when I got my first Barbie doll, as my party favor. Later on, when I got to be thirteen or fourteen, she would always try to help me look good. My mother was making a lot of my clothes back then, and they were awful. But Julia would lend me her clothes, teach me how to do scarves and put things together—all the stuff that's so major when you're a teenager.

Julia sewed, too, and one time she made this absolutely gorgeous dress for herself. I still remember the fabric: white crepe with pale pink and yellow flowers. It was a summer sheath, very elegant, with a row of gold ball buttons all the way down, and one of those mandarin collars, remember when those were popular? [Softly.] And she finished the hem with *lace*. I watched her make it; I just fell in love with it. And when she finished it, she said, "Here." She had seen that I liked it and she just gave it to me.

That was Julia. The generosity—and also the wonderful messages she was giving me. Because I considered this a very, very grown-up dress, and it was like she was acknowledging that I was growing up. That maybe I could be like her.

More than anybody else, I think, my sister gave me this really good sense that growing up was okay. You know, that things were basically good and that you managed, and the things that you worried about when you were fourteen were resolved by the time you were eighteen, and the things you worried about at eighteen were resolved by the time you were twenty-one. It was a sense of *I* can do it so *you* can do it; I can manage so you can manage. [Very quietly.] Things will be okay. That was the message from her all the way along.

And I needed that message. Because all along, things between my mother and me were very tough. Julia understood my mother, connected with her in a way I never knew how to. They had this special thing between them—they're still very close. But I couldn't get in, and my attitude from a very early age was that I'm not part of it, so I don't *wanna* be part of it. My mother thought that my sister was—toward perfection. And I was definitely a problem. The line was always that Julia was generous and giving and I was selfish and sneaky and irresponsible. I was more *this* than Julia and more *that* than Julia. And more always meant less.

My father was different. I adored him; he was my big protector. But from the time I was very young, I had the clear sense of wanting to leave my mother. Because I was always setting her off, and I was fearful of her. She lost her temper easily. Sometimes she hit. When things got really bad, my father would take me for walks, and sometimes we would walk toward the playground where there was this big empty field. I was maybe eight or ten at the time. And I would say, "Dad, I just feel like screaming for five minutes." And I'd scream and he'd smile, and then we'd go back.

Julia tried to help me, too. She couldn't stop the hitting. At the point where my mother's hands were flying, my mother was really not in control. But I could never tell what would piss her off, and my sister somehow *did* know. And she tried to tell me, to ward it off. Or if my mother discovered something, was upset about something, Julia would try to mediate. But beyond that, there was a sense of comfort. [Tears in her voice.] She would sit with me. She would talk to me. Try to give me some perspective. She didn't understand why she got along with my mother and I couldn't, but it wasn't like it's 'cause "I'm so wonderful and you're not." Never that. She was trying to get me through it.

There was something else about my sister that I tremendously respected. Julia was smart, really sharp; she had opinions and she expressed them. This was the late sixties, you know, and I remember all these dinner-table discussions about politics where my sister would really stand up to my parents on all the hot issues. I watched her; I was so proud of her. But then, when she got to be a junior at Northwestern, something very significant happened.

Up until then she had been living at home. Now she wanted to get her own apartment. And my mother said *no way*. Her thing was that your parents take care of you and then your husband takes care of you, and that's that. They argued and fought and my mother finally pulled out her big card and said, "If you leave, you can never come back." And Julia gave in. She never got her apartment. She stayed home and very soon after that—when she was barely twenty-one—she got married. I watched all this. I remember feeling furious. Even more determined to get out. I couldn't *wait* to be autonomous.

Two years after she got married, I started college. To cut to the chase, I became sexually involved with a man, my mother found out, she told my father, and a major family crisis broke out. My mother was telling me, "You've got two choices: You either marry him or you break up with him," and I said to her, "No, I have a third choice, which is goodbye." And I left for Julia's. I needed to talk to my sister.

There's a scene in my brain. [Takes a deep breath.] I went to see my sister to talk with her about moving out of my parents' house. Because she always knew what to do; I knew she would help me. And what she said to me was, "You can't move out." And I thought to myself, *This is not happening.*

"You can't support yourself," she went on. You can't do this, you can't do that, you can't do *it*. And as she talked on and on it came to me that, my God, this is not about me. This is about *her*. She is reliving something. I can't trust what my sister is saying to me. And I thought to myself, *Nope.* I have this vivid memory of removing myself; of letting her have her say but all the while just withdrawing from her, mentally and emotionally, and knowing that I would not be coming to her again for advice and help. I was on my own.

And I went home and threw all my stuff into a bunch of plastic garbage bags and had a friend pick me up. I never lived at home again. I was seventeen.

There was a lot of damage done. I felt betrayed by my sister. I felt she could give me nothing I wanted or needed. For a while, we just didn't talk. I had a room in this big group house in town; it was the seventies, and I was involved in all kinds of activities, meeting lots of people. Then one day Julia came over and gave me a cat. [Smiles.] And after that, she started calling me up when she was going to be in town and we would meet for dinner, go hear some music. It didn't happen very often, but it happened.

There was no big moment of forgiveness. But over those next few years I began to see, very clearly, that I was doing all the things she had always wanted to do. I left home, and lightning didn't strike me. After college, I married a guy my parents really liked, who was good to me. I was putting together a career. And she had married too quickly, to someone I don't think she was ever happy with, and it seemed that she wasn't going to be allowed to be all of the wonderful things she could have been. [Softly.] I began to see her as caught. And her not supporting me as all part of feeling so caught. There had never been any malice.

But there was still something between us. I had the good life. What Julia had left was my mother. She still had the corner on my mother. We got into this pattern where if I had a problem with my mother, I'd call Julia to see if she had more information than I did, or could smooth things out. She would be in the middle—and it wasn't a helpful middle. I began to feel that she *enjoyed* being a go-between. Because that's a very, very powerful position. But the game just went on and on, and it was only about a year ago, actually, that I stopped playing.

What happened was that I had a very major confrontation with my mother, in which I was able to tell her that I loved her but that I would no longer allow her to treat me the way she had been treating me my whole life. [Stops to collect herself.] I—I had gotten some therapy to get me to this point. It was a very long and emotional scene—lots of yelling and crying—but it was very important in that it was the first time I had been able to say any of this to my mother. I felt scared and also very good. And when I left my mother's house and got home, I didn't call my sister.

Real conscious. I *wanted* badly to call her. But I thought, there's no way. I wanted my mother to deal with me, one-on-one. I didn't want Julia in the middle anymore. [Firmly.] I just wasn't gonna do it. I needed to remove my sister from the equation. What happened was between my mother and me; it had to stay there and it had to be resolved there. And it is getting resolved, little by little. That's a whole other story. But Julia was very upset. She had had a special relationship with my mother and a special relationship with me. And now my mother and I were finally talking to each other. Where did that leave her?

Also, I had disagreed with my mother, and there wasn't hell to pay. In fact, since our big confrontation, my mother has begun expressing approval of me in lots of ways. I hate to say this but my mother is a snob, she's into money, and the fact that I have this big house is a big deal to her. She talks about it. And you know, Julia lives in a little row house; they have constant money problems. So Julia became very snappish toward me. I could hear this tight-ass note come into her voice whenever we talked.

And the truth is, that tightness hasn't really gone away. I've tried to ignore it and I've also tried to defuse it, by being real careful not to use my new relationship with my mother against her—you know, acting like I know things that she doesn't know. That's *not* what it's about. But still, there's a tension I feel coming toward me, no question. I don't know if I'd call it jealousy, but like this little knot of resentment. [Sighs deeply.] There's an ease missing. And it makes me sad.

I've almost despaired at times. But not totally. Just a couple months ago, at the very end of the summer, I invited her up to our lake house, just us and our kids. No husbands. And she came down and I rode bikes with her boys and she taught needlepoint to my girls and we picnicked on the beach—we're wonderful aunts to each other's children. [Smiles.] I felt a little bit of relaxation beginning to happen. Then on the third night, we put the kids to bed and went out on the deck, and we just started talking. And we talked until six o'clock in the morning.

We covered a lot of territory. Obviously. [Laughs.] But it was great. We talked some about our parents and what it meant to be their children, and we shared memories, things during childhood. Mostly the good ones, giggly stories. We talked about our grandfather. And I told her how much she had helped me when Sara was born. I mean, this was my first kid and I was very nervous, very insecure, and Julia already had two kids and was this incredibly calm, nurturing mother. I would call her up and shriek, "The baby book said babies do this and Sara's doing *that*." And she would say [softly]: "Ellen, *Sara didn't read the book.*"

And I recounted that story to her, and I told her, "You know, that was very comforting. That was a wonderful thing to say." I told her how she had always done that—given me permission to just do my best. To live my life.

But as we talked, I had this feeling that she wanted something. And finally, about two o'clock in the morning, she asked me about the therapy I had gone through. And I told her about it. How it had changed my relationships, not just with Mom but also with my husband, and how important that had been, and what came out, ultimately, was that she and *her* husband were having problems. Major problems. Well, I already knew that, everybody in the family knew it, but now she was telling me.

And as she talked about it I started to feel, real strongly, how much she had done for me when I was growing up, and how much I wanted to help her now. Give something back. And I just wanted to say, Julia, damn it, you're such an amazing, extraordinary person, I love you, come live with us, *get out now.* [Cries for a moment.]

But of course I didn't. I just kept giving her lots of support and telling her how positive my experience had been. And I tried to convey that whatever she might need, at any point, I would be there to help her get it or find it or do it. I meant it, and it felt good to say that. And that whole evening I think we felt really close. There was that trusting feeling again.

And it—it gives me some hope. Because, you know, we had put the old agendas and family dynamics away and that night we were just who we are—two women together, two women with families and lives. Two sisters who really know each other.

## Terry and Marie: Excuse Me, I've Gotta Call My Sister

My evening with Terry and Marie, two sisters from South Philadelphia, was not so much an interview as a piece of sister performance art. I would venture a question and Terry, thirty-two, would fire back a wisecracking answer while Marie, thirty-six, would dissolve in laughter. Or they would simultaneously spout the same one-liner. Then, as often as not, they would turn to each other and intensely debate the question at hand—Whaddya think? No, that's nuts!—and as they did this they frequently touched, smiled, hugged and hooted. They were clearly crazy about each other, these daughters of working-class Italian American parents, and their bond went deeper than joke-trading and shared hilarity. Each woman felt that a regular "fix" of sisterly interaction was essential to her emotional well-being, to her sense that somewhere in the world she deeply, unalterably *belonged*. Seeing and hearing them together, there was no reason to doubt it.

MARIE: Sometimes we'll go four days without talking.

TERRY: But sometimes four times in one day. Or if I can't reach her, I'll fax her at work.

MARIE: We do a lot of answering machine . . .

TERRY: You should hear her messages—they use up the whole tape. "How are you? Where are you? You're not there? Call me back. Having a fit, going nuts, remind me to tell you the story about Betsy, remind me to tell you what Joey did in school, remind me to tell you what Mommy said the other day."

MARIE: Then she'll call me back and say, "Okay, *you owe me stories*." And we'll meet for lunch and I'll have this list on a piece of paper, and we'll go down it.

TERRY: Or I'll visit and we'll stand up in her kitchen and eat ice cream out of the pint, and we'll go over everything.

MARIE: Because if we don't tell each other these little stories, I mean, we *have* to know these little stories . . .

TERRY: That's our bond.

Q: Were you this close growing up?

TERRY AND MARIE [in unison]: Best friends.

TERRY: We did everything together.

MARIE: We did. We were really in cahoots together. Sisters against the world.

TERRY: Like Marie was overweight back then and my mother didn't want her to eat junk. So I felt bad for her. I mean, she wanted those cheese puffs and Tastykakes so bad! [Both laugh.] So I would go. There was a candy store around the corner and she'd give me the money and an extra dollar for myself, and I'd run out and get the candy. And I'd put it in the milk crate outside the door, 'cause if I walked in with it, my mother would say, "So what's in the bag?" After they went to sleep, we'd sneak down to the milk crate in the middle of the night. And then we'd eat the candy in our beds.

MARIE: Heaven. Wasn't she a doll?

TERRY: But come on, who else are you gonna be nice to? I mean, we grew up together, same bedroom and all, and it was just us—no other kids in the family. It just makes sense we'd be close.

MARIE: Yeah, but you know, a lot aren't. We had a real sense of family. Parents, grandparents, cousins. There was a lot of hugging and kissing growing up. I grew up feel-

ing that everybody loves me, my grandparents love me
and my parents love me and Terry loves me. We always got lots of praise from both of our parents—to
this day we do. Just this week I was talking to Dad,
telling him about an argument I had with my boss, and
he said, "I'm so proud of the way you handle yourself." And he's said that to me since I was three. So we
always felt a lot of—all those "self" words. We had
'em. Self-esteem, self-confidence.

TERRY: Which was lucky, or I could've come down with a
real inferiority complex. I mean, look at her! She's always been the perfect one. I was The Thin One, but she
was The Perfect One. Listened to the teachers and the
principals, to Mommy and Daddy. She went to college
right after high school, I didn't go to college. I just
wanted to go to France, have fun and get money. Then
she married a nice boy from the neighborhood, the guy
she'd been dating since she was fifteen. And I didn't
get married till last year, and all along dated all different types, all different colors.

MARIE: See, she was more daring, more adventurous . . .

TERRY: [To Marie.] But what I'm saying is that it would have
been easy for Mommy and Daddy to say, "Why can't
you be more like your sister?" or, "Look how Marie
does it." But no, never. They always made sure we
knew they were proud of the both of us. Like with report cards it was "You got a C, that's okay. If you did
the best you could, a C is fine."

Q: What happened when boys entered the picture?

TERRY: Jealousy. *Pain.* Not 'cause we wanted the same guy,
but 'cause when Marie got a boyfriend, she didn't
spend all her time with *me.* [Turns to Marie.] Remember? I told you, "You don't love me anymore." And
you were so wonderful. You said, "But honey, there are
different *kinds* of liking. I'll always love you most, and
I've known you the longest. But the way I love you is

different from the way I can like a boy." That really helped me.

MARIE: But you know, I think the bond between the two of us *was* closer. He was a boyfriend, but still, I knew Terry longer. I would take her with me on dates—daytime stuff, not Saturday nights—and he complained a little but I thought, The hell with him. He's gonna have to deal with it because she's my sister. What's he gonna do about it? [Conspiratorial laughter.]

TERRY: He married you! [More laughter.] But you know, when they did get married, I was hysterical. I was up there, maid of honor, and when I heard them say, "I pronounce you husband and wife," I started crying and I couldn't stop. I remember standing in the receiving line, carrying on like a crazy person, because I was going home that night and she was never coming home again. And Mommy and Daddy telling me, "Sweetie, you're still gonna *see* her. Some people get married and they move to Boston or California or wherever. Your sister is moving ten minutes away."

MARIE: Anyway, I slipped her the keys.

TERRY: Right! She gave me the key to their new apartment. So it was great from then on. I was constantly over at that apartment. I'd come over right after school with a girlfriend, and we'd make shepherd's pie or spaghetti so when they came home from work, dinner would be all ready. And I'd bring my boyfriends over, too. Marie got me a sofabed for my birthday, to keep right there in her apartment just for me and my boyfriends! So it was my second home. And Danny—Marie's husband—he just kind of got used to me.

MARIE: Get out, he adored you. But it was a little hard in the beginning. He was a little jealous. Don't you think? Because here we were married, and we're supposed to be a couple, and *she* was still around. [Terry nods, grinning.] One time I went out with Terry to the mall when

Danny wanted me with him, and he had a few beers and when I called him from the mall . . .

TERRY: He hung up on her. She was *so* upset.

MARIE: But he doesn't have any sisters or brothers, see, he didn't understand why we couldn't just, you know, fade away from each other. He still doesn't, totally. He'll see me calling her up and he'll say, "What do you have to talk to her about *now?*" [Peals of laughter.]

Q: And what's your answer? Why do you think you enjoy being together and talking with each other so much?

TERRY: Nobody else can tolerate us. [Joint guffaws.]

MARIE: She has that quickness—sharp and smart and funny. You have to be quick! And, well, we're just on the same wavelength. Built-in. She knows how I think. I don't even have to say it. She just knows.

TERRY: We have the same attitude on things. Okay, so we'll go to somebody's house for dinner, and somebody will say something. Just some annoying comment, and we'll go like this. [They exchange meaningful glances.] Just a look and we both know . . .

MARIE: That we're gonna talk about it that night when we get home, I'll leave a message on her answering machine that says . . .

TERRY: "Did you *hear* what that asshole said?"

MARIE: Or we'll each leave a message on the other's machine—you know, crossing—saying the same thing. "Do you believe what that jerk said?" I'll say, and her message'll be, "That jerk-off at the party, *just amazing* . . ."

TERRY: We also know how the other one would react to things—what she's sensitive to, even if I'm not. So if we're at a party and I overhear some guy say some stupid thing to Marie . . .

MARIE: She'll call me later and say, "Okay, stop crying now. He hurt your feelings, but you're gonna be fine."

TERRY: She does the same. I mean, it's very eerie. It's wonderful. We're different, but she's like a bookend—an extension of me. And it's like a standard. When I'm starting to get to know somebody who could maybe be a friend, I'm already comparing them. I'm thinking, is this just like talking to Marie? Is there that little "click"? I have my little checklist: sense of humor, bright enough to catch things, knowing things that are unsaid, warm and loving and not afraid to show it. Like if we're walking down South Street with a million people looking, can I kiss this friend on the cheek or will she run screaming down the block? And most of my friends are a lot like her—okay, some aren't as quick, but you can't have everything.

MARIE: We also have the same kind of relationship with our husbands that we have with each other. Well, minus the sex thing. [Shrieks of laughter.]

TERRY: But you know, I knew that the person I would spend my life with would be so much like Marie. Because we were so close, I got to spend all these years with somebody who I could just let my hair down with and totally be myself with. Not that I really thought about it, it's just that any man I hooked up with would *have* to be very much like her for me to have a comfortable life. In lots of ways, Jack is a male Marie. If I hadn't found somebody like this, I would probably rather live alone.

MARIE: I see her influence as going on right now. Kind of as a model. See, Terry was always more verbally adventurous than me. Much more with the mouth. The way girls aren't supposed to be, right? And how I never learned to be—especially on the subject of saying no. Sure, I'll do the car pool for the next eleven years.

Forty people over for Thanksgiving? No problem! But now I'm starting to really watch her, learning how she does it. How to say what I think, which she does in this beautiful, honest but compassionate way. She doesn't wishy-wash. She's very brave that way. And wise.

TERRY: [Obviously moved.] I didn't know you felt that way. Because I still feel like the baby. God, I'm *wise*. [They laugh, and hug.]

MARIE: I told you she's a doll.

TERRY: I think *she's* a doll.

Q: Has there ever been a time when either of you felt that the other was *not* a doll?

MARIE: Never.

TERRY: Once. [Marie looks at her, surprised.] Okay. It was, what—three or four years ago. When you started losing all that weight. Remember? And that's what *I* had. You had the husband, you had the college degree, you had the house, you had the baby. Let *me* have the thinness. Now you're going to take this away from me, too.

MARIE: But you'll always be cuter.

TERRY: See? That's why I can't stay mad at her. But for a while, I went around thinking, All this perfection is annoying. At least she could be *fat*. Now we're both The Thin One; I've gotten used to it. Pretty much, anyway.

MARIE: What can I do?

TERRY: Eat more Doritos.

Q: What do you get from your relationship that's most important to you?

TERRY AND MARIE: Nothing. [Peals of laughter.]

TERRY: Okay. I think of the times I've been really down—like just before I met Jack and I was thirty years old and dating nobody and everybody in the family was saying, "Whatsa matter, pretty girl like you not married?" And I would cry to Marie, and she'd just listen and . . .

MARIE: I always wanted to snap my fingers and make it perfect, but I couldn't. All I could do is say, "Keep on talking, I love you."

TERRY: And that's what I get. Unconditional love. I know that no matter what, no matter how much disagreeing, she'll never change the way she feels about me. I'll swear that till the day I die. She was always there— always, always, *always*—and she's nuts about me. She makes me feel perfect about myself.

MARIE: See, I have this fantasy. One day we just won't go to work and we'll just get together. We'll sit around the house and talk about nothing important, just look at old letters, watch *L.A. Law* that we taped. Eat ice cream out of the pint! No husbands, no kids, no mom. Just be together. Just be in the same room with each other, and enjoying it. And that's really it—you know, my definition of what makes this relationship so great. I don't know how else to say it.

TERRY: Yep. It's real.

MARIE: It's a chemistry.

TERRY: And it's always been.

MARIE: Always.

Postscript: When I talked with Terry later, she told me that as soon as she got home from this three-hour interview, she called up Marie. They compared notes about the experience (and the interviewer) for another hour.

## Lucy: The Princess Factor

Tall, fit and energetic, sixty-one-year-old Lucy exudes both
confidence and a touching vulnerability. The daughter of a
private-school headmaster, she grew up in what she calls
"WASP heaven," an environment in which foreign travel was
frequent, an Ivy League education was assumed, and the ex-
tracurricular lessons for Lucy and her younger sister and
brother—piano, drawing, riding, violin—never stopped. But
beneath a veneer of privileged harmony, Lucy's childhood
was an angry and lonely one. From as far back as she can remember, she was locked in a painful, self-diminishing struggle
with her sister that she could neither win nor escape from—
and that continued to derail their relationship long after they
left their childhood home. Only in the past few years have
they begun to repair the damage.


When I was eleven, Beth got a pony for Christmas. Every girl's dream, right? It was from my grandmother. When
my mother told me about it in advance—to prepare me, I
guess—I remember being very excited. I thought, If Beth is
going to get *this*, then I must be going to get some incredible, wonderful, magical present. I thought about it end-
lessly. I couldn't wait for Christmas morning. When it
finally came, I remember bursting into the living room and
there, leaning up against the wall right beside the tree, was
*my* present. It was a mattress.

Beth got a pony and I got a mattress. That happened.
I've really never gotten over it.

But that was how it was. From the very beginning, Beth
was the princess in our family. When she was very little,
she had some serious illnesses and there was always a
sense that she was fragile, needed to be coddled, needed—
well, extra. Special nurturing. And I was the one who *didn't*
need the nurturing. That was real clear in my family. I was
the manager, the organizer, the capable one who got the job
done. I carried the suitcases. I remember that so well: One
summer we traveled through Europe and Dad carried

Mother's suitcases, and I carried Beth's. I wasn't even two years older than she was.

So Beth grew up thinking she was something very special. And that made things between us very hard. Well, I do have some good memories. Every summer we'd spend nights together out on the sleeping porch, and I can remember lying out there and cooking up fantasies about who we were going to marry. And we played dolls and jacks, did the hand-clapping songs, all those little-girl things. But I remember her as a very bossy, manipulative kid. She could be very cranky and snotty. Very centered on herself. She was going to do whatever she wanted to, and the hell with you.

And I had no defender. My mother saw Beth as this poor little thing, so nothing was ever her fault. Nobody would ever say anything to her because the family line was, "This is just the way Beth is." Once in a while I would explode, and then I would be called aggressive. So I learned that it didn't pay.

As a kid, I think I felt a lot of rejection. I did get some warmth from Dad, but he was very, very busy. And Mother, well, she was the headmaster's wife, so she was involved with all these duties and little luncheon parties and teas and things like that. But even when she was home, there was a coolness and a detachment about Mom. [Very quietly.] I never could hug my mother. There was never that. There was always a feeling that she was fragile and might break. She was constantly going to bed or lying around on a chaise lounge that she had up in her room, always with some vague illness. Now I think that a lot of her illnesses were depressions. But at the time, it just made me feel lonely. I felt like I couldn't reach her.

And what she had to give seemed to go to my sister. I remember how we both took piano lessons, but Beth was the one who had the "touch" on the piano, the musical talent in the family, according to my mother. I got awfully tired of hearing about how Beth had that "touch." Same thing with art. Beth was considered the poetic one, the literary one, the actress. I did all those things too—and I loved them. But I was considered the brain, the mathematical and scientific one.

So when we went away to boarding school for high school, she got to go to a special place, a *wonderful* school, where they believed in the "whole child" and really pushed the arts. And Beth wrote beautiful poetry there, went on camping trips, learned the violin. And I was sent to this very traditional, academically oriented girls' boarding school. I was very jealous.

Beth was also incredibly pretty. Life isn't fair, right? [Shakes her head, laughing.] But she was. Very small and slim, with wild curls all over her head. Big blue eyes. And I was tall and had straight brown hair and I think I was the least cute of the three kids. People were always telling me how cute my younger sister was. I remember when we were both in a big school operetta, *The Pied Piper of Hamelin*. Beth was selected to be the mayor's daughter because she was so adorable, and I was just one of the crowd's daughters. This happened over and over: I was always in the plays, but Beth always got that featured role.

So there was just this feeling—eyes would always go to Beth. She would be the chosen one.

The whole "pretty" thing was actually awful. I remember a couple of critical scenes around that. One was when I was about twelve. I had developed early and had gotten my period early and got bad skin and gained weight and all this horrible stuff. I felt so terrible about myself and my body. And at one point I remember saying to my mother, "Am I pretty?"

And she said, "Well, no, you're not, really."

And I said, "Well, is Beth pretty?"

"Yes, Beth is pretty."

And then she said something about how I was striking or attractive or something. But it was too late. I just felt hopeless.

The other thing I remember happened in college. I had developed a weight problem—and of course Beth hadn't—and at one point I came up to visit her at her boarding school. And during the course of that weekend Beth reported that one of her friends had said to her, "You know, your sister is prettier than you are. Too bad she's so fat." And I was *delighted*. [Laughs.] Delighted to hear that she thought I was prettier. I could always lose weight. But still, it took me a long time to believe that I was attractive. I was into my twenties before I could *feel* that, really experience that about myself.

Once I finished college and got married, Beth and I didn't see each other for long stretches. I was in Pittsburgh and she was in Tulsa; we were both raising children. It was a hectic time. But you know, the times we would get together, I would be conscious of a couple of things. One was wanting to be closer. Even in college I realized that away from the family scene, we could have a good time together. We always had a lot to talk about, and we could really get to giggling sometimes. Beth could be very funny. And I really had the sense that she admired me—wanted to be with me. She was always ready to confide in me, ask my advice about kids and work and all.

But I was also conscious of something in me that held me back. A kind of anger. Because in many ways, very little had changed. I remember one very tense visit to our place that she made with her husband. They stayed for a week and didn't make any contributions, and we had thirty dollars in the bank and we were expecting our first child. And when I finally asked her, "Aren't you going to help me buy groceries?" she said, "Am I *expected* to?"

I never confronted that type of thing. You know, "That's how Beth is." It never occurred to me that anything *could* change. So I would just keep my distance, emotionally and otherwise. And yet I felt sad about it. But I kept the walls up, more or less, until Mother died two years ago. After Mother's memorial service, Beth and I took a drive all over the town we grew up in, and we revisited a lot of places. The street where we grew up and the school and the library and the drugstore with the soda fountain, where you could get the most wonderful ice cream sodas for fifteen cents. Most of it was still there. And we talked about a lot of family things, and we had a real special time together.

That day, Beth asked me whether she could come up and visit me at our cabin in Maine, where we spent summers. I hadn't invited her for a long time, because I always found it so difficult to be with her in situations like that. I would always be the one who was doing the organizing, taking charge. [Softly.] But you know, Mother was gone, and my dad had died years ago, and my brother, Stephen, was always—very much of a loner. We were rarely in touch. And here was Beth reaching out. So I said, "Okay. Come this summer, with all the kids. We'll have a kind of family reunion. It will be lovely."

And they came and it was horrible. My kids and I painted the cabin, and she and her kids fished. We got in the groceries, made the dinners and cleaned up. They never helped. Beth brought all her problems to the island; she never had enough money, could I possibly lend her some? Same old dumb roles! I also saw the most eerie thing happening. With her kids. I saw that she was protecting her youngest daughter in just the way Mother protected *her*. Molly came to the cabin with all her needs. She wants everything. She needs this, she needs that, and when I watched Beth turn everything upside down to give it to her, I was infuriated. Princess Molly. I mean this girl is darling and charming and I love her dearly, but she is just so damned *spoiled!*

But I couldn't tell Beth any of this. I just kind of nagged people to do more, hinted around that they should do this and that. And everybody was clearly resenting me, I could feel it. Finally Beth told me that, "You know, Lucy, we didn't come up to the cabin to do all these things and be organized by you," and all of a sudden *I* was the bad guy on this trip, when I felt I was the one who was trying to keep it all together. So they left early and everyone was furious.

It was a kind of crystallizing experience. So bad that I knew that if something didn't change, I would never be able to spend time with my sister again. I had nothing to lose. So I wrote her a letter, and for the first time that I can truly remember, I was direct. I expressed my resentment. [Anger in her voice.] I told her that I didn't like being put in the bad-guy role, that it really hurt, and how I felt about the unequal division of labor between her family and my family. I told her about all the things I had tried to do to make the reunion special—I mean I had really *killed* myself before they ever got there, fixing up the place to make it festive, making pillows, flowers in everybody's rooms—and how nobody had even mentioned it. Not word one.

And she wrote back. A very, very angry letter. It really dipped into a lot of old stuff. About all the ways I had hurt *her*—how all her life she had felt I didn't like her, that she always wanted to be with me more than I wanted to be with her. A very accusatory, defensive letter. I remember feeling, So now I'm the bad guy *again!* I felt defeated—that there was just no way to get past all this junk with her. I felt angry and cheated and really miserable about it.

Then, about a week later, she sent me another letter. I still have it. She wrote, "Lucy, I didn't say this in the first letter, but I think it was wonderful that you put together the reunion for us. The time we had together really meant a lot." [Quietly.] That was really all she said. But I thought, It's *something*. For her—for us—it was a lot. And I wrote her back and basically said, "Look, Beth, we've both hurt each other in the past. This is how you've hurt me and we each remember things differently, and this is how I remember some of the things you brought up, and this is one of the terrible things that I did to you once, and I still feel bad about that and I hope you'll forgive me." And I enclosed a forgiveness poem that had helped me a lot.

And it was kind of amazing. She called me up about a week later and said, "Thank you for writing, Lucy. I'm really glad you sent me the poem." So that whole exchange kind of opened up something between us.

We haven't seen each other since the reunion. But I feel like we've begun to work on being close. We've been trying to move it along. We're talking. I feel like Beth is always going to be who she is, and I'm going to be who I am, but we're beginning to learn how to talk about it instead of crying or getting mad alone in a room. And one of the things I've been able to tell her is how the absolute number one issue for me in our relationship is equality. [Earnestly.] How I don't want to always take responsibility for everything. How I begin to put up walls when I feel I'm doing that, because it makes me feel that she doesn't give a damn about me.

And so when I invited her back to the cabin for this summer—yes, I did that!—she said, "Well, let's have a meeting beforehand to discuss how to split up the work." And I said, "Wow. I think that's a wonderful idea, Beth. And you know what? *You* call the meeting. *You* be in charge of that. Let me know when the meeting will be and I'll be there." [Laughs.]

Will she do that? I don't know. I really *hope* she will. I'd like real intimacy with my sister. I feel deeply drawn to her and I love her deeply. But we're grown-ups. I won't drag around her suitcases anymore. So I guess this summer will be a real test. Of what's possible for us.

There's another piece of it, something that I think has made me able to reach out to Beth more. I remember once showing some poetry to Mother and having her say that it was very nice, but then two weeks later hearing her say to someone else what a wonderful poet *Beth* was.

But just in the last few years, I've taken some workshops on creativity connected with my job, and one of the things I got from them was the understanding that I write well. And I'd always thought that I didn't write well. I'd been programmed out of that. So I got that sense of "Hey, I can do these things, too." And so I'm finally beginning to let myself out of that box of being the mathematical and scientific one. Really, you know, I could care less about math and science!

I think that I am, in many ways, a creative person. And I've started to write poetry again.

\* \* \*

The stories of Lucy and Beth, Terry and Marie, and Ellen and Julia attest to the remarkable diversity of the sister bond. Each of these relationships is marked by its own distinct style and rhythms, enduring themes, reasons to connect and reasons to clash, each element issuing from a sister pair's unique mix of childhood and adult influences. The dozens of other sisters I spoke with only reinforced the futility of trying to standardize sisterly relationships: Each one is implacably and complicatedly individual.

Such significant contrasts notwithstanding, a strong and consistent common theme that emerges from these interviews is the *primacy* of this relationship in women's lives. Whether a satisfying emotional tie is easily and consistently achieved, as for Terry and Marie ("She's like a bookend"); whether it has ebbed and flowed over the course of the relationship, as for Ellen and Julia ("I've almost despaired at times—but not totally"); or whether closeness is still only a powerfully felt wish, as for Lucy ("I'd like real intimacy with my sister; I feel deeply drawn to her"), the desire for a sustaining connection—and a willingness to work for it—tends to persist in the face of rivalries, disappointments, mother knots, and a host of other barriers. While not every woman I spoke with felt as fundamentally hopeful about her sister bond as did the women in this chapter, those who did not—usually because of persistent unresolved conflicts—deeply felt the absence of an affirming tie. There was a sense of impoverishment, a tendency to feel, as Louise Bernikow so eloquently expressed it, "like a sisterless child."

But are brothers really so different? The wish for intimacy is hardly exclusive to sisters: Most men want to be closer to their same-sex siblings, too. But as we will see in the next chapter, the specific aims, dominant themes, strengths and vulnerabilities that men bring to their brother bond shape the character of "fraternity" in distinctive ways—and make the encounter between brothers like no other sibling experience.

# 6

# Brothers: Love at Arm's Length

Who can fathom the relations of brothers? I love you, Lawrence, and to this day I consider my life as tied to yours as to anyone else's in the world, to my wife's or to my son's, to our sister's or to our mother's. You are more a part of me than any of them.

Ethan Canin, *Blue River*

I am Joseph, your brother, whom ye sold into Egypt.

Genesis 45:4

Joseph, the second youngest of Jacob's twelve sons in the Old Testament story, was not an easy brother to love. Not only was he his father's favorite—made cruelly clear by the bestowal of the coat of many colors—but he had a penchant for rubbing it in. What sort of boy regales his siblings with last night's dreams of suns and stars bowing down to worship him? Not surprisingly, his brothers despised this teenage narcissist and "could not speak peaceably unto him." Yet when given the chance, neither could they bring themselves to kill him. They merely wanted him out of their sight—and their father's. So when the opportunity arose to sell him into slavery in Egypt, it seemed like an excellent solution.

Of course, younger brothers are not so easy to lose. Joseph prospers in Egypt—by becoming the "favorite son" of the Pharaoh—and by age thirty is ruler of the land. When his brothers later travel to Egypt to seek refuge from famine and come before Joseph, they do not recognize him. But Joseph knows his brothers, and he throws the lot of them into prison. Behind bars, however, his siblings begin to talk among themselves, and when they express guilty regret over their youthful abuse of Joseph, he overhears them—and begins to weep. Then, when the brothers refuse his orders to leave behind Benjamin, the youngest, in order to save themselves, Joseph understands that his siblings have truly changed. He reveals his identity; they beg his forgiveness; Joseph joyfully kisses each of them. The former spoiled dreamer, now a successful and somewhat isolated middle-aged man, chooses brotherhood over getting even.

When the Bible is invoked to illustrate the brother bond, the story of Joseph and his brothers is not the most frequently cited saga. Instead, the tale of Cain and Abel is widely viewed as the quintessential "brother story," one defined by endless, hopeless and finally fatal struggle over a father's favor. Rivalry, beyond a doubt, *is* a significant dimension of the brother relationship. Throughout their lives, brother pairs tend to be far more competitive than either sister pairs or brother-sister duos.[1] Yet fraternal conflict is by no means a static given. The brother pairs I interviewed had, by and large, far more in common with the sons of Jacob than with the sons of Adam.

Like Joseph and his siblings, early struggles were common, sometimes protracted, and in many cases emotionally wounding. Yet at some point—usually after the age of thirty-five—a subtle shift often occurred. One or both brothers began to consciously long for a more nourishing sibling connection, and the armor began to crumble. Rivalry rarely disappeared entirely, but it no longer so thoroughly dominated the relationship. Such change never happened quickly or easily, and for some brothers, it did not happen at all. But for many, there was a moment when battle-weariness overcame them and the thought and the feeling arose: There must be more to being brothers than *this*.

*This*, for brothers close in age, usually went way back. It might have begun over sports, or over school, or over girls, or over who was coolest or had the best comic book collection or told the funniest jokes, but always it was about *who's doing better, me or my brother?* Among those I interviewed, this "keeping score" reflex tended to operate even between otherwise companionable brothers, with the younger of the two often feeling at a chronic, insurmountable disadvantage. (One younger brother tried to solve this "elder power" dilemma by reg- ularly reminding his brother throughout adolescence: "I'm better at basketball at my age than *you* were at my age.")

When brothers were more than three or four years apart, serious competition usually didn't emerge until early adult- hood. From that point onward, the contest most frequently centered on our culture's leading indicator of adult masculine adequacy—career success and its accoutrements, money and status. Indeed, research indicates that brothers tend to be most contentious when they are at appreciably different occupa- tional levels.[2] Many men I interviewed readily acknowledged that a brother served as a kind of success yardstick against which they automatically and perpetually measured their own degree of worldly triumph, in the process deriving—or losing—a significant measure of self-esteem.

Driving much of the rivalry between brothers, both in childhood and adulthood, was the underlying struggle for pa- rental love. But while sisters tended to feel more acutely the pain of maternal favoritism, the brothers I spoke with were more apt to yearn for, and battle over, a father's nod of ap- proval. This father was nearly always perceived as a critical, hard-to-get parent, the keeper of a conditional love that could be won only by meeting the father's particular standards for manly success. Almost inevitably, one son managed this more successfully than the other, and received some version of the "coat of many colors." Sometimes the empty-handed brother responded by trying to wrest the coat away, by putting enor- mous energy into diminishing his brother in the eyes of their father or in the eyes of the world.

In other cases, however, the man who couldn't measure up simply dropped out of the sibling contest. Particularly in two- brother families, this brother was sometimes the "black sheep," the designated troublemaker or ne'er-do-well who, in many cases, battled an alcohol or drug problem. This black- sheep brother only made his more successful sibling, the fam- ily "white knight," glow more brightly in comparison—which often led to a vicious, no-win relationship cycle. The "good" brother, guilty about shining at the expense of his "bad" coun- terpart, often tried to compensate with endless gestures of aid: lending him money repeatedly, helping him find work, bailing him out of various forms of trouble. Such relief measures rarely helped the troubled brother, because they tended to mire him more deeply in dependence, and they rarely helped the relationship, because ultimately each rescue mission only reinforced the gap between the strong savior brother and the hapless "loser."

Fathers also influenced the brother bond by their conspicuous absence. Even though the theme of the "absent father" has been much explored in recent years by Robert Bly and others, I was unprepared for the vast numbers of both men and women I interviewed who reported losing their fathers early on to alcoholism, workaholism, divorce, desertion, emotional withdrawal, or some combination of these factors. While both sexes expressed profound pain over this abandonment, the men experienced a double loss in their growing-up years. For they lacked not only a loving father, but also their designated gender-role model—the man who was supposed to teach them how to be a man. Numerous studies indicate that fathers are primary role models for their sons *only* when the fathers are nurturant and affectionate.[3] Otherwise, a boy will seek a readily available substitute. For some of the men I talked with, that replacement model of manhood was an older brother.

This rarely turned out well. The luckiest boys attached themselves to a brother who at least treated them kindly and protectively, and to that degree provided a measure of "good fathering." But as a mentor for masculinity, such a big brother was set up to fail. For he, too, was the son of an absent father; he, too, had received a paternal education in manhood that was dominated by lessons in physical and emotional distance—and little else. Research on father absence indicates that eldest sons of such fathers typically look to equally confused peers as their primary gender-role models, while simultaneously trying to be as thoroughly *unlike* their mothers and sisters as possible.[4] The likely result is an exaggerated, stereotypical version of masculinity that, in turn, becomes a younger brother's model. One man remembers admiringly watching the poses and postures of his older adolescent brother, and learning that "the way to be was, 'You can't touch me, I'm a rock.' He was incredibly hip and he managed to convey that there was nothing, *nothing* that he really cared about. And I admired that in him because he was able to get things that way—you know, make people dance around him."

Brothers often give brothers firsthand experience in the meaning of masculinity in our society—including an initiation into violence. A major study of domestic violence involving more than 2,000 families found that in every age group, boys were more frequently violent toward their siblings than were girls, and also were more severely violent, that is, brothers were more likely than sisters to kick, punch, beat up, attack with an object, or threaten a sibling with a knife or gun. Not surprisingly, then, the highest level of violence occurred *between* brothers, and was especially likely in all-boy families.[5]

Sibling violence is rarely taken seriously in our society, for we tend to shrug it off as the inevitable squabbling of inevitable rivals. And in fact, between brothers well matched in size and strength, little lasting harm may result. But when the physical "power gap" between brothers is large and victimization is repeated and severe, some researchers speculate that sibling violence may well engender a form of learned helplessness, wherein the tyrannized sibling comes to approach other relationships and situations expecting exploitation and defeat.[6] This may be particularly likely to result from brother-brother violence because our culture's tolerance of male aggression leads many parents to refrain from intervening, dismissing one son's attack on another as mere evidence that "boys will be boys."

For the "bully," meanwhile, such brother-battering may amount to early training in child abuse. A Washington State University study found that individuals who had acted violently toward a sibling in childhood were more apt to be violent toward others in adulthood than were those who had been abused by a parent in their early years,[7] perhaps because the experience of perpetrating violence on a peer is more apt to produce a sense of "winning through intimidation" than the experience of being abused by a larger, stronger parent.

Among the men I interviewed, those who suffered at the hands of an extremely violent or destructively competitive brother were apt to simply avoid him in adulthood. There was little interest in redefining or strengthening the relationship;

indeed, such men felt they had little bond on which to build. Most adult brothers I spoke with however, remembered much more than youthful acrimony. Alongside scuffles and one-upsmanship, many men could recall episodes of boyhood fun, exploration and sometimes illicit adventure with a brother, enjoying him as a sidekick or a partner in crime, and often relying on him for a sense of "strength in numbers" among the boys in the neighborhood.

As adults, most such brothers kept in touch, usually maintaining their early connection through structured activities—sports, vacation trips, joint building projects, season tickets to local team games. When I asked these brothers, "What do you talk about when you get together?" the typical answers were not too different from what one would expect of any two friendly male peers: work, sports, politics, lots of joking around. A number of men expressed satisfaction with this kind of fraternal bond, emphasizing the fun and camaraderie that were shared and the unspoken sense of solidarity that issued from joint activity. Others, however, wanted more.

The "more" that these brothers wanted was, nearly always, more intimacy. These men expressed a desire to share more of their inner lives with a brother, to find out what he was feeling as well as what he was thinking and doing, to get some help in "figuring myself out." This quest for a deeper fraternal connectedness converges with the very recent initiatives by some men to consciously question the tenets of the male gender role, especially those that urge men to keep a wary distance from other human beings. Moreover, as Sam Keen observed in his best-selling *Fire in the Belly:*

> There is much about our experience as men that can only be shared with, and understood by, other men. There are stories we can tell only to those who have wrestled in the dark with the same demons and have been wounded by the same angels. Only men understand the secret fears that go with the territory of masculinity.[8]

If what Keen says is true—and who hasn't felt the powerful sense of connection that springs from shared experience?—it is not surprising that many brothers are beginning to seek closer ties. Having grown up together, brothers uniquely share and understand the "secret fears" of masculinity that were filtered through the peculiar lens of their own family experience, through the particular model of manhood that their own father embodied, or through the conspicuous *lack* of a model that forced the brothers to covertly study each other, try out different personas and fake it the best they could. The potential for a relationship of rare empathy with another man lies just beneath the surface of the brother bond, and men who sensed that potential wanted to tap it.

Those who tried reported feeling both discouraged and exhilarated by their quest. Most men found that being vulnerable with a brother was not easy. There was the "rivalry response" to contend with: How does one suddenly stop competing with one's earliest and most enduring competitor? There were issues of trust, of pride, of a profound fear of foolishness. There was also the issue of reciprocity. Any man who wanted to deepen his relationship with his brother found himself face to face with a sibling who had learned similar taboos against intimacy, similar injunctions to maintain status, similar imperatives to do or say nothing that even remotely felt like "losing it." So it was not enough merely to want a different relationship with one's brother—one's brother had to want it, too.

At best, progress was slow, full of false starts and backtracking, requiring much patience with oneself and one's brother. When a deeper connection was made, however, the rewards often exceeded a man's expectations. As one man described his altered bond with his older brother, "The fact that I have someone who knows exactly who I am and he loves me anyway—is amazing to me. Nothing in my life gave me reason to think I could have this."

## David: When Winning Is Losing

David, an energetic, affable and very thoughtful man of thirty-seven, joined the family business last year with his eyes wide open. From the moment his father asked him to help revitalize the faltering bottled water company that his thirty-year-old brother, Alan, had been running, David knew that many of their old sibling issues—power struggles, older-younger resentments, father favoritism—would be forced out of hiding. The question that emerged was not whether David and Alan would compete over company management, for the ethic of winning was woven into the family fabric. The question was whether rivalry would destroy their partnership—as business owners and as brothers.

Achievement and loyalty. Growing up, those were the big values drilled into all three of us—especially by my father. But if one had to be sacrificed, it would be loyalty. No question.

My father had this kind of vision. He saw us as "the Cohen boys," some sort of team or force that would go out into the world and slay dragons, as a united family front. [Chuckles.] But he didn't really *do* much to make that happen. He worked all the time in his father's business, so he was out of the house most of the time. It was very rare for him to be home on a Saturday or a Sunday, and a lot of the time he didn't have dinner with us. So this "close family" thing was just kind of a fantasy he liked to talk about.

At any rate, loyalty didn't matter as much as doing well. We all grew up knowing that the best thing you could do was to get good grades, and then get into a good college, and then get into a good profession. And the thing was, I was the student. I was the great student. Steve, who's two years younger than me, was the athlete. And Alan, the youngest, well, he always worked very, very hard at everything. But Steve could beat him at any sport, and in school, he never got more than B-minuses, C-pluses.

And from grade school on, my father would ask me—in front of both of my brothers—"So, are you the smartest kid in your class?" And I'd say no and reel off a couple of names of smarter kids, and he'd say, "Well, *why* is he smarter? Are you *sure* you're not smarter?" And he'd take opportunities to show me off. For my bar mitzvah, instead of just reading from the Torah, I did the whole service as if I were a cantor. [Smiles ruefully.] Not exactly the way to my brothers' hearts.

As kids, though, Alan and I weren't that competitive. He's seven years younger than me, so when we were growing up, I never felt we were peers in any way. If anything, I felt a kind of noblesse oblige. Sort of like, "Hey, he's a kid, I'll cut him a break." I remember him as a cute, affectionate little guy—and a real brat. He was the baby. He got everything he wanted, more or less on demand. I remember very clearly wanting to play the guitar in high school, and really having to fight to get a guitar, and then to get lessons. But when Alan came along and decided for some reason that he wanted to play the trumpet, my parents went out and bought him a brand-new trumpet. A *beautiful* trumpet. And he never really played it. I *still* play the guitar. [Laughs.]

To be honest, though, I wasn't your model big brother. By the time I was thirteen or fourteen, I had gotten really very distant from my whole family. I imagined myself to be a rebel, a real individualistic, nonconformist type. I got so I was really uncomfortable being seen in public with my brothers. And at home, I had the only bedroom on the second floor, so I had my own little den of iniquity up there. I would come home from school and go up there and play my music and not even *see* my brothers. That was a long period, where I just did my own thing and more or less ignored both of them.

Looking back, I can almost pinpoint when the competition began to show up. It was the summer Alan graduated from college and I had decided to go back to business school, so he was studying for his law boards at the same time I was studying for my business boards. And for various reasons, we both lived at my parents' house that summer. We spent a fair amount of time together, and some of that was good. We were both under a lot of pressure to do well on these exams, so for the first time there was a feeling that we were in the same boat. But I also remember some nasty arguments.

They were all competitive, comparative type arguments. Who was better at this or that? One I remember was really stupid. It was about, um, clutching. [Laughs.] We were in the car and Alan was driving and he was really riding the clutch and I told him he was overclutching and we both got angry and didn't talk for the rest of the car drive. [Shakes his head.] Then there was another fight—more to the point. We were insulting each other over how to study and what schools the other one would or wouldn't get into, and finally Alan got very huffy and he said, "Well, we'll *see* who does better. We'll *see* who earns more money." As it turned out, I got into my first-choice school. Alan didn't.

The other issue that summer had to do with sleeping privileges. Who was entitled to, uh, sleep where. [Laughs, a little embarrassed.] My parents lived in a condo with only one real extra bedroom, so if more than one of us was there, somebody had to sleep on the couch in the den. Okay, but who? Alan had been living with my parents all year, so he argued that he had already staked a claim to the bedroom, and I should take the couch. But I argued that I was only there for a short time, so I should get what I wanted because he had run of the place the *rest* of the year.

We got into huge fights about that. What it was really about, I think, was who was entitled to what in our family. I guess Alan's perspective was that I was running some returning hero routine. And my perspective is, or was—I've tried to moderate it—that I'm the oldest and certain privileges *do* accrue to the oldest. I mean, I'm not talking about being sole heir to my parents' fortune or anything. Just little privileges. Getting to sleep in the bedroom of my choice.

After that summer, things were okay between us—he was in L.A. working in my father's spring-water business and I was in Palo Alto heading up sales for a computer company, so we didn't see each other much. We'd talk on the phone sometimes, but not that often. It would be pretty rare for us to just call one another out of the blue. Maybe once a year we would do that. Maybe once every two years. But things were okay. Then, last year, my father asked me to join the family firm, to beef up sales. Now, looking back, I think he was trying to fulfill his old "Cohen boys" fantasy.

But the thing was, he didn't consult my brother first.

I remember the first phone call Alan and I had about it. He was very worried. He wanted to be sure that if I was coming into the business, I would be working for him. And

I said that temporarily that might be okay, but that ultimately, "I would want to run the company as much as you do." And he said, "That's a problem." And I said, "Yes, it's a problem." And it was the first of a series of long, intense phone conversations about sharing power and turf—who's going to be in charge of what. I found out from those talks how much alike we actually are—bullheaded and control-oriented and we like to be *right*. [Chuckles.] But finally we agreed that we'd be coequals, vice presidents in different areas. And I thought it was settled.

Then, just before I joined, I went to a conference where Alan was giving a talk. I was looking through the conference program and saw that he was listed as COO—chief operating officer. *Unbelievable.* He had changed his title on me! I waited until his talk was over and asked him to come up to my hotel room and I confronted him with it. And he basically said, "So what? What business is it of yours?"

I said, "Damn it, Alan, we've had these long discussions about sharing power and this is clearly a power play." And he shouted at me, *"Dad and I run this company!"*

And we had this long, loud battle in the hotel room, yelling and stomping around. It would have fallen apart at that point except that my father stepped in and said he would retire in a year's time so that Alan could be CEO and I could be president. Until then, Alan would go on being COO—and I would somehow swallow that.

We're just eight months into it. [Takes a long breath.] It's been very hard. Alan is very jealous of his power, and I can understand some of that. Up to now, he's been able to shape the company in his own image and here I come along, big brother from the outside. And I'm probably not the easiest person to work with. I *do* like to take charge. I don't like to be taken charge of. If that's an oldest-brother symptom, I've got it. Plus, because of this achievement ethic that my father has instilled in us, I always feel—challenged. I always feel that I have to demonstrate my competence, my intelligence. I have to prove myself. If anything, I've always felt that I wasn't pushy enough because I had this father who said, "Push, push, *push.*"

And in this particular situation, I feel it even more. Because my brother is constantly rubbing in my face: "I'm the COO and you're *not*." So I'm trying to carve out my own position and stand on firm ground. But I have a feeling that my brother perceives it differently. Perceives it as a major threat whenever I do that. I see myself as just sort of running the treadmill to maintain my place. Treading water to keep my head above so I can breathe. But it probably comes across as trying to drown him. Trying to prevent *him* from breathing.

And so we're having real problems. Serious. I've watched him exclude me from decisions. Go out of his way not to share information. I'm constantly concerned that he's figuring out ways to marginalize me. That's not a good feeling. [He is silent for a moment.] It's real interesting. He has a huge stake in the company, yet whenever I lose a sale, he's—almost complacent. It's like, "Oh, well, that's okay." Because the reality is that the more sales I bring in, the more power I have. From a business standpoint, he needs the sales, because it brings in money.

But at a personal level, I think he'd just as soon see me fail.

We also have trouble just trying to talk to each other. Alan says whenever he tells me about a problem, I make him feel worse instead of better. He says I'm hypercritical. But generally when someone describes a problem to me, my reaction is, "Oh, they want to pick apart the problem and find a solution." So that's what I do, and sometimes it involves criticism of the way he's handled something. Then he gets all upset. So I'm trying to shift gears. I'm beginning to get that he doesn't want answers as much as support, a little empathy for what he's dealing with. And respect.

That's a big one. My brother really, really wants my respect. He has run this company for five years and he really wants me to acknowledge that. But I've got to say this: I don't see how he could be where he is without being my father's son. My father brought him into the company at the age of twenty-five, with no experience in this industry— whereas I got all my business experience on my own. You know, he's really doing a pretty good job. But I do tend to look at him and I see my father favoring him, spending more time with him, giving him all kinds of breaks, and I think, Little spoiled brat, who does he think he is? I don't know if I can ever change that, totally. But I'm trying to see his point of view. I *want* this to work.

You know, I had all these fantasies about coming down here and having these great conversations with Alan on weekends, hanging out together. And it hasn't happened. [Sounding discouraged.] My brother has never even invited me over to his house. It hasn't been nearly as much fun as I thought it would be.

And yet I always have this feeling that if we could just get past some of this stuff, we could be close. Or closer. You know, Alan is the godfather of our oldest son. But Alan also has two kids, and we're not the godparents of *either* of those children. A few years ago I asked him about that, and I remember being stunned because what he said was, "I didn't think you really cared about being a godparent." And then he started crying. We both sort of cried about it, actually, and after that we had a good conversation.

And it made me think that I've never actually asked Alan how he felt about me when we were growing up. You know, whether he really resented me, my distance—always shutting him out. I think now that he probably did.

Right now, I'm trying to focus on the idea that sometimes you have to get farther to get closer. You know, you have to get to know each other to resolve old problems. At this point, we're having a major blowup about every other week. It used to be once a week, so we're doing a little better. [Smiles faintly.] But every fight is over the same issues: who's right, who's smart, who does things best, who has Dad's ear. We need to figure out the psychodynamics of what is happening between us—all the little tripwires in our heads that the other one keeps touching off. And try to step around them, or do whatever works.

Maybe we can do that. But I can't count on it. Just a few weeks ago, in fact, we sat down and discussed a buy-sell agreement, where one of us would buy out the other in case it turns out we can't get along. And at one point Alan said,

"Maybe we can't get along as business associates. Maybe we just have to be brothers."

And I said, "Alan, *forget* about business. I don't think we're doing that well as brothers."

Because that's really how I see it. Our business issues *are* brother issues. We need to start there. And I told him that. I said "Alan, you know it and I know it. If you became CEO today and I became president and our power in the company was absolutely and precisely equal, we'd still be fighting over who gets the key to the men's room."

## Pat and Danny: Can We Talk?

Pat, fifty, and Danny, forty-six, clearly get a kick out of each other. Throughout my interview with them there was lots of joking, easy laughter, and reminiscing about growing up in their large Irish Catholic family in inner-city Philadelphia. Today, the brothers still live around the corner from each other; both teach high school, play tennis weekly and consider themselves best friends. Yet as the three of us talked over tea in Danny's basement family room, it became clear that there were realms of experience these brothers never spoke about—silences enforced by gender, their ethnic heritage and a family history of alcoholism. Were they ready to break their code of cheerful stoicism and get to know the man behind the tennis partner? Maybe.

DANNY: Remember the Irish sweet potatoes?

PAT: [Laughing.] Yeah.

DANNY: In my mind, that marks the beginning of—I don't know—feeling like brothers. I always connect them up. It was the day you were leaving to go into the service. I was in the eighth grade. I remember vividly how my teacher kept the whole class after school that particular day and I remember getting real agitated about maybe missing you. *Real* upset. And when she finally let us out I ran the whole way to the candy store to get some

Irish sweet potatoes. They were pretty disgusting—sort of coconut cream candies shaped like potatoes—but I wanted to give you a going-away present. It was real important to me. And I made it home just in time.

PAT: [Nodding, smiling.] I remember you flying into the house with this huge candy bag. I have the same memory exactly.

DANNY: But that's the first time I can remember having strong feelings for you. That departure is very vivid. It's strange. Because before that, I don't remember feeling much of anything.

PAT: Well, our family wasn't exactly big on emotions.

DANNY: Not a lot of physical expression, especially. I rarely saw our parents kiss or hand-hold or hug.

PAT: I don't *ever* remember seeing them touch.

DANNY AND PAT: They're Irish. [Both laugh.]

DANNY: I think our family lived by another very Irish trait, and that's the tendency to want to keep the peace. Keep everything calm—not by working it through but by simply not letting stuff erupt. No anger allowed. "Let's agree everything is okay here." That was definitely how we all learned to operate.

Q: Was there anything going on in your family that was clearly "not okay"?

PAT: [After a small silence.] Yeah. Both of our parents drank. My dad did most of his drinking when I was young, and then after he quit, my mother got into it heavy. Her drinking probably affected Danny more than me—he was still in grade school at the time.

DANNY: Yeah. I have recollections of grade school, early high school, being really worried about how much she drank. Mostly, she tried to hide it. But I remember once she passed out on the steps coming home from a party with Dad and another couple—it was awful.

PAT: I never knew about that! You never told me that.

DANNY: No. Probably not.

PAT: You know, I always thought of Dad as having the big problem. Lots of bar drinking, lots of fights. I remember being just a little guy—seventh or eighth grade—and trying to get between him and these guys he would pick fights with. *Big* guys. [Shakes his head.]

DANNY: No kidding? I never knew that.

PAT: Huh. They talked a lot about sending us all to St. Vincent's Home and . . .

DANNY: *What?*

PAT: Yeah, pack us up and farm us out.

DANNY: Oh, wow!

PAT: Terrible.

DANNY: *Geez.*

Q: Have you ever talked before about growing up with alcoholic parents?

DANNY: Occasionally. Uh, not frequently.

PAT: You know, we could do it more. I've thought about that.

DANNY: Huh.

Q: Growing up with these tensions and secrets in your family, how did the two of you get to be friends?

DANNY: Again, for me, I date it back to Pat's going into the service. He would come home on leave and the house would be, you know, a different place. He'd bring buddies over and they'd sit around the kitchen table and drink beer and sing songs and I remember really, really liking it. Being fascinated with him and his friends and their stories of being out in this bigger world, traveling, meeting new people.

[To Pat.] And you let me in on it. That was a real important piece of it. I wasn't an official participant, but I felt welcome to hang around and hear the stories. So that made me feel like I could be—part of your world. Even if I had to go to bed earlier. [Both laugh.]

PAT: But in my memory, we didn't really start to be friends until I got out of the service and you got out of high school. We more or less stopped doing things with the whole family, and we'd go off on our own a lot.

DANNY: Right. That's when it got really intense.

Q: In what way was it intense?

DANNY: Well, we had a large circle of good friends, and we had a lot in common. Pat and I would go out with them and we'd play a lot of sports together. A *whole* lot of tennis. I can remember just gobbling dinner down and rushing off to the tennis courts. That was during the tennis boom when it was hard to get courts.

PAT: Our life revolved around that. Sports and . . .

DANNY: The lake.

PAT: [Grinning.] Yeah, going down to the lake . . .

DANNY: Summertime especially. We'd go all afternoon. Swim and play games there. And then we'd organize a mass trip to a movie downtown and you know, twenty of us would go to the movies.

PAT: [Laughing.] Every week. Every *day*. There wouldn't be enough hours in the day to do everything.

DANNY: Yeah. And that's when we first got to know each other, I think.

Q: What did you find out about each other?

DANNY: Well, that I liked *doing* things with him. If I can think of traits . . . [To Pat.] Uh, I felt good doing things with you. Hanging out with you. [Silence.] Yeah. Hmm. I'm having trouble getting more specific than that.

PAT: Yeah. Well, it seemed like it was fun whenever I was around you, too. More like peers by then. Though I like to think I still had a good influence on this little guy. [Both laugh.]

DANNY: But there's truth in that. I can think of times when I was sort of pulled and led by you, and I think the whole peace movement was . . .

PAT: Peace days. Yes.

DANNY: . . . something that I really admired you being so involved in, and that really sensitized me. That was his direct influence.

PAT: Yeah, we talked a lot about the issues, and eventually we shared a house together. Remember? There were five of us . . .

DANNY: Pretty antiwar-oriented house.

PAT: The commune. [Laughter.]

DANNY: We were part of the now infamous "Rizzo's Raiders" who came down from Philly for the big 1970 demonstration to shut down Washington. [Both laugh uproariously.]

PAT: I'm going to tell the jail story. [Danny lets out a mock groan.] We went down to D.C. together with a big group, and the night before the demonstration we got a very intensive training about wetting your handkerchief to put over your nose for the tear gas and writing a key phone number on your wrist because the expectation was that all of us would get locked up. Then we got assigned to a certain intersection, where we were to go the next morning and sit down in the middle of it. Bring Washington, D.C., to its knees. [Joint chortling.]

DANNY: So the next morning—like at five-thirty a.m., the sun wasn't even out yet—Pat and I went out with another guy, Greg, to our assigned intersection. And before we ever got there a car pulled up and two plainclothes policemen jumped out and grabbed Pat and Greg and slammed them up against the car and frisked them and threw them in the cop car and for some strange reason I'll never understand, just left me standing there. They drove off and there I was.

And I remember thinking, Man, a guy can't get himself locked up! And I wandered around for a while by myself and finally I used my "one phone call" dime to call my uncle who had this real straight Department of Labor job and I wound up at his Bethesda home for a full dinner. Meanwhile, my brother was languishing in jail. [Both laugh.]

PAT: Seventy-three people in my jail cell and he's eating steak. [Chuckles.]

DANNY: Uh, well, I was concerned about you. But to be honest, I was more concerned about myself. I was alone and got gassed once, and I was frightened. So the next day, my uncle put me on a train. He sent me home. Um, I heard from Pat after I got home.

PAT: [Grinning.] So much for brotherhood! But actually, it was a real nice thing to have someone in my family to share those values and vision with—and Danny was definitely the *only* one who did. The other four siblings were all very—well, more conventional. I think those days kind of laid the foundation for the relationship we have now.

Q: How would you describe that relationship?

DANNY: Well, I see our relationship as symbolized by how we've purchased cars. [To Pat.] I remember a time when you wanted to buy a car and didn't make enough money to get a loan, and I happened to be in a position to sign for you to get a car. And I remember being in the exact same position—wanting to get a car and *you* being the one to sign. And I see that as the way it's gone—lots of helping out, back and forth. Real equal that way.

Q: You haven't talked at all about rivalry. Do you feel any?

DANNY: On the tennis court—no question. I think we're both very competitive people, and it comes out mostly through sports. We still play a lot of sports together. I really play hard and I really *like* beating somebody. I don't know that it's about beating Pat specifically.

PAT: Hmmm. I feel that it does get more complicated for me to beat him. Because I need to use anger at somebody to play my very best. So it gets complicated to beat my little brother. [To Danny.] So when you beat me, it's not because you're better. [Both laugh.]

DANNY: I'd say that most of what we do together is just fun. Like this spring, we took my sons down to Clearwater to watch the Phillies play. And we're two members of a twenty-member decathlon group. Let's see. We spend time down the shore with our families.

PAT: We don't do much, just the two of us.

DANNY: I don't feel a great need to do that. How about you?

PAT: [Silent for a moment.] Maybe. I mean, yeah, I could see doing that once in a while.

Q: When you do get together, what kinds of things do you talk about?

DANNY: [After a long pause.] I can't really say.

PAT: We talk some about work, some about sports. But actually, I like to think it's been opening up the last couple of years. We talk some about good books, trade 'em back and forth. It's begun to get real interesting and varied in my mind. Lately we've been talking some about the men's movement. We've, uh, even joined a small men's group.

DANNY: Uh, well, I'm a would-be member. I haven't attended a meeting yet. [Laughs a little uncomfortably.]

PAT: I started it a few months ago with three other guys, and Danny's the next to come in. [Softly, to Danny.] I'm really hoping you will. Because it's a little—well, not scary, but there's always the pull to back off, not be so open. I have this idea that if you're in the group, I'll feel the challenge to keep on being open.

DANNY: Yeah?

PAT: I mean, just that you're not supposed to talk about when you're not feeling good or when you're anxious or when you're depressed. You just don't talk about those things. There's the men's part of it—it makes you weak. But there's another, family part of it, where you're not supposed to express those things. "Everything's okay here." And I could see where Danny and I could give each other a lot of support for fighting that old junk. [To Danny.] Same boot camp!

DANNY: [A little stiffly.] He is very open to different ways of thinking. [To Pat.] That's a prominent trait with you that I admire.

PAT: Well, I admire how you have changed just over the past year—with assertiveness and expressing anger. I'm impressed. Coming from our family, I don't know how you do it.

DANNY: [Pleased and embarrassed.] Hey, thanks. You recognized it.

PAT: To me, it feels like our relationship is developing. Right now, we're maybe more willing than able. [Chuckles.] Sort of moving from preverbal to verbal.

[Danny nods, looking down.]

PAT: But I think that's pretty neat, given our history.

DANNY: Hmmm.

## Joe: Be My Brother, Be My Dad

When Joe, thirty-eight, talks about his brother, Michael, forty-one, his voice resonates with affection, exasperation and admiration—all of them deeply felt. From the time they were teenagers growing up in New York's Little Italy, Michael was the primary figure in Joe's life, at once mentor, rescuer, and above all, stand-in for the father by whom Joe felt abandoned. But when Michael became a wealthy, world-renowned cancer specialist, new complications arose in their relationship. How could Joe possibly feel jealous of the guy he loved most in the world? Even more fundamental, what happens when one's brother no longer has the time nor the inclination to be one's father?

If he walked into this room right now, you'd know what I mean about Michael. He's a very imposing guy. Six feet tall and bald, but it looks better on him than on me. Huge shoulders, immense arms, enormous barrel chest, a bit of a gut now—but he wears it well. He's a real presence.

And you'd *like* him. He's quick; he's a very, very funny son of a bitch. [Chuckles.] And there's a genuine joie de vivre about him—not the theatrical kind that some people put on. He's just a very enthusiastic, hospitable, generous kind of a guy. You talk to him, you feel good. He's got that ability.

Looking at my brother now, you'd think he had been somebody's favored child. But that was me. I was the sick one, the baby. I had asthma, I had bronchitis, I had mastoid ear problems, I had all kinds of things. My mother favored me incredibly—horrendously, looking back. I remember somebody giving us boxing gloves when we were kids, and I wanted to box with Michael. So my mother made Michael get on his knees and she rigged it a few other ways so that basically I pummeled him—and this was in front of the whole family and a bunch of relatives.

This kind of thing happened constantly. To say that my mother tortured Michael—that may not be too strong a word.

And she ran the show, because my father rarely made an appearance. He would work all day at his store, come in, have dinner, fall asleep on the couch for a half hour and then go back out. Nobody really knew where he was going. Growing up, I was very angry at him for that—for never showing up. Now I understand him better, but back then, I had no respect for him whatever. He loved money, loved to throw it around, he was into conspicuous consumption. A real nouveau riche kind of a guy. He always had a Cadillac—almost new. We lived in a poor neighborhood, sort of sleazy and marginal, and we were always the richest people in it. And everybody knew that, because there was always this Caddy parked outside.

For most of my childhood, Michael was just my brother. He was a lug. He had no importance in the world. I didn't care for him, nor did he for me. Then, in his senior year of high school, he just kind of—bloomed. He became class president. He got into school plays, he formed the Spirit Club, and he got very social. Girls liked him. *Everybody* liked him. Everybody started treating him like he was something special—so I figured he must *be*. I was a freshman then. And at that point I decided—very consciously—that I wanted to be like Michael.

I was serious about it. The very next year I ran for class president, and lost. So then I got into drama. To me, acting was what sexy people did, *artistes,* and I did manage to become president of the Thespians—as Michael had. But I never got the parts he did. Michael always had the romantic leads, but I never got leads. [Sounding frustrated.] I just didn't *look* as good as Michael did. I always had these little character parts. And then I used to get horrible, horrible stage fright.

Then he went off to Notre Dame, full scholarship, and he became an even bigger deal. He would come home with stories about dating glamorous women, he had his own car, he was premed. And now my mother and sisters would be, "Oh, Michael's home, Michael's home." Now Michael was the star, the returning hero. So now the roles were reversed. Now he was going to be a *doctor,* now he was achieving, which is what Italian families do through their kids. And he was playing into my father's concern with money and status. So Michael was making it.

I can't entirely explain this, but at this point, I felt a little jealousy but mostly admiration. See, I always assumed that everything he did, I could do. [Laughs ruefully.] I used to *love* knowing that my brother was doing well. I figured I could learn his social skills, and I knew I was as smart as he was. So I would simply benefit from the path he had already blazed. I didn't realize at the time how extraordinary a guy he was. It was just going to be a matter of time before I got to where he was.

The other thing was that, with my father basically out of the picture, I really looked to Michael to kind of—show me the world. Define manhood for me, I suppose. Plus, now that he wasn't living at home anymore, we were getting closer. So when I was eighteen and he was twenty-one, we took a trip to Mexico. Just the two of us. And that was my introduction to sex. Or was supposed to be. [Laughs.] We were walking down a street in Tijuana, I think, when some guy crawled out of a corner and said, "Come to a nice party, meet some nice women." Michael had done this kind of thing before, but of course I hadn't. And we went in and I can still remember this one young woman, dark-skinned, big almond eyes, just—oh, my, gorgeous.

But I thought we were just going to kind of flirt around. I mean, "Momma's Boy" was my middle name. When I realized that Michael was going to stay, I was scandalized. He was actually going to *do* this. And he was encouraging me to do it, too. And I remember thinking, Oh my God it's a sin, and it's dangerous, and it's illegal, and somebody might knock you upside your head, and these were all my images. And he just laughed and said, "Okay, go back to the hotel," and I scurried back.

But what I really got from it, I think, was that this was okay with Michael—so in some way it must be okay. And a couple years later, on another trip with him to Italy, I did sleep with prostitutes.

The women stuff—I think it's one of the areas where he failed me as a "father." It was all such a wilderness then, and I really looked to my brother for advice. And his advice stunk. He basically said, "Don't get pushed around. And the only way not to get pushed around is to take the reins. There will always be power struggles. Don't lose them. Lose one, and you've lost them all." I see now that he watched that happen in spades with my parents—my mother really did overpower my dad.

My brother was a big bar guy, too, which was why I became a big bar guy. He was always a big drinker, heavy. He got me served when I was underage, we drank a lot together, he helped me get a bartending job one year. And for a number of years, I had a real problem. Because when I drank, my inhibitions went, and suddenly I wasn't this short, shy, awkward guy anymore. Then I, too, was the hail-fellow-well-met, and I, too, was funny, and I, too, was everybody's buddy, and I, too, was confident, and I, too, was *just like Michael.*

[After a reflective silence.] I'm convinced that is why drinking played such a big role for me, for such a long time. That, and the fact that Michael sanctioned it.

And that's really the story of my maturation, I guess. Or retardation. [Laughs.] If Michael said it was okay, it was okay. If Michael had said it was *not* okay, it would not have been okay. It was really as simple as that. He sanctioned drinking, so drinking was okay. If he sanctioned prostitutes,

prostitutes were okay. If his attitude toward women was hard-ass, then hard-ass was okay. I used to be angry at him about some of this until I realized, at some point, that my brother didn't have a father either. He didn't have *anybody* to go to, to show him what was what. At least I had him.

And in many ways, he was a terrific "father." Between my junior and senior year in college, down here in D.C., I began collapsing. My life went to pieces, and I stayed in pieces for a long time—I was a very troubled guy throughout my twenties. And of course, my history was that whenever I had been sick, I had someone to go to. With my childhood physical sicknesses, I had my mother. And so now, when I had these new kinds of sicknesses—head sicknesses—I went to Michael. A substitute parent.

And he accepted that, somehow. He would get on the phone with me—not just once or twice but I mean *years* of phone calls—and say, "Don't worry, you had an anxiety attack, this happens, you'll be okay, I'll get you some medication, you can go into therapy. I'll get you a referral." On the one hand, my brother likes taking care of his own—he's a Godfather—but I really did push the limits.

I remember one time in particular. I was in my late twenties, having what I hoped would be the last of my nervous breakdowns. And my brother went way out of his way to come down here to visit me. He took me out to dinner and listened to all my problems, and then he basically said, "Hey, Joe, this is not the end of the world. You've got a lot going for you. *Everything can change.*" Then he started lining up people for me to meet, job connections on the Hill, all kinds of stuff to help me.

And I remember telling him that night that, you know, Dad was actually a nice enough guy, but that he was not my father. I said to my brother, "You are. You've always been."

And you know, even with all his macho stuff, I think I learned from Michael a capacity for intimacy with other men. He's a very, very vulnerable guy, very easily hurt—especially by women. And it's amazing, but he's always been able to talk about that stuff. He told me years ago, for instance, that back in college he was actually terrified of women, that he only *seemed* to be good with girls. I remember him telling me, "You think I'm this big stud, but believe me, I'm not. I've been rejected *thousands* of times." He was never sexually successful, he told me, until he was in medical school.

So I've never had that sense that I guess a lot of men have, that talking about these things is taboo. And I look for friends I can talk to. I mean, if someone wants to play tennis or share intellectual interests, that's nice, but the above-all thing for me is somebody you can be honest with. It's hard to find guys like that; there are only a few. But the ones I've found I cultivate like hell. And it was Michael, more than anybody else, who led me to see how important this is. How *he* learned it, I can't imagine.

But my feelings toward my brother are horrendously complicated. While I was in the depths of my decade-long collapse, Michael was busy getting very, very big. He had been making doctor's money, which was very good—much more than I'll ever make as a drug-abuse bureaucrat—but his salary was always, you know, within reach. But by the time I hit my thirties, he had started to ascend the heights. He was in demand; he was becoming a superstar. Half a million a year. Then a lot more than that. My brother was on the cover of a couple of very big magazines; he was on national TV. And suddenly one house wasn't enough; he had to have a cottage in the Hamptons. [Resentment creeps into his voice.] And then a Volvo wasn't enough; it had to be a Porsche. *And* a Mercedes. It all went through the roof.

And I started feeling very angry at him. [Very quietly.] I mean, all my life, my dream—my innermost, deepest, most private and secret dream—was to attain some measure, somehow, of renown that would put me on the same level as Michael. Now that wasn't possible. Never *would* be. My income today is approximately one-twentieth of my brother's. I'll admit that I could never bust ass the way he does. My brother is the king of the ass-busters. But ever since he got rich and famous, basically, I've been fighting this chronic irritation, this sort of disgust about how greedy and sleazy and social-climbing he is. Partly, it reminds me of my father.

But mainly I'm just jealous as hell and I don't know that I can totally resolve it.

My brother's stardom has had other fallout. I'm not as—as primary to him anymore. Most of my life I've had this huge need for Michael's attention, a sort of "I want mine." Exclusive time. Now that's almost impossible. Starting a few years ago he began to call me on his car phone, which really pissed me off. Now I'm getting crammed into the free time. He should be *making* time for Joe. Or I'd come up to New York for a visit and expect to have dinner with him, and he'd say, "Terrific, we'll go to this little French place and there'll be nine of us, and you'll *love* these people." But the real moment of truth came last year, when I came up to the city to celebrate my birthday with him.

I *always* come back up for my birthday. A lot of that has to do with being single, and wanting to celebrate my birthday with family. So I came to visit about a week beforehand, and I just sort of assumed that on my birthday, I'd be doing something with Michael. I had not specifically said, "Can we do something?" I had just expected that we would. So it comes my birthday, and I finally blurt out something about it since nobody else does, and Michael tells me that he and his wife had already made plans, weeks ago, to go out with friends who were about to leave the country. There was no getting out of it. He said he was sorry. And I was furious.

I brooded about it all weekend. I was hurt, and I was embarrassed to be so hurt. I mean, I was thirty-seven, for God's sake! But I couldn't stop feeling hurt. And finally I told him, "Let's go have a drink, I gotta talk to you." And we go to the top of some hotel and I start talking and I realize my voice is shaking, I'm so upset. And I tell him that he *knew* it was my birthday and he *knew* I was going to be in New York, and so, in effect, how *could* he. A real guilt trip.

And he just sat there and looked at me a minute. And then he kind of leaned in and said, "Look, Joe. You have a right to be upset. And I *am* sorry. But by the same token, *you* should have been more explicit about what you wanted. I cannot and I will not anticipate your every need." And he went on in that vein. And I just got more furious. I didn't want to share responsibility, I wanted an *abject apology!* [Chuckles.] But I could see that wasn't going to happen. And it was a very important talk for me. Because what I got from it, once I got some perspective, was that my brother was saying to me, "Look, I want to support you, I want to spend time with you. But that is *it*. Don't expect me to be your daddy anymore."

That was a year ago. And I'd say we're definitely attempting to push our relationship in a different direction. Not as intense. More equitable, less dependent. I'm trying to rely more on other people, rely more on myself. I don't call him as much anymore. It's not an estrangement; just more distance.

But it's hard. I mean, I'd never really detached from Daddy before. [Smiles ruefully.] So I miss him. I miss the son of a bitch in a lot of ways.

But you know, we've had such a close relationship—so tested and true—that I have a kind of faith that we'll get past this phase. Because the attachment I have to him is partly the father stuff, but there's another big part of it, too. It's knowing how vulnerable *he* is. See, that's the key to Michael. Here's a guy who, when all is said and done, is a very commanding presence. He's wealthy and respected, he likes power, he likes to be in control, he likes to be the center of attention. In every visible way, he's a very, very formidable guy.

I think I'm one of the few people who know how easily he is hurt. How much he needs everybody to *love* him. Liking him isn't enough. [Smiles indulgently.] You've gotta *love* Michael. I think it goes all the way back to our childhood—he had to achieve, achieve, achieve to get the coddling that came to me without lifting a finger. So Michael's always been a puppy. You pat him on the head, tell him he's a big deal, he'll follow you anywhere. You want me to be a doctor? I'll be a doctor. You want me to be rich and famous? I'll do it. But *love* me.

So when I hear my brother criticized, I feel it viscerally. It seems like slapping an old lady. Or a child. I think, *Say it again, and I'll put my foot down your throat. Say it again, and I'll put your eyes out.*

It's really amazing, isn't it. How you love the people who will show that side to you. You know who they really are. So that's a piece of it, too. Of why—why there is nobody I love more than Michael. There is nobody I have *ever* loved more. He's necessary to me.

\* \* \*

Joe's story was unique among members of brother pairs I spoke with. No other man I spoke with described a comparable level of empathy with a brother, or such a willingness to be emotionally vulnerable with him. And while his story may be exceptional, it underscores the necessity of viewing gender in the context of the entire spectrum of influences on the sibling bond. In Joe's case, a number of critically shaping influences—among them a vacuum of parental nurturing, Michael's extraordinary example of emotional openness, and Joe's childhood history as "the fragile one"—allowed these brothers to dispense with the interpersonal caution that characterizes most fraternal bonds. At the same time, Joe's and Michael's tie incorporates many quintessentially brotherly elements, in particular Joe's enduring, profoundly felt rivalry with Michael in the career arena; a bond reinforced by joint travels, nights on the town, and other "outward bound" activity; and the powerful education in manhood that Michael imparted to Joe as a consequence of their father's nonpresence in their lives.

Observations of the distinctive qualities of the brother bond and the sister bond raise the inevitable next question: What happens when sister meets brother? As Deborah Tannen observes, "We don't expect family . . . who grew up in 'the same culture' and speak 'the same language' to . . . have different views of the world."[9] Yet when one person grew up female in that family and the other grew up male, such divergent views are nearly inescapable and are apt to be profound, encompassing not only different experiences of intimacy and separateness, but also of power. As we will see, the "gender lessons" that families impart are quite literally unforgettable, and they exert a shaping influence on bonds between brothers and sisters.

# 7

# Sisters and Brothers:

## Trying to Connect

And my brothers . . . must represent half the world to me, as I must represent the other half to them.

Alice Walker, *In Search of Our Mothers' Gardens*

I am an only child. I have one sister.

Woody Allen

Among the Fore of Papua New Guinea, a man refers to his sister as "my mouth."[1] I had recently interviewed several members of sister-brother pairs when I came upon that metaphor, and it seemed to me startlingly apt for our culture as well, encompassing both the central source of power and the central dilemma of many brother-sister bonds. On the one hand, the image of one's sibling as a part of oneself speaks to the deep mutual identification that a number of sisters and brothers I interviewed experienced, a felt sense that one's opposite-sex sibling embodied one's own unexplored or inaccessible male or female side. As one man said of his sister, "I sometimes feel she's the female of me." Such a sensed connection lent both comfort and excitement to the relationship, a deep belonging and a trace of mystery.

Yet for a man to cast his sister as "my mouth"—not, for example, "my arm" or "my head" or "my eyes"—suggests something very specific, and often troublesome, about the role many sisters play within this relationship. Sisters, in fact, do much of the "mouth work" for their brothers. That is, they tend to initiate most of the communication that occurs between sister and brother, and they tend to speak more freely the language of connection that helps to sustain relationships. Among members of sister-brother pairs I talked with, most acknowledged that sisters more frequently made the phone calls, wrote the letters, and organized the get-togethers between them. Once contact was made, moreover, a sister was more apt to ask the open-ended questions, to articulate feelings and, at times, to dare say the unsayable in order to try to deepen the bond.

Many brothers I spoke with highly valued the "connector" role their sisters played in their relationship. A number, in fact, viewed the sister bond as a rare opportunity for an intimate tie, regardless of whether that potential had been realized. As a family member, a sister was seen by many men as one of the few people capable of truly understanding him and his history; as a woman, she was viewed as one of the few people he could be—or could imagine being—emotionally vulnerable with, without fear of ridicule or pity.

Of course, not all brothers I interviewed felt the presence of such sisterly support, and among those who felt it, some men felt uninterested in, or uncomfortable with, a sister's bid for a sustaining connection. Nonetheless, among the men I interviewed who had at least one brother as well as a sister, the sister was more frequently named as "the sibling I feel closest to," a choice documented in a number of research studies as well.[2] One man expressed it succinctly: "She extends not just a hand, but both hands. Herself."

Women with brothers, however, tended to experience the bond very differently from men with sisters. More anger, more frustration and more longing emerged from my interviews with these sisters. More than anything, women with brothers expressed enormous weariness at being the designated "mouth" for the relationship, and they wanted their male siblings to share more fully that gender-typed role. This meant, in part, that they wished their brothers would simply initiate more of the interaction between them, but many sisters also longed for a different *kind* of conversation with their brothers. Many wanted to explore more intimate topics—family emotional history, current family dynamics, personal psychological stumbling blocks and growth—than their brothers felt comfortable with. Significantly, far fewer sisters than brothers reported that they could "talk about anything" with their opposite-sex sibling.

Sisters also wanted their brothers simply to listen to them, especially when all was not well. One woman spoke for many sisters when she said, "We can now talk about a lot of things, including his problems. But my brother has trouble hearing *my* pain." Given these perceptions of emotional boundaries and of lopsided nurturing, it is not surprising that women who had siblings of both sexes were more likely to elect a sister than a brother as the one they felt closest to—just as men were more apt to choose a sister. This by no means meant, however, that women had written off their male siblings. Among the sisters I interviewed, most cared deeply, even fiercely, for their brothers; many were committed to trying to deepen the bond and were saddened by the distances they sensed between them. But they wanted their brothers to meet them in the middle.

Beyond the gender gap in communication and caregiving habits, many adult sisters and brothers face a deeper source of friction: parents' preferential treatment of sons over daughters. Sisters do not easily forget the deprivation of such favoritism. At the age of eighty-two, Anna Freud Bernays published a magazine article titled "My Brother, Sigmund Freud," which began as a stiffly worded appreciation of her brilliant, recently deceased sibling, whom their mother had called "my golden Sigi." But in the course of dutifully recording Sigmund's many childhood manifestations of genius, Anna described the story of her own piano lessons, undertaken with passionate enthusiasm and impressive discipline at the age of eight. As she came to the point of her anecdote—retold more than seventy years after the fact—she could not entirely suppress her bitterness toward her privileged brother:

> Though Sigmund's room was not near the piano, the sound disturbed him. He appealed to my mother to remove the piano if she did not wish him to leave the house

altogether. The piano disappeared and with it all opportunities for his sisters to become musicians.[3]

From this passage a number of questions emerge: To what extent did this blatant favoritism shape the lifelong animosity between Anna and Sigmund? Further, how did this parent-assisted, wildly successful power play against a sister—only one of many—contribute to Freud's vision of the "natural" inferiority of women? And how must it have shaped Anna's vision of herself, her power to control her destiny, her importance in her family and in the world?

One might be tempted to dismiss Anna Freud's deprivation as a mere artifact of Victorian sexism. But while parental gender bias was not a universal phenomenon among those I interviewed—some reported that parents went to great lengths to treat sons and daughters equally—the majority of members of opposite-sex sibling pairs reported that one or both parents overtly valued and favored a son (particularly an eldest son) over a daughter. There were some striking ethnic differences: Both my interviews and the research literature suggest that families of Irish, Italian, Latino and Asian origins may be particularly apt to practice blatant "son worship," with brothers often getting many varieties of "more"— attention, praise, education, privileges, freedoms—at the direct expense of their sisters.[4] By contrast, African American and Native American families tend to be notably equitable in their treatment of boy and girl children.[5]

My interviews indicated that class also plays a role in the ranking of daughters and sons. Women who grew up in working-class households more often reported being made to wait on their brothers—clean their rooms, iron their clothes, serve them at the table—than did their middle-class counterparts. Significantly and dishearteningly, generation made almost no difference: Sisters and brothers in their twenties and thirties were as likely to report parental gender bias as those in their fifties and older. Furthermore, such bias almost never reversed direction. Among those I interviewed, only one brother reported feeling less valued or privileged than a sister.

Such inequitable treatment is documented as well in recent birth order research that takes note of gender differences. Several studies indicate that among laterborn children, boys tend to receive more parental affection and caregiving, as well as more education and support for learning, than do girls.[6] A study of firstborn adolescents, meanwhile, found that parental involvement and support was high for firstborn boys regardless of the sex of their younger siblings. For firstborn girls, however, parental support was high *unless* they happened to have brothers. Then, attention from both mothers and fathers was consistently rated "low."[7] In light of such findings, it hardly seems coincidental that among the twenty-five highly successful businesswomen profiled by Margaret Hennig and Anne Jardim for *The Managerial Woman,* not a single one had a brother.[8]

What is the impact of growing up "less than" one's sibling, based entirely on the accident of sex? Several women I talked with spoke of careers and talents they never pursued because family money and encouragement flowed to a brother; others spoke of a deep, enduring sense of unworthiness and powerlessness that permeated many realms of their adult lives. Still others identified this childhood education in sexism as the roots of an unshakable distrust and resentment toward men. One thirty-eight-year-old woman told me that her decision never to marry was directly linked to her childhood experience as involuntary "maid" to her three brothers. She expressed her position succinctly: "I will never live with men again."

Several women—and men as well—talked of the ways in which a parent *still* lavished more attention or rewards on their son, in the process continuing to diminish their daughter. One woman told me, "To this day, if I'm talking to my mother and my brother walks in the room, she'll cut me off in the middle of a sentence and ask him what he needs." When such adult favoritism was blatant and unremitting, a sister was apt to still bitterly resent her "anointed" brother, particularly if he seemed to uncritically accept—or even expect as his due—the privileges accorded a perpetual golden boy. Favored brothers, for their part, were often saddened and hurt by a sister's anger or emotional withdrawal, but frequently expressed uncertainty about how to repair the relationship.

\* \* \*

Yet the greater status conferred on male children by many families—and by the culture at large—pushed some brother-sister bonds in a different direction. A number of younger sisters I spoke with remembered idolizing a brother throughout childhood, thrilled by some mix of power and significance and unexplainable "cool" that seemed to shroud their male sibling. This opposite-sex hero worship was an overwhelmingly older brother–younger sister phenomenon. While several younger brothers I interviewed reported admiring an older sister, none described anything approaching the level of passionate sibling worship—often coupled with a meager sense of self—reported by a number of younger sisters. The memory of one thirty-two-year-old "kid sister" was not unusual:

My brother could occupy my thoughts. Alone, I could think about how great Chris was. And anything he did, I would just sit back in awe. Building model cars, I would just want to sit there and watch him do that. If he was taking the dog for a walk, I wanted to go along. I'm sure that did a lot for his ego. It sounds corny, but just to be in his *presence*. [Laughs.] Graced by my brother Chris.

Not surprisingly, research indicates that brothers tend to have a greater psychological impact on their sisters than the reverse.[9] Perhaps perceiving their brothers' greater social power, as well as coveting their more adventurous, less rule-bound lives, many women reported that as girls, they not merely admired but desperately wanted to *be* like their older brothers. One African American woman recalled a phase during which "I dressed in jeans and army jackets, just like him, I cut my hair in a short little bush, and I copied his walk—a real straight, smooth walk, kind of like a glide. I did a pretty good imitation." Because of this worshipful identification and attachment, many women I interviewed believed that the way an older brother treated them—protectively or exploitatively, appreciatively or disdainfully—had a decisive influence on their female self-concept and later intimate relationships. In the only study to date on the older brother–younger sister bond, Marilyn DuHamel found that in the development of body image, self-image, feelings toward men, and style of relating to men, the majority of her younger-sister subjects believed that an older brother had been as influential—and in some cases *more influential*—than either of their parents.[10]

What happens when this age hierarchy is reversed? Research indicates that throughout childhood, older sisters lavish more attention and nurturing on younger brothers than on younger sisters—and far more than older brothers give to siblings of either sex.[11] Many younger brothers I interviewed did remember their sisters as quasi-motherly figures whom, in many cases, they still viewed as a key source of emotional sustenance within the family, particularly if their mothers were no longer alive. Older sisters varied in their response to this role. Generally, those who had voluntarily "played mother" to a younger male sibling in childhood were more apt to freely, even gladly, offer emotional support to an adult brother—especially when they felt they got some back. But sisters whose early caregiver role was assigned rather than sought were likely to resent deeply a brother's adult needs, even though—or perhaps because—they often felt compelled to go on meeting them.

An older sister's impact on her brother's adult relationships and feelings about women depended heavily on her position in the family. If she had no older brothers who were clearly favored, and if their parents didn't otherwise teach him that girls were "lesser," a younger brother was apt to view his sister—and female peers in general—as strong and capable unless proven otherwise. Sometimes, sisterly lessons in female equality were overt. My younger brother Phil recently told me, to my surprise and gratification, that his views on women were heavily influenced by the years of frequent, impassioned arguments I had with our parents in my late adolescence and early twenties on the subject of women's rights. "The idea that everyone had equal intelligence and ability—back then, that was new stuff," Phil told me. "So I grew up on that, hearing your opinions, the parents' opinions. I never said much, but I really listened. And at some point, I decided that I agreed with you."

\* \* \*

Perhaps the most disquieting and least talked about issue between brothers and sisters is that of sex. Among those I interviewed, a few acknowledged twinges of sexual attraction toward a sibling, but not a single individual, female or male, reported ever having acted on such feelings, at any time, to any degree. While such demurrals may accurately reflect respondents' experience, it is also likely that the powerful societal taboos surrounding sibling sexuality make the subject extraordinarily difficult for individuals to talk about, much less acknowledge in their own histories.

For when privacy is guaranteed—as in studies that use anonymous questionnaires—between thirteen percent and seventeen percent of siblings report having had a sexual encounter with a sibling, ranging from mutually consenting childhood exploration to outright rape, which is almost always perpetrated by an older brother on a younger sister.[12] One study of nearly 800 college students attested to the extreme secrecy surrounding this issue: Only one in eight participants in sibling sexual activity had ever told *anyone* about it—and those who had been most severely exploited tended to be both most silent and most emotionally wounded by the experience.[13] Such findings suggest that we urgently need to revise our current assumptions about incest as a primarily paternal crime to include the reality of sibling sexual abuse, and to make intervention and supportive services far more widely available to victims.

Simply because sibling sexual activity occurs, however, doesn't mean that every brother and sister harbor some deeply repressed illicit desire for a sibling. On the contrary, many opposite-sex siblings I spoke with considered one of the most pleasant aspects of their bond to be the *absence* of sexual tensions or assumptions that underlie so many interactions between men and women in our culture. A forty-eight-year-old man who has achieved a gratifying level of intimacy with his older sister pointed out that "outside of my wife, she is probably the only woman I can talk to about what I'm feeling. If I did that with most women, they'd think, 'Hey, what's he comin' on to me for?' Think about it." To many individuals, in fact, an amicable bond with a brother or a sister seemed to offer the best of both worlds: the challenging, invigorating differences offered by an opposite-sex relationship, and at the same time the comfort of a pal with whom one "went way back," a man or a woman one could appear before without first changing clothes or rehearsing conversational gambits.

Granted, for most of those I interviewed, such a state of sister-brother harmony was more ideal than real. Some, though, were working toward it, and among those who felt most encouraged, a number of common themes emerged. Brothers who were making progress toward intimacy with their sisters nearly always spoke of taking a more active role in sustaining the bond and, among those who enjoyed a favorite-son status in their family, of making a conscious effort to relinquish that role. Sisters talked of confronting their own anger about family gender bias, halting their one-sided nurturing and, in some cases, acknowledging their own part in keeping the relationship stuck in emotional distance. One woman who had spent years railing against her older brother for "never talking to me about real stuff" only recently realized how much she had invested in being the protected younger sister. She can admit now, "I didn't really want to know anything about my brother that wasn't heroic. I didn't *want* to see his vulnerable side."

For both sisters and brothers, relinquishing old roles and old expectations is apt to be hard and continuing work. Such "habits of being" have not only the force of years and the power of family behind them, but in most cases the authority of an entire culture. Unquestionably, throwing off that weight takes two.

## Ben: Stuck Love

A highly analytic man who has thought extensively about family issues, Ben, thirty-three, is nonetheless stymied by the current tensions between him and his thirty-one-year-old sister, Diane. On the one hand, he acutely grasps and sympathizes with her gripes: Ben acknowledges being the favored child of their highly ambitious, achievement-oriented parents, and understands how profoundly his sister has suffered from this lopsided family reward system. He also deeply values his

bond with Diane, and is saddened by the distrust and bitterness he has long sensed from her. But somehow, despite all of
the insight and caring at his disposal, Ben can't yet approach
his sister with all he knows—and especially with all he feels.

If you asked my sister what made her angriest in her entire childhood, she would probably tell you about the bat
mitzvah. When I had my bar mitzvah, it was a *huge* deal.
You know, it was my day in the sun. We had a hundred and
twenty-five people at the house, a catered dinner, I got
presents, I got loads of attention. And so my sister told my
parents that she wanted a bat mitzvah—this was back when
they were first coming in in St. Louis. She wanted it *badly.*
And the answer was no.

"Girls don't have that," my parents told her. "It's not appropriate." Finally, they put something together where on a
Friday night, we all went to the synagogue and she got her
name called out and she read some short thing, and then
the immediate family went out to dinner. No cause for
great excitement. And my sister, for years and years afterward, was just furious. She couldn't forget it; she thought it
was, you know, horribly sexist. And she was right.

But I think it was kind of symbolic of the way our parents
dealt with us, all along the way. The main battleground, no
question, was achievement. For my parents, that was critically important. To a very, very extreme degree. This was *the*
measurement. Report cards were scrutinized; the standards
were extremely high. And my sister did by far the best. I
think we had six report cards a year—I remember that because it was very important stuff—so from junior high
through high school, we got thirty-six report cards.

In all that time my sister got a total of one B. She graduated from high school first in her class.

Our younger brother, Scott, was no competition for
her—he was very bright but the running joke was that he
never read a book till high school. *I* was the competition. I
actually tried *not* to be. I mean, I would have been a fool to
try. [Grins.] Being smart was real important to me, but my
thing was never to push myself hard enough to find out
whether I had limits. I was gonna make *sure* I didn't have

any by not finding out what they were. [Laughs.] So instead I kind of cultivated this image of an extremely smart, somewhat eccentric, very creative type, but not necessarily on a straight and narrow path. My grades tended to vary a lot, depending on whether I felt like doing the work.

And I think this made Diane furious. Because no matter what she did, the family mythology was that, yeah, she was bright, but that mainly she did so well because she worked extremely hard and got along well with teachers. Because she was a good girl. It made her furious—with some justification. I think she felt that, for a lot of years, her achievements got written off, while mine got written up. I would do some interesting paper that wasn't quite on the assigned topic and would get all kinds of approbation for being creative and intellectually bold and so forth. So I think she felt for years and years that the message, the implied message, was that she was not the smartest. Not even *as* smart—as me.

And my memory of her, all through our childhood, was just how *angry* she seemed. She would have these amazing temper tantrums. And I don't remember my parents ever acknowledging her feelings. My father called her Princess Black Cloud. Her anger was kind of a family joke.

In those days, though, I think she was mostly angry at my parents, rather than at me. We actually were pretty close, right through college. You know, we were close in age and had a lot of common interests, so we kind of served as confidants and reference points for each other. There was a bit of a coconspiracy element, too—kind of an unspoken grouping against the common, dominant authority figure of our parents. My father, especially, was a very controlling, "do it my way" kind of person—we called him The General. So I remember having a lot of conversations with her, sort of talking about our family and analyzing, you know, who was doing what and why, and generally agreeing that the parents were difficult. So I think we had, back then, some sense of common cause.

But there was even deeper stuff. At that point, I think we dealt with each other as very close friends. We talked about things that I wouldn't necessarily talk to many other people about—you know, sex, drugs, rock 'n' roll. There weren't any taboo subjects that I can remember. One of the best examples was when I was in my first year in college and I was, um, involved with a woman who got pregnant and had an abortion. And I invited my sister up for a weekend not long after that and I talked it over with her—about the emotions, the emotions attached to that.

And you know, I'm probably not that open a person generally in terms of confiding—talking with real emotions. [Clears his throat.] Probably with Diane as much as anybody. Definitely not with my brother. I always have the sense that he feels the emotions, but he tends to put up barriers. I think when he feels like sharing something, actually, he shares it much easier with my sister than he does with me. Because Diane can be very supportive that way. She's a wonderful listener. She can really draw you out.

I think things began to come apart between us after she graduated from college. For the record, my sister went to Harvard. I refused to even apply there, which made my father furious. But to give you some idea of the magnitude— she went to Harvard, she had the highest grade point average in her class for the first year, and she finished Harvard in three years. Then she took her medical boards and got a perfect score. You know, she got an *eight hundred.* You're talking about a sort of—brilliance. But no sooner did she get those board scores when my parents started talking about how they hoped she would "slow down," and not, you know, compromise her future family with a demanding career.

Meanwhile, I had graduated from Williams the year before, and I had done well enough to get into med school myself. And my parents were making a huge deal about my future career as a doc. Great expectations. And it was at that point that I perceived her kind of—moving away from me. The beginnings of a coolness.

At least we had sense enough to go into different specialties. [Smiles slightly.] She's an ob-gyn and I'm an internist. And our identities in medicine are very different—or at least they started out that way. Diane was—still is—very interested in the research end; she loves the intellectual challenges of medicine. She's already published a bunch of stuff. And true to form, I moved in the opposite direction and became much more oriented toward, if you will, activism. Doing work that has political content. So I've been working in a clinic up here in New Hampshire, immunizing poor kids, doing education and so forth. But from a very early point, I've perceived her as kind of trying to— move in on my turf, if you will.

My sister has gotten very involved in women's health issues, especially around reproductive rights for indigent women. Now she's a real spokesperson in this area. And I have to say that's really irritated me—you know, it's really kind of raised the hairs on the back of my neck. I mean, if she wants to academically achieve, *fine*. She's always done that. But now it's like she's saying, "I'm as politically conscious as *you* are." And even throwing it in my face a little, from my point of view.

Then I decided to get married. Stop the presses! [Chuckles.] My mother, from day one, got really, really involved in the wedding. Not planning it so much as just *talking* about it—obsessively, you could say—and I think my sister got to feeling that every third word was about the wedding. I think she really resented that once again, everything was revolving around me. Me, and not her. Then, after we got married, we had Amy, and then our *baby* became a huge, huge topic. And things just seemed to deteriorate more. I'd call Diane up and she'd snap at me in sort of really unpleasant ways. And the other thing was that—I know this sounds ridiculous—but I began to feel that my sister and my brother were ganging up on me. At one point Scott was living on our third floor, and Diane would come up to visit and what she would literally do was go straight up to the third floor without even speaking to me. Making clear, more or less, that I didn't *exist*.

And you know, I have always defined myself as a sort of very independent, well-insulated person, you know, nobody's going to get to me. But I was becoming conscious that I was upset with my sister. Feeling rejected, I guess.

[Looks down for a moment.] I was really, really angry at her.

About six months ago, I was down in Boston for a conference and I asked Diane to spend the evening with me. And she told me she had been up all night before with a delivery and she was really frazzled—but that we could get together for dinner, and then I could stay over. So, okay, she was obviously exhausted. But on the other hand, I had been storing all this stuff up for a while and I had it in my head that this was the time we were gonna finally sit down and try to *do* this.

And so we went out to this restaurant and I basically told her all the things she had done and hadn't done that were upsetting me. I told her I didn't like that she hadn't been putting any effort into our relationship. I told her that I didn't like her snapping out at me, and that she just wasn't being real sensitive. And that was pretty much it. My basic orientation was that I was angry at her.

And, basically, she told me where to go. She basically said, *"Who's being insensitive?"* That I knew how strung out she was, how much pressure she'd been under, so how could I bring all this up now, and in this way? She was extremely, extremely angry. Yelling at me, right there in the restaurant. And she ended up telling me that if this was going to be how I approached her, she wasn't sure she wanted to have a relationship with me at all. We walked back to her place and didn't even speak. Then, the next morning, she did say, "You know, I was really exhausted last night, and I really *do* want to have a relationship with you. But I'm still angry about last night." But that was it. We haven't talked about it since.

What now? I don't have a clue. The coolness between us is even—frostier. She's stopped snapping out at me, but the whole tone is now, sort of, stilted. Not personal, not tuned in. I report on my stuff, she reports on hers. [Sadly.] I mean, it's been a really long time since we've done—the kinds of things we used to. You know, just sit around and kind of look at our lives, in relation to our family, figuring everything out.

And the thing is, I can't do that with anybody else. But we seem to have lost that. [Shakes his head.] And I really don't know how to get back there.

I mean, obviously she's angry at me. I get all these veiled allusions. Almost every time I talk to her—especially when we're with the family—some story will come out about our past that features her as the injured party compared to me. I mean, *lists* of stuff. How I was allowed to chew gum and she wasn't, because it wasn't ladylike. How she had to cross her legs, even when she was wearing pants, and obviously I didn't. How Dad would give us all tennis lessons and spend the first half hour with me, the second twenty minutes with Scott, and she'd get five minutes at the end. She still thinks about all this stuff, still sorts through it all. It all still has a tremendous amount of relevance for her.

Lately I've been thinking back on all the times it's been so important for her to win. Not just to be as good as me, but *better*. The report cards, SAT scores, medical boards, Harvard. Like it would prove that she really *had* it—whatever that was. [Softly.] You know, I really feel like she's spent the last ten or fifteen years wanting—wanting that imaginary conversation that will never happen, where my folks will sit down with her and say, "You know, Diane, we were *wrong*. You really *are* the smartest." And of course, they will never say that. And I think that's why, in the end, she's so furious at me.

I've never really told her that—that I think this is what it's probably all about. You know, we've never really talked about it. Not directly.

But, uh, I guess I'm fairly convinced that she wouldn't want to get into it. So, okay, maybe that's a self-fulfilling prophecy. Maybe I'm not really being fair to her and not giving her a chance to tell me what's really going on. But because of the infamous dinner, I guess I'm feeling burned. I mean, I felt like what I did, more than anything at that dinner, was asking her to reaffirm our relationship, by trying to lay things on the table. Be honest. And look what happened.

I mean, okay, obviously my timing could have been better. She felt I was a little insensitive, and maybe I was. Maybe I shouldn't have kept an agenda for so long. I mean, I don't think I've been the perfect person in the relationship. But I feel like the main thing, now, is that I've tried. Now *she* has to decide she wants to re-evaluate our relationship. Until then, I'm inclined to let sleeping dogs lie for a while. Maybe her anger will dissipate. You know, over time. That could happen. It's always a possibility.

## Kate and John: This Is Family

Kate, twenty-six, and her brother, John, twenty-seven, share the same athletic good looks, quick smile, and way of nodding—thoughtfully and appreciatively—while the other is speaking. Born just eleven months apart, they grew up as "best friends" within a close-knit Southern Baptist family; even today, they seem to possess unusual empathy and respect for each other, as well as a kind of quiet, hang-loose comfort in each other's company. While their intimacy has clear limits—there are many realms of their inner lives they simply do not share with each other—their mutual admiration is thoroughgoing, their mutual caring profound. If Kate and John face a problem, it's that few others in their lives can quite measure up.

JOHN: I've never lost that sense of wanting Kate to—to *be* there. Because she always was. I grew up on that. Being close in age was part of it, but much more it was the basic way our family operated. I don't think we totally saw ourselves as individuals, growing up. It was almost like we had a family identity.

KATE: [Nodding.] Even when I was little, I always had the feeling that our family was a lot different from other families. There was a lot of warmth. We were always together. Church together—three times a week till we were eighteen. Goin' as a family to each other's meets and games. We took a lot of trips . . .

JOHN: . . . and if somebody didn't get to go, honestly, it was *bad*. I mean, I always thought of us as The Six. So you'd really miss somebody.

KATE: It'd be no fun. But the other thing was, you were never allowed to disrespect anybody. Sometimes that had a disciplinary side to it, that I think carried over from Dad havin' been in the military . . .

JOHN: She's right. I mean, the belt would come out, and that was always pretty frightening, looking back now. But as far as the brothers and sisters went, I don't remember feeling that doing things for you all was—you know—forced on me. We had our fights. But I more remember feeling a lot of pride in what everybody was doing. Especially around the sports stuff.

KATE: [Grinning.] We *loved* watchin' each other play.

JOHN: So Kate would come to all my softball games; I would go to all her gymnastics meets. That meant a lot. When you're fifteen and your sister comes to your games, it means more than when it's your mother. I mean, it's much more interesting when your sister comes because, hey . . .

KATE: . . . she didn't *have* to. [Both laugh.]

JOHN: I think a lot of the energy behind our closeness as a family, though, comes from an upbringing that was church-related. Because the church teaches love and unity among everyone, and the lessons you learned on Sunday, you were encouraged to express right there in the family. It was like a little microcosm of how you were supposed to behave. So I think that had a profound effect.

KATE: There was one time, though, when I really struggled with doin' that.

JOHN: [Looks at her, surprised.] Yeah?

KATE: Yeah. When we were little, you know, it was just you and me for a long time. And then Gary came along and kinda messed up things between us. My first reaction was, "Ugh! Who *is* this thing?" 'Cause now it was like, you and I would be out in the driveway playin' basketball, and now Gary would come out and want to play trucks, and you'd go over and play with *him*. [A brief silence.] I mean, of course, I learned to love him. But at first, it was like, "Hey, we were doin' *good*. What do we need *him* for?"

JOHN: That's interesting—that you felt that. I never felt Gary's coming as an intervening thing. Or Bonnie's, later on. I always felt there was a kind of special thing between you and me, regardless. I mean, we were more or less raised together, almost like twins. So we shared experiences that we probably aren't even aware of—Mom made the same mistakes on both of us, and did the same good stuff, too. We were in the same place at the same time.

KATE: Then, all the moves. That just kind of cemented things.

JOHN: [Nodding.] Great point.

KATE: I mean, by the time we got to high school, we had moved from Decatur, Georgia, up to Roanoke, then Roanoke to Knoxville, then back to Decatur. And when you move around a lot, your brothers and sisters are your friends. They're your *core*. I mean, I remember being new in school and I'd see him in the hall and it would be like, ahhhhhhh! There's John!

JOHN: That was probably even more important for me than for you.

KATE: Yeah. It's funny, even though he's a little older, I've always kinda taken care of John. Like in school, um— now I'm going to get upset. [Takes a deep breath.] But I always, I always wanted to make sure [voice wobbling] that he was okay. Make sure . . . [Her voice breaks; she can't go on.]

JOHN: Well, maybe I can add to that. [Softly.] See, Kate was always the more sociable one. She was always accepted by the kind of upper-crust crowd. And I was a real late bloomer when it came to the social stuff. I was more the bookworm, more the—nerdy element. I think what she's trying to say is that maybe . . . [Now his voice breaks. He puts his face in his hands and shakes his head.]

KATE: [Almost whispering.] See, I was always, I just wanted to make sure he had *friends*. Make sure he was included in things. It was important to me that he didn't feel left out. And, you know, I guess I was in the "in crowd" because I was a cheerleader, and the cheerleaders are always the popular girls, so I just kinda traveled in that circle. But half the time I *didn't*, 'cause, you know, I was hangin' out with John.

JOHN: And she did. She never shunned me to look good with them. The bottom line is that it would have been very easy for Kate to ignore me. It's typical sitcom fodder, you see it in *The Wonder Years* all the time, where one sibling is embarrassed by the other one. Very common. But Kate never made me feel like an outcast. I never felt like she wasn't my sister. I always felt like she loved me. I felt that she would have forfeited her stand with those people to reach out to me—if it had come to that.

KATE: In a second. And everybody knew that.

Q: You've always felt very connected to each other, but you're also very close in age and have a lot of similar interests. Have you ever felt competitive with each other?

JOHN: I think at some point we took off in different directions, maybe to sidestep the competitive element. Kate was always athletic first, scholastic second. With me, I took all the books home to try to get A's, that was my big thing. I also loved sports, but my athletic talents were very mediocre, especially compared with Kate's. She was an *extremely* talented gymnast. So we just . . .

KATE: But John, I'd say a big part of that was Mom and Dad. You know, how they strived to really—to equalize everything. *All* the time.

JOHN: That's right. They went to extreme pains . . .

KATE: I just remember the college thing. I went away to college so it cost—*extreme pains* is the word, financially—but it was important to them to make it all fair for everybody. So even though I wasn't the great student in high school, and they could've said, "Hey, she doesn't really need that," I *knew* I was going to college. There was never a question.

JOHN: I can relate to that on the athletics end. I mean, even though Kate excelled more—I mean, a *lot* more—than I did, we each got the same support. They came to my softball games the same as they came to Kate's meets. Even though Kate won blue ribbons at her meets.

KATE: You just got supported. Period.

Q: You still live within a few miles of each other. These days, what do you do together?

KATE AND JOHN: Falcons games! [Both dissolve in laughter.]

KATE: We've been doin' that since we graduated from college and moved back here, near Atlanta. Stuff like that's fun because we both get a big kick out of it. So we'll get there at, like, ten-thirty in the morning and read the paper and take in the scene—even though the games don't start till one. [Joint chuckling.] We can spend the whole day together, it's great.

JOHN: Working out, that's another thing. Goin' to the gym. That's *real* important to both of us. And we kinda motivate each other that way. You want the other one to be proud. There are times I'm workin' out at the gym, even by myself, and I think, nope, can't leave yet. *Kate* would do another rep. [Both laugh.]

KATE: [After a moment.] You know, but we're not doing this stuff as much as we used to. We're even busier, jobs and all, and ... [Sighs.]

JOHN: I got married last year. That had to be the biggest change. Your time isn't your own, not as much as before. It's—it's, uh, definitely harder now. Gettin' together.

Q: If you had more time together, how would you spend it?

KATE: Just hangin' out with him. Talking about stuff ...

JOHN: Well, but—we really haven't talked that intimately as far as like, intimate problems, per se. We never really have. I'll admit that. I mean, Kate and I will talk and I will definitely want to know everything that has happened, and I will pay attention and care. If she has a problem, I might say something to help her through it, something in passing. But its kinda like, "Spare me the details," you know?

KATE: I'll ask John about certain things, like exercise. But personal stuff—yeah, he's right. I'd talk to a friend first.

JOHN: It doesn't mean we don't support each other. She knows I'm there when she needs me. But there are just some things we don't want to reveal. Maybe for fear the other person will lose respect. I mean, we idealize each other a lot. I think we idealize our whole family a lot. So we kinda avoid having a mushy kind of relationship ...

KATE: We've never been that way.

JOHN: . . . and I'm glad for that. 'Cause I think some of that stuff *should* be private. I mean, you just want to work it out yourself.

KATE: Huh. [A small silence.] Well, but there's a sort of an understanding we have—without talking a whole bunch. Like, I feel I'll always know how he'll react. How he's feelin' is many a time going through my head. You know, 'cause he's a part of me.

JOHN: [Nodding.] There's a lot of bein' on the same page. I sometimes feel like Kate is the female of me and I'm the male of her.

KATE: Yes!

JOHN: For one thing, we look alike. [They look at each other and giggle.] We have similar values; the same things that would warm Kate's heart would warm mine. But I also feel that we both have qualities that, well, I don't express as much as she does. She likes to help people a lot, that's what makes her a good teacher. I want to develop that more—the reaching out to people, the compassion—and I see Kate helping me do that. Just by being a model, watching how she does it. Blending tough with soft.

KATE: Hey. That's nice.

JOHN: And see, it carries over, too, to how I look at other women. Kate sets certain standards for females. Kate is incredibly versatile—she just flows with the situation. She can work out and sweat, and yet later on dress up, put makeup on and look beautiful. She can do both of those things; there are many women who can't do both. They cannot sweat. Or they refuse to. Or if they do, they might not put makeup on later.

KATE: Wow. [Laughs.] And here I thought I was just a jock.

JOHN: But I'm serious. And your personality, same thing. I like your aggressiveness; I like the blend it has with tenderness. So many people are either pushovers or pushy. But Kate knows how to blend the two. And believe me, it's gone into my appreciation of what a woman should be.

I'll be honest. It affects my marriage. There are times when I see Kate working out, and I'll think, Why can't Barbara come to the gym? And there are times when Kate will come with me to a Falcons game even when she's real busy, and I'll think, Why can't Barbara support me that way? So I do draw direct comparisons. It's an issue.

KATE: Well, I've had the same type problem. Even more so. I mean, John is a very special, a very select kind of a man. You know, respectful of me in every sense of the word. Very appreciative of me, proud of my accomplishments. And he *listens.* Picks up on where I'm comin' from. Whatever I add to a conversation is always important to him.

But out there, I mean, there are a lot of guys who just don't have an *idea*. D'you know? They don't have an *idea* of how to behave with a woman. Had John been a different kind of man, they probably would be more tolerable to me. But because of the way he is, I just can't put up with them. So I have a long list of what I call intolerables. Untouchables. That's the measuring stick he was talkin' about.

JOHN: But still, even when you do find the person you want to spend your life with, even then, my feeling about Kate is that she'll always be one of The Six. Our Six. And Kate, bein' part of that, will always have a special meaning to me that's different from other people.

KATE: Like with Christmas comin' up. Everybody's got boyfriends, girlfriends, wives now. But The Six always come to mind first. You wanna make sure everybody's comin' home.

JOHN: [Nodding.] I remember one time Daddy said to me, "I love you with all my heart." And I remember thinkin' at the time, But what about Kate and Gary and Bonnie? Don't you love *them?* [Chuckles.] But what he was really sayin' was, I don't hold back.

And with Kate, that's how it is. I don't hold back. Even now. My feeling is, there's enough to go around. Plenty to go around. [Quietly, with conviction.] I don't have to divvy up this heart.

## Margaret: Her Brother's Keeper

Margaret, a quick-witted, expressive woman of forty-nine, can hardly remember a time when she didn't deeply resent her forty-seven-year-old brother, Mickey. From the time they were small children growing up in an Irish American enclave of Evansville, Indiana, she was his designated caregiver-cum-troubleshooter. Worse, despite sacrificing her childhood to "do for the family," Margaret's parents seemed clearly to favor her brother over her. As young adults, a new source of contention emerged as Margaret became aware that she was gay, while watching her brother metamorphose into "a notorious Lothario" who consistently treated women poorly. Then, just a few years ago, their family situation shifted dramatically, confronting Margaret and Mickey with the challenge—and the chance—to see each other in a different light.

When I was a child, the worst thing you could be accused of was being selfish. As in "How can you think of *yourself?* How can you want anything just for *you?*" That may be Irish or Catholic or some of each—but I heard a lot of it. Because from the time I was five or six, I was my brother's full-time baby-sitter. Around the clock. If I went anywhere, *anywhere,* I had to take Mickey. If he needed something, I had to provide it. I was never allowed to go out by myself, with my friends. And if I ever tried to object to that, stick up for myself, open my mouth to complain about anything, I was accused of selfishness. And then I'd get a smack across the mouth.

What I had to do—it went beyond baby-sitting. I was absolutely *responsible* for my brother. So if he did something, it was my fault. And he was forever getting into trouble. Borderline incorrigible. We went to the same parochial school, and I don't have to close my eyes to remember being called down to Sister Celestine's classroom, and there was Mickey sitting in the back row, crying, with his face all blue from writing on it with ballpoint pen, and there was Sister C, who was known for humiliating children, yelling and screaming at him, and there *I* was, all of ten years old, supposed to explain to her satisfaction exactly why my brother had just decorated himself with a Bic. [Shakes her head, exasperated.] This went on all the time. This was normal life.

And I pretty much accepted that it *was* my fault—whatever bad happened. At home my mother's big lines were "Margaret, you're older. You should *know* better. It's up to *you* to set an example." What it really did was serve to get Mickey out of her hair. And looking back, yeah, there was a lot of pressure on her. My father was chronically depressed and out of work a lot, and so a good bit of the time, she was the breadwinner. But even when he did have a job, things weren't much better. He'd come home, hand her the paycheck, sink into a chair, disappear behind the newspaper and eventually fall asleep there. And she had four little screamers underfoot.

But whatever her reasons, the upshot was that I just hated Mickey. I felt smothered. He was like a life sentence. I can't remember a single time in our entire childhood when I enjoyed him.


But the resentment I felt—there's another important piece to it. When I was about four, the war had just ended and my father couldn't find work, and we literally had no place to live. My mother and father and Mickey and I. And I can remember—this is probably my first vivid childhood memory—just walking the streets of the town of Evansville, Indiana, looking for a place to live. And what we finally found was one bedroom in a boardinghouse. And that room had one bed, two chairs, and a hot plate sitting on the radiator. That was it.

So I guess my parents worked out pretty quick that there wasn't room enough for all of us. Mickey was small enough, being two years old, where the two chairs pushed together could be a bed for him. And my parents took the real bed. So. [A silence.] About a block and a half away was a Catholic girls' boarding school called the Mercy Memorial, run by the Benedictine nuns. So at four years of age, it was arranged that I would go there to live.

And they dressed me up in the little uniform, which was a black smock with a stiff collar, but of course I was too young to go to school. All I can remember is just being alone. Always alone. My mother used to come and visit me sometimes, and we would play checkers together. Then she would leave and I would cry.

[After a silence.] That event, I've come to realize, has had a dramatic effect on me in a whole lot of ways. But it definitely had a profound effect on my relationship with my brother. Because I do remember feeling, even as a little kid, Why does *he* get to stay with them, and not *me?* I felt that they must love him more. And it was a feeling, unfortunately, that just kept getting reinforced. It's a thread that goes right through our relationship. That there has been one set of expectations and reactions to me as the eldest and as a female, and a whole other set for my brother as a male and younger. And I've really, really resented that.

With my mother, there was always just a lot more fussing over Mickey. In the late sixties, both of us went into the Air Force—it was during the Vietnam conflict, and I had just gotten my nursing degree. And when Mickey left, my mother was very, very upset. She cried and became depressed and whatever else. She really mourned. And it may not have been an inappropriate amount of mourning, but ultimately it seemed that way to me because when *I* left, it just didn't happen.

I remember it very well. I got a hug and a kiss and a stand at the doorway, waving. But there was no real emotion expressed. None of the weeping and wailing that went on when Mickey left.

I felt my father favored Mickey, too—both my brothers, really—more in terms of what he wanted for them. The two boys, Mickey and Jamey, passed every school year by the skin of their teeth, and Anne and I were the overachievers. So my father loved to say, "I wish my sons were my daughters and my daughters were my sons," by which he meant that he wanted his sons to achieve and he couldn't care less what his daughters did. My *brothers* were the ones he wanted to see go to college. As it turned out, I was the first Reilly to get a college degree. Five years of night school, but I did it. And Mickey never did. Now I'm realizing that he probably resented *me* for that.

The other part of this whole incredible double standard had to do with sex. When my brother got to be around eighteen or so, he turned into a real Lothario. And my father, basically, advised him that he should sow his wild oats in any way, shape or form that he could, which was diametrically opposed to what was communicated to me. Whenever I brought anyone home, my father was *extremely* critical. Usually there would be at least one if not more funny names for them. So there was The Farmer. The Bum. Ichabod Crane. You get the drift. And Mickey would usually join in the name-calling.

So the message was that anything I tried to do in the boy department was a bad thing. It was something that would get me put down, laughed at. Humiliated.

I really believe that my brother, along with my father, formed a goodly basis for my feelings and my ability to relate to men. I mean, both of them were extremely poor role models. My father—there are simply chunks of my childhood when I just don't remember him being there. For a period when I was a teenager, he did just split. He was gone.

And it was from my brother, I think, that I got the notion in my head that the primary thing that men were interested in was sex. Mickey had a great reputation for lovin' 'em and leavin' 'em. You know the type—the brains tend to hang suspended between the legs. Well, while my brother was in the Air Force, he got a woman pregnant. And he disappeared immediately and wouldn't pay child support, so he was arrested and landed in jail. He got out of jail, met a new woman and got *her* pregnant.

So I saw that he used the women that he went with. Hurt 'em in the process. And between my brother and my father, what I saw was that men are—not there. They are just *not there*.

And you know, it was in my early twenties that I began to be aware of my attraction to women. I'm not saying there's a connection—I don't know. But up until then, I didn't consider myself to be gay; it never entered my mind. I dated guys, and I was even engaged to one. But I always felt very cautious with them. Afraid. [ Softly.] *Very* afraid of sex. Some of this was maybe just the crap that the nuns had beat into my head. But then, when I met Patricia, that all kind of disappeared. There was right away more of a sense of tenderness and affection than I had ever gotten from any of the relationships I'd had with men. And certainly more than I had ever gotten from the men in my family.

For a whole lot of years after that, Mickey and I just went our own ways. We'd go for protracted periods with no contact whatsoever. I can't say I exactly pined for him. But then a bunch of things started happening in our family in a fairly short space of time. Five years ago, both of our parents died within several months of each other. And shortly after that, our little sister got a brain tumor. She almost died—several times. Very scary.

But the other part of that is that once Annie got out of the hospital, with my parents gone, taking care of her was really up to us siblings. Now we all live within a twenty-mile radius, okay? [Her voice rises in irritation.] But *I* was the one who was always over there. Everything from cleaning the house to fixing the meals, and meantime, I was working full-time. This went on for months. And I didn't mind helping. What galled me was that my brothers weren't being asked to do anything, nor did they offer to. The boys [laughs]—excuse me, my brothers—did *nothing*.

And what it brought up for me was all the ways in which I was still the handmaiden to the family. Still the one doing the waiting on, the caring for, the fixing up, the making better. And then I started thinking about my job. I mean, I'm a *nurse*. [Laughs shortly.] I'm still dealing with this, actually. I've been a nurse for twenty-eight years and I'm only beginning to realize just how programmed I was into that profession. [Very angrily.] I mean, I was born with a nurse's cap on my head! I didn't really choose it. From the time I was five I have been taking care of other people, and from five I have been indoctrinated with the idea that this is what you *do* in your life. You do for other people—especially your brother, in my case—and *you do not think about yourself*. And I'm up to here with it. I am fed up.

And I can't even hide it anymore. Just last week, at the school where I work, it had been a terrible week, I mean, every time I turned around, somebody was bleeding; I would open my office door and somebody would throw up on my floor. So finally I got a chance to escape to the faculty lounge, and I was just sitting down with a couple of colleagues when the principal comes rushing in to tell me that someone has just gotten bashed in the mouth.

And I slammed my hand down on the coffee table and I yelled, "My God, in my next life, I will *not* do this again! I will *not* choose this profession! All the things I hate most about the traditional female role are embodied in this profession!" And at that moment I realized—I will not be doing this very much longer. I *can't*.

That's the work part. But there's also the Mickey part. Just this past summer my brother came over one day, I forget why, but the upshot was that he specifically wanted me to know that he was *there* for me. If there was ever anything he could do, you know, all I had to do was pick up the phone. Now that was new. Him wanting to do for *me*. I was surprised. But I liked it very much. [Chuckles.] And he's expressed that since. And he's also gotten much more openly affectionate toward me, and with Jamey and Anne, too. I mean, when I see my brother now, he'll give me a bear hug that will last until I want it to stop. And he'll say, "I really love you." I can feel it—that it's genuine. But it's new.

I guess maybe what's happening is he's seeing that, well,

we're kind of *it*. We're the ball game. Our parents are dead, our sister almost died, both of his marriages broke up, his only kid ran away from home a couple of years ago and stayed away several months. So I think all of that's really sobered Mickey. I think he'd really like to repair family relationships.

And I have to say that I'm really responding very warmly. [Smiles a little sheepishly.] I mean, I guess I could still be ready to kill my brother for not showing up when my sister was sick. I could kick him in the butt for that and a few hundred other things. But you know, we're getting older. He may be aware of that; I know I am. Our parents are no longer here, so it's not like we're vying with one another anymore for recognition or goodies from them. I feel like now, I can *choose* where I want to go with my siblings.

And with Mickey—hmmm. [A thoughtful silence.] I get the feeling that we're going *somewhere*. I mean, it means a whole lot that he's reaching out to me. So I'm working toward this idea of sitting down and talking with him about—a lot of stuff. I'm not there yet. I'm not sure whether he is.

One of the things I would really like to tell my brother is that I'm gay. [Lets out a long breath.] Oh, wow. That's a biggie. I mean, this is a very, very vital part of my life that I have pretended does not exist, that I have denied, that I have never been able to discuss, all of these years. None of my siblings know. Or rather, I haven't *told* them. They probably do know. They are not stupid people. But whether I will ever feel comfortable discussing my relationship with Patricia with Mickey—I don't know. In many ways, he's a very rigid person. His world is pretty black and white. My fear is that he will reject me as the aberrant, and I will therefore lose my new relationship with my brother.

But I think I also know, in my heart of hearts, that it would probably make us closer. If he knew. If I told him. I could imagine that. [Very quietly.] But I'm not there yet. It's still real scary.

The other stuff I'd like to talk with Mickey about are some of the things that we've experienced together. The childhood things. We've really never talked about them. It's funny, because he talks about himself as the black sheep of the family—the one who was always in trouble, got kicked out of schools, didn't go to college. He sees me as the paragon, the parents' perfect kid. And I always *was* held up as an example to him. But I'd like him to know that I didn't want that role, that it was forced on me. That I hated it. That I never wanted to hurt him.

And what I'd also like him to know is how, all along, I felt that *I* was the black sheep. That *I* was the outcast. [Almost whispering.] That, by God, it was painful for *me, too*. I mean, I think that we both had a hard, hard time growing up in our family.

So I'm thinking about all of these conversations that I want to have with my brother. Not yet. I have to be a little readier than I am right now. But I have the sense now with Mickey that I never had when we were kids, which is that both of us *want* some kind of relationship with each other. Nobody's making us. That feels pretty special to me.

So I think, if we can ever find a time and a place to sit down and talk to one another person to person, that we maybe have a fighting chance to get close. I think the potential's there. Maybe not to be best friends. But you know. [Smiles to herself.] We can be brother and sister.

\* \* \*

One of the most striking aspects of Margaret's bond with Mickey is its fluidity. No sooner does this relationship seem to take a clearly defined shape—as an archetypal "caretaker-ward" bond, or a classic clash of opposites, or a case of resentment toward a favored brother—than it has already begun to evolve, slowly and subtly, into something else. From a stance of ferocious mutual resentment in childhood, Margaret and Mickey seem to have moved toward genuine mutual appreciation and, at least on Margaret's part, an emerging wish for intimacy. One can't help wondering what direction their bond has taken since the time of this interview—have they edged still closer by now, or has some new event or misunderstanding divided them once again?

Margaret and Mickey's relationship, of course, is not

unique in its adaptability. Nearly all of the sibling bonds explored in depth in these chapters have undergone significant
shifts over time, in patterns of intimacy or conflict, levels of
dependence or autonomy, roles adopted or shed—and sometimes in all of these realms. The widespread nature of such
evolution prompts a number of questions that are addressed
in the next chapter: Why are adult sibling relationships so sus-
ceptible to change? Under what circumstances are they most
apt to shift course? And perhaps most critical to those of us
who have siblings, what factors influence the *direction* of
change, thereby nudging some brothers and sisters toward
deeper levels of understanding and connection, while pushing
others further into antagonism and silence?

# 8

# Turning Points: Chances for Change

Each of us is moving, changing, with respect to others. As we discover, we remember, remembering, we discover; and most intensely do we experience this when our separate journeys converge.

Eudora Welty, *One Writer's Beginnings*

Go crazy on her sister was the last thing Susan expected to do at the family reunion, though looking back now, she thinks she probably should have seen it coming. All the "kids" in her family had just arrived at their mother's Philadelphia home for the biannual summertime event: Janet, thirty-nine, had flown in from Seattle; Richard, thirty-six, had driven up from Gainesville, Florida, and Susan herself, thirty-two, had simply walked around the corner and down the block to reach her mom's house. Since her siblings had last spent substantial time with her, Susan had become a mother and was now pregnant with her second child. As it happened, Janet was pregnant as well. We're gonna have *so* much to talk about, Susan remembers thinking as they exchanged hugs of greeting, and she found herself looking for an opportunity to spend some private time with her sister.

She got that chance the very next day, when their mother asked Janet to drive over to New Jersey to pick up another relative and Susan offered to go along. They bundled Susan's eighteen-month-old baby into the car and set out on their errand, Janet at the wheel. Within five minutes, she had made a wrong turn. "So I told her to just turn around, take Vine Street to the bridge, and we'd be golden," Susan remembers. But when her sister immediately and firmly disagreed, she could feel her temperature rising. "I said to myself, *Now I live here in this town.* She wants to get to New Jersey and I can tell her how to get there. She's lived here, but she hasn't *been* here—not for a long time. This is *my* city now." And when she suggested again, irritation now edging her voice, that Janet had better turn around or they would end up at the airport, her sister turned to her and said icily, "If you'll recall, Susan, I didn't *ask* you to come along. I was perfectly happy to make this trip myself."

At that moment, Susan remembers, "something blew up inside me." No *way*, she thought to herself, was she going to sit and take this crap from her sister, not for one more millisecond. "And so I demanded to get out of the car. Right then. On the highway. With my baby, and my five-month-pregnant self. And she said something like 'Oh, just sit there, don't be silly,' and I yelled at the top of my lungs, *'Let me out of the car, or you're gonna get hurt!'* "

The force of her own fury took Susan by surprise. "I mean, I don't think I was really going to beat her up. But I did know I was going to make some kind of effort to hurt her, one way or another. I was really *going* to. And somehow she knew it. She pulled right over and let me out. And I walked back to the train station carrying my kid, and I got myself home."

For the remainder of the family reunion the sisters did not speak, and it was several weeks before Susan understood what had really happened inside that car—and months more before she could pick up the phone to talk with her sister again, to begin to repair and renegotiate their relationship. The blowup wasn't, of course, really about directions to New Jersey, or even about sibling "turf" issues. What kept occurring to Susan as she reviewed the scene over and over in her mind was "how Janet treated me in that car—that tone of 'just sit there and be quiet and let me handle it.' Like I was a kid. And I really needed her to see me as *not a kid.*

"She's always been the big sister, and I've always been the little one," says Susan, whose strong, elegant features and air of quiet confidence make the adjective "little" seem absurdly ill-fitting. "And I've always known she cares about me. But for as long as I can remember she has always assumed that not only could she advise me, but she could correct me, contradict me, restate it, rethink it, show me a better way." She shakes her head in exasperation. "It seemed I was always trying to get her to understand and respect what I was doing, but then she would redo it *her* way."

And for Susan, this particular visit represented her chance finally to capture that elusive sisterly respect. "I don't think I realized it at the time, but I was counting on our pregnancies to equalize us in her mind," she says. "We were both carrying our second child, so I felt that here was an area where, *finally*, I had some hope for authority. Pregnancy, childbirth, babies, all of that. Now I could be talked to, and listened to, as an equal." Plus, Susan points out that by the time of her ill-fated car trip she had been through "too much adulthood" to be treated like a child. "I had lived too long without my sister," she says simply. "I had married, had children, and made a whole lot of decisions without her. I just didn't *believe* that anybody had the right to tell me what was what anymore."

Now that Susan and her sister have begun the process of talking through these issues, their bond is very slowly becoming more balanced, more like that between two adults than between authoritarian parent and dutiful child. And that is why, her temporary loss of dignity notwithstanding, Susan is still glad she jumped out of the car on that steamy summer afternoon in the middle of Philadelphia. "All those years, the worst of it was just sitting back and *taking* it," she says. "When I got out of that car, I stepped over the line."

Sibling relationships change. The shifts may be subtle or dramatic, welcome or not, the result of conscious plan or against all expectations, but in most cases, sibling bonds continue to evolve throughout the life span. This still is not a widely accepted perspective. The popular perception remains that relationships with brothers and sisters are somehow finished products, molded in early childhood and hardened into permanent shape by the time we leave our parents' home. Adult sibling interactions, by this logic, can be little more than knee-jerk replays of early attachments and rivalries; for good or ill, we're "stuck with" what we've got.

Yet when individuals are asked to describe the course of their *own* sibling histories thus far, many can readily identify points along the way when a relationship with an adult brother or sister noticeably changed—either for better or for worse. In one of the few studies to date on turning points in the "sibling career," conducted by Helgola Ross and Joel Milgram, fully eighty-five percent of respondents aged twenty-two to ninety-three reported that a critical incident had either significantly enhanced or eroded their relationship with a sister or brother.[1] Another study found that even within a given two-year period, the majority of adult respondents reported significant change in their feelings of acceptance, solidarity or resentment toward a sibling.[2] In my own interviews, this pattern emerged strongly as well: Of eighty individuals aged twenty-six to seventy-nine, only sixteen reported "no significant change" in their adult sibling ties thus far. Least likely to report change were those with extremely close *or* extremely troubled relationships.

Sibling bonds keep changing because, among other factors, individuals keep changing. Those who study adult development propose that far from being psychologically calcified at age eighteen, as was once widely believed, we continue to be influenced by significant events, ideas and relationships throughout the life cycle. While controversy remains over whether adults actually move through predictable age-linked stages (the Trying Twenties, the Midlife Crucible, etc.), hundreds of studies have now substantiated a wide range and degree of personality change during the adult years.[3] Such findings by no means imply that the impact of childhood experiences is unimportant, but rather that, in the words of life span development theorist Paul Baltes, it is "the community of life events"[4] that jointly determines the self at any given moment. We bring these continuing developmental shifts to our sibling relationships, so that, as in Susan's case, a growing perception of oneself as a capable adult rather than as the perpetual "baby" of the family is apt to prompt the renegotiation of a bond with a "parental" sibling. In reciprocal fashion, the very process of interacting with adult siblings in new ways is likely to spur further change in one's continually evolving identity and personality.

But individual capacity for change only partly explains why adult siblings so frequently reconsider and revise their relationships. The sibling bond is not just any relationship in our lives, but one embedded in an organism with its own distinctive life cycle—the family. As the family moves through time, it inevitably confronts a number of pivotal transitions. Some of these shifts are predictable, such as marriage, the birth of children, the illness and death of elderly parents, the children's departure from home, and retirement. Other turning points may take a family entirely by surprise, such as a parent's or sibling's divorce or one's own, a geographical move, a sibling's illness or death, a family member's coming out as gay, a major career success or setback, or the facing of a family member's addiction.

Whether these critical events represent growth or loss to the family, and whether they are billed as "happy" or "sad," all of them represent change and therefore tend to disturb the family's often delicately balanced equilibrium. Roles shifts, triangles form and dissolve, expectations change, new needs arise. Consequently, few family relationships remain the same—including those between brothers and sisters.

Unquestionably, siblings can and do rework their ties without the benefit of a major event. The slow, undramatic accumulation of small influences over time—a new friendship, an experience in therapy, the reading of a thoughtful article, exposure to other "sibling styles"—may gradually reorient one's priorities or one's self-concept, in turn encouraging a shift in a sibling relationship. Family turning points, however, tend to be particularly potent change agents because they are such forceful catalysts for confronting underlying, unresolved issues between adult sisters and brothers.

Much of the time, in the interests of getting along, we tend to collude with our siblings to keep these outstanding issues fuzzy and unspoken. We try not to notice a sister's penchant for criticism; we repress annoyance at a brother's chronic need to be right. They, in turn, suppress their irritation at some of our less lovable qualities. When a family faces a major transition, however, such cover-up tactics tend to fail us. Because emotions tend to run higher than usual during times of stress, and because at such times family members' demands on each other tend to intensify or shift, the real contours of a sibling relationship—particularly those defining attachment, separation, rivalry and power—are often brought into clear relief. Susan and Janet, for example, had been doing a radically unbalanced "you lead, me follow" sibling dance for years. But it had remained only semiconscious until a major turning point—Susan's entry into parenthood—pushed her into a fuller awareness of her need for, and right to, sisterly respect, and of the assumption of inequality on which her bond with Janet was based. Once she saw the relationship clearly, she was motivated to try to change it.

Turning points in the sibling life cycle can be valuable opportunities to revitalize, repair or deepen bonds with sisters and brothers. But such transitions also can sharpen existing strains and conflicts, in some cases even prompting a severing of the bond. Whether a turning point leads to renewal or rupture depends, to a significant degree, on the pre-existing investment that each sibling has in the relationship. Given a fundamental level of attachment before the crisis, siblings often are highly motivated to address the unresolved tensions it illuminates, in some cases because the crisis itself jolts them into a new awareness of their need for brotherly or sisterly closeness. Meanwhile, for sisters and brothers whose bond is already extremely hardy, a major turning point may simply reaffirm it through the satisfying experience of pulling together as a team. Conversely, if a sibling tie has already been frayed by serious resentments, or if it has always been very distant, a stressful transition may serve as the breaking point. In such cases, a crisis tends to lay bare the "truth" of the bond, and the siblings may well lack the commitment to engage in a long, difficult process of relationship repair.

The degree of comfort and skill each sibling brings to the "change project" will also influence its outcome. Unlike spouses and friends, adult siblings grew up in the same childhood family, which means that they probably learned very similar rules about how individuals are permitted to conduct

themselves under stress. If the "family way" included tolerance for change and the collaborative resolution of differences,
adult sisters and brothers obviously will have an enormous
advantage in negotiating a family transition and a consequent
shift in their bond. If, however, siblings learned from their
first family that change was tantamount to disloyalty and that
difficult feelings were to be swallowed—or denied altogether—the process of maneuvering through a crisis is apt to be a
much tougher challenge. Still, family legacies don't always
dictate outcome: Among those I interviewed, some siblings
who were highly motivated to preserve their bond consciously
worked to "rewrite" their old family rule book so that they
could begin to communicate more openly and directly.

The outcome will depend, too, on the way the particular
issues raised by a turning point interact with the particular
family system siblings inhabit. A good example is the divorce
of parents, which a quarter of a million adult children face
each year.[5] If an adult brother and sister have long identified
or allied themselves with different parents—if one is clearly
"Dad's boy" and the other "Mommy's girl"—then their parents' divorce might well spark or sharpen sibling divisions, as
each feels pressured to side loyally with his or her chosen
parent. Yet if that same sister or brother faced a very different
kind of transition—say, the birth of the sister's child—the
event might spur little or no conflict between them, or it
might even nudge them closer. (Unless, of course, producing
children is a "hot" family issue.) The critical factor is the particular *meaning* of a given turning point to a family, and an
awareness of such meanings may help siblings move more
successfully through their shared transitions.

Finally, the outcome of any turning point depends on the
particular issues individual siblings bring to it, and whether
these issues harmonize or clash. Siblings far apart in age, for
example, may be at different stages of adult development
when a family crisis occurs. The illness of an aging parent
may elicit very different responses from a recently married
twenty-seven-year-old woman who is trying to establish
boundaries between her childhood family and her emerging
adult one, and her thirty-six-year-old sister, who years ago

may have balanced those competing domains and may, in addition, be a mother herself and therefore identify more readily with a parent's needs. Consequently, such sisters may vehemently disagree about how much care they "owe" their parent—and about how those responsibilities should be shared between them. Similarly, gender differences in coping are apt to emerge. Many crises and transitions center around additions and losses to the family, or around situations of increased need for family support. Therefore, some of the most critical issues they raise center on attachment, separation and caregiving—among the very issues brothers and sisters are apt to grapple with most differently. Such differences do not mean that siblings cannot successfully traverse a passage, only that one cannot assume that because "we're family," one's own issues surrounding a turning point mirror or mesh with those of a sibling.

Of the many family-linked passages one faces in adulthood, few are more likely to generate change in the sibling bond than marriage—either a sibling's or one's own. In Ross and Milgram's study of sibling turning points over the life cycle, marriage was among the most frequently cited critical events triggering significant change, and among those I interviewed, nearly every individual reported a shift in a sibling bond after marriage or entrance into a highly committed intimate relationship. Such widely reported change reflects the fundamental reordering of family bonds that accompanies this turning point.

Marriage represents a move away from one's family of origin—for some, the first major move—and requires a significant transfer of family loyalties. Yet as one shifts one's identity from that of childhood family member to member of a couple, allegiance to that first family rarely disappears. Instead, individuals typically attempt a conscientious and delicate rebalancing of time, energy and obligation. As pioneering family theorists Ivan Boszormenyi-Nagy and Geraldine Spark observed, "The struggle for all adults is to balance the old relationships with the new: to continuously integrate the relationships with early important persons with the involvement and committedness with current relationships, namely one's mate and children."[6]

As individuals attempt to balance sibling and spousal bonds in particular, the word "struggle" seems a very apt one. Ross and Milgram found that among those who reported shifts in their sibling bonds after marriage, fully two-thirds felt that the direction of that change had been negative. Many of those I interviewed also reported a deterioration of sibling ties after marriage, with the majority of comments along the lines of "we're just not as close as we used to be" or "I feel like I don't know him that well anymore." Most chalked up this postmarital intimacy gap to increased geographical distance or, even more commonly, time problems—the losing battle to find enough hours in a day or weeks in a year to meet the myriad new demands of marriage while also maintaining a one-on-one tie with a sister or brother.

But a mere sense of increased distance is rarely the only sibling by-product of marriage. Particularly among closely attached sisters and brothers who spent a lot of time together through adolescence and early adulthood, the marriage of one frequently leaves the still-single sibling feeling abandoned, bereft of the special "buddy" who had once been so readily available—who, in fact, had *always* been in his or her life until now. Among those I interviewed, sisters were more apt to feel—or at least to acknowledge—this deep sense of loss than were brothers, yet few individuals of either sex had ever spoken of such feelings to a sibling, for fear of seeming competitive with a new partner or simply "too needy." Kate and John, for example, the closely connected sister and brother who discussed their relationship in the preceding chapter, had never talked directly about the feelings and challenges represented by John's recent marriage until the evening of our interview. John was the one who brought up this delicate subject:

> JOHN: [To Kate.] You've never said anything about this, but I'd say that me getting married two years ago has had a huge impact on us. I've had that perception crystallized by Mom. A few months ago she told me she thought you were a little, uh, bothered by the fact that

Barbara is now in my life. And you know, I'd never be so presumptuous as to assume that I was that important to you. And so it took Mom to tell me.

KATE: [A little uncomfortably.] Well, yeah. It's kinda like the Gary syndrome. You know, it was just you and me, and then—well now, who's *this?* [Laughs.] That's how it was.

JOHN: Huh. Well, sure, I guess I can see . . .

KATE: [Quickly.] I mean I was very proud of you, and real happy that you'd found somebody. But by the same token, now, all of a sudden, well, now *Barbara*'s going to the Falcons games with us. Or else you just can't go at all. Okay. All of a sudden, I'm not in the picture anymore. [Speaking softly, with effort.] And that hurt. It hurt a lot. Especially in the beginning, when I wasn't seein' anybody on a regular basis. It was just hard to face—that you know, this is the way it's going to be. That this is important to you. So I'm just gonna have to deal with it.

JOHN: [To interviewer.] You see, coming back from college, we lived at home for a couple of years. For a while we were both unemployed, so we went through a nice little crisis together. Then we both got jobs in retail, so we had that in common. And we both enjoyed working out, so we had *that* in common. We did a lot together for a couple of years there. So I guess it's been, you know, an adjustment for Kate.

KATE: [After a small silence.] But you know, John, it's *still* hard. Many's the night I just feel like goin' over to your house, and maybe just watch TV or listen to CDs with you guys. But Barbara—I still don't feel very comfortable around her. I feel I'm more of an intruder. [Pause.] I just wish I could fit into the relationship better.

The impact of an intimate partnership on sibling bonds also depends on an obvious yet enormously critical factor—

whether one's sibling and one's partner happen to *like* each other. When they do, already close sisters and brothers are much more apt to stay in touch, simply because there are no third-party impediments to continued contact. Somewhat emotionally distant siblings, meanwhile, may find themselves edging closer to each other simply because the friendship between spouse and sibling-in-law often spurs more family "getting together" that, in turn, provides more opportunities for the siblings to connect. Lucky individuals *each* find intimate partners with whom their sibling gets along, and those who are truly blessed find that the partners like each other, too—opening the way for a four-way friendship that, in the process, ensures continuing sibling contact.

Of course, such collective congeniality is by no means guaranteed—or probably even very likely. Several individuals I spoke with reported that their spouse was notably critical of one of their siblings—often a sibling whom they had idealized—which in some cases spurred their own clearer-eyed re-evaluation of that brother or sister. While such a re-evaluation sometimes led to the establishment of a more balanced sibling bond, just as often it only prompted painful loyalty conflicts—and anger at the "sibling-basher" spouse. As one woman whose new husband regularly criticizes her older sister observes:

> I've always felt there was a tug of war between the two of them for my allegiance—but especially on Jim's part. He's pointed out a lot of flaws in her that I'd never seen before, and partly I resent that because I don't *want* to see them. But also, you don't want somebody you love downgraded in front of you all the time! On the other hand, I want to keep my relationship with Madeline without making Jim feel I've abandoned him. There's got to be a way to do this without feeling so *pulled*.

In other cases, conflict arises because a sibling objects to a spouse. Research suggests this is particularly likely to occur when an individual marries someone notably different from his or her childhood family's class, ethnic or religious background, because the new partner is less apt to share that first family's fundamental values and enthusiasms.[7] When this "misfit" is glaring, some siblings find themselves avoiding or severely limiting contact with the new couple, in the process surrendering a meaningful connection with an adult sister or brother. Others, especially those from families who don't easily admit newcomers, may try to isolate a sibling's spouse by casting him or her as a family outsider. In a quirky, moving essay about the enduring emotional pull of one's first family, Joan Didion notes that her brother cannot understand her husband's failure to join in her childhood family's twin obsessions, namely, sale-leaseback transactions and mentally unstable people. And so, Didion observes, "My brother refers to my husband, in his presence, as 'Joan's husband.' Marriage is the classic betrayal."[8]

Conflict can also arise when two people who marry hold vastly different views of the importance of adult sibling bonds—or of appropriate styles of expressing sibling solidarity. Ethnicity often plays a strong role here: One study found that forty-seven percent of middle-class, married Italian Americans saw at least one sibling daily, compared to only four percent of their WASP counterparts. Italian Americans further reported that in times of trouble, they were as likely to seek help from a sister or brother as from a spouse, while few WASPs viewed siblings as their primary source of crisis support.[9] One might expect, then, that an Italian American and a WASP who married each other would hold significantly different convictions about appropriate adult sibling interaction. So, too, might a couple from different class backgrounds, since working-class adults report keeping in closer contact and feeling fewer tensions with their brothers and sisters than their middle-class counterparts.[10]

Such contrasting attitudes and styles sometimes work to siblings' benefit. A man from an emotionally constrained "touch-me-not" family, for example, may watch his wife interact with her brothers and sisters with unreserved affection, and gradually may find her demonstrative style rubbing off a bit on his own sibling interactions. But dramatically different sibling styles can also spark marital trouble. Because behaviors toward family members are so deeply rooted and long-standing, many people are convinced that their own sisterly or brotherly style is the "normal" one, while a spouse's approach is simply wrong, deviant and should be changed. Such judgments are particularly apt to be made when an individual views a spouse's sibling tie as too close—and thereby in competition with the marital bond.

Some siblings, of course, *are* in fact too tightly tied to each other. One may chronically rescue the other, for example, or they may be mutually dependent to an extreme degree. But in other cases, the mere intention to keep in regular touch with a sibling after marriage, or a consistent show of warmth toward an adult brother or sister, can deeply threaten a spouse who is unaccustomed to such family connectedness— and may prompt him or her to try to dilute it. For Kate and John, Barbara's very different "family vision" has already made an impact on their accustomed style of sibling camaraderie:

JOHN: It's not just a suspicion on my part. It's a concrete fact. Barbara is jealous of my willingness to spend time with my sisters and my brother.

KATE: Remember the concert?

JOHN: [Nodding.] There was a Willie Nelson concert here last summer, and Kate asked me to go. Well, Barbara wasn't so thrilled with that. So me, the great diplomat, decides that I'll go with *both* of them. We'll be the big happy trio that night. But as it turned out, Kate and I had fun, but Barbara was just like really . . .

KATE: *Miserable.* She looked at her feet the whole night.

JOHN: She was just fed up with the fact that Kate had to come. She could not *imagine* that we could all go together and have fun. She couldn't grasp that.

KATE: But you know, I think it's very hard for Barbara to understand the kinds of relationships that our family has. They're just real different . . .

JOHN: From hers. Right. It's not that she didn't have love in her own family—but it wasn't the same. More, uh, formal. She finds it really odd the way we hug and stuff. Like if we're saying goodbye after a visit, I'll definitely go up and hug Kate goodbye.

KATE: Always.

JOHN: It's very natural to do that. But for Barbara, it's odd. So what it comes down to is, well, it *is* hard for Kate to just pop over. [To Kate.] You know, I'd love it if you could just come over. Just to do anything. Reminisce. Read about the Falcons. Look at an old yearbook. But that's hard to do because Barbara, well, she wants to be hospitable, but . . .

KATE: [Softly.] So John, *talk* to her.

JOHN: [Speaking at the same time.] I mean, it's important for me to still have things to do with you. And there's definitely a potential for things to split apart . . .

KATE: [More urgently.] So let her *know*. Until you say to her, "Hey, this is how I see it, this is what I'd like, this is what we could try," how's she gonna know, John? How's anything gonna change?

Kate and John are at a pivotal juncture in their sibling relationship, and the direction they will ultimately take is still uncertain. In large part, the outcome turns on the way John chooses to answer a critical question: How much will I risk in my marriage to preserve my bond with my sister? A key question for Kate, meanwhile, is whether she can remain patient and positive toward her brother while he continues to grapple with this conflict, or whether she will begin to feel too angry and rejected to do so much longer. Kate and John bring real strengths to their dilemma: Neither flinches from talking about the enormously sensitive issues surrounding this stage of their relationship, and the two have shared an emotionally close and committed bond since childhood. Until now, however, their solidarity has been taken for granted, thoroughly enjoyed yet largely untested. Now they have to choose connection.

While the addition of a family member through marriage can profoundly alter the ground rules, expectations and habits of connection on which the sibling bond is based, the experience of family loss typically confronts siblings with still more dislocating shifts and unanticipated challenges. Indeed, in Ross and Milgram's sibling life-cycle study, the death of a family member was the single most frequently reported "critical incident" prompting change in the sibling bond. Sometimes this experience of loss brings remaining family members closer—but not always. Because family relationships are so delicately hinged on each other, the loss of one member tends to make us more keenly aware of our needs from the remaining others, and also of the ways in which they imperfectly meet those needs. Consequently, long-buried wounds and grievances often rise to the surface. When the loss in question is a parent, the ability to resolve those reawakened issues with a sibling is particularly critical. For a parent's death—particularly the last parent's death—renders the sibling relationship more voluntary than ever before. With a mother and father no longer there to urge closeness, mediate arguments or provide a focus for family get-togethers, many adult siblings confront the stark question: Is my relationship with my sister or my brother still worth pursuing?

For many, the wish to stay connected is strong. Once parents die, many of us become acutely aware for the first time that our childhood family is not "forever" but rather a fragile, perishable entity, and that from now on, we and our brothers and sisters *are* that family. Siblings not only help us to feel that we still belong, but they also give us the chance to hold on to a "piece" of the parents we no longer have with us. For to some extent, we retain our parents *through* our siblings, both through the genetic link and through the process of memory-sharing. As long as we still maintain a connection with a brother or sister, we are never entirely orphaned.

Ironically, however, the circumstances surrounding a parent's death often fuel tensions between siblings rather than bind them closer. In part, this is because events both preceding and following a parent's death often require a heightened degree of sibling cooperation, respect and sensitivity, so that the absence of such caring is apt to become more obvious than usual. When the last living parent becomes seriously ill, for example, siblings frequently become responsible for his or her care. Yet rarely is that responsibility shouldered equally, particularly in families of both sisters and brothers. Numerous studies document that not only are sisters far more likely to be caregivers for ailing parents than are brothers, but contrary to popular perception, they perform *every* kind of service, from mowing a parent's lawn to managing finances to providing emotional support, more frequently than do brothers.[11] Even in all-sister families, however, one sister is apt to take the "head nurse" role, and caregivers who feel unsupported by their siblings are apt to feel deeply resentful—especially those who feel that the parent they are caring for actually favors a do-nothing brother or sister.[12]

By contrast, siblings with a history of mutual cooperation are apt to pull together still more tightly during the time of their parent's illness. A sixty-two-year-old woman I spoke with remembered the day—now nearly twenty years ago—that she "lost it" with her seriously ailing, extremely obstreperous father and called her older, out-of-state sister in tears. "She was on the train almost before I got off the phone," she says, and she remembers that act of support as the basis of her unshakable conviction that "I can count on my sister for anything."

After a parent's death, many siblings face a new, emotion-laden crisis: the dividing up of family possessions. Once again, among brothers and sisters whose bond is already relatively harmonious, this process is apt to be handled with minimal furor. But for those with serious unresolved resentments, the settling of a parent's estate can be a traumatically divisive crisis. Particularly for siblings whose parents played favorites, the disposition of family belongings is apt to have powerful symbolic value. If more of a parent's things—money, real estate, furniture, prized family pictures—go to a brother or sister perceived to be favored, the "loser" is apt to view it as a sign of less parental love and turn his or her rage and hurt on that sibling, who, now as always, seems to "get it all."

Meanwhile, for siblings whose bond has always been distant or hostile, the splitting of family possessions may simply disintegrate into a greedy free-for-all, exposing the fundamental lack of caring between them. One thirty-two-year-old man who had always resented his older brother's cool distance from the family recalled that, a week after their mother's death, the brothers met at her house to divide her belongings. Before a word had been spoken, the older brother took out a screwdriver and began dismantling the dining room table, announcing, "This is really all I want, and I'm taking it now," to which his brother recalls spitting out, "You've never been a part of this family, so why would I expect you to be a part of it now?" Two years later, the brothers speak to each other only when absolutely necessary.

While the impact of a parent's death on siblings is peculiarly marked by such emotionally charged events, as well as by the elemental link between the parental bond and the sibling bond, in fact the death of *any* family member triggers significant shifts in family relationships. Whether we lose a parent, a sibling, a spouse or a child, a hole opens up in the family. We can never fully close it, yet we can't help trying. Whatever we got from the person now gone—nurturance, identity, companionship, rocklike strength—we now may seek in another family member. To complicate matters enormously, others in the family are apt to be doing the same thing, under the weight of collective grief and stress. In this free-for-all scramble for solace and stability, alliances shift, old roles crumble, family rules are questioned, new and urgently felt expectations rise to the surface. Anyone who has ever lived through a family loss recognizes this fundamental truth: No one is ever the same again. Nor is any sibling bond.

It was family loss, more than any other single influence, that propelled me toward a different relationship with my brother Phil. Nearly seven years ago, our brother, Bob, died. Two years later—almost to the day—our father died. For more than a year after that second loss, I consciously avoided sitting down, for fear that I would not be able to get up again. People tended to assume that my depression stemmed from my father's death, and they were partly right. While anger and frustration had dominated my bond with my father for most of my life, in the months before his death we had just begun to edge toward one another, and I felt the sadness of a cut-off chance.

But it was Bob, my difficult, electrically charged, transparently vulnerable younger brother, whose absence from the world I felt most intensely and unceasingly, and with renewed force in the wake of my father's death. At the time, I didn't know why I was so devastated by losing Bob, and it would be years before I would understand just how deeply bound to each other my brother and I had been, beneath our obvious conflicts and contrasts. But then, in my scrambled emotional state, there was much I didn't know.

I didn't know, for example, why I was suddenly feeling so angry at Phil. *Furious* at Phil. This was very new. I had, until then, been conscious only of a sense of benign big-sisterhood toward my youngest brother. Now I catalogued his failings: He almost never called me, and when we did talk, it was the usual edgy dance—a nuts-and-bolts rundown of recent activities followed by a speedy exit. I didn't see Phil in person for months at a time, and when I did, it was usually at a Mom-sponsored event. Most indefensible of all, he rarely mentioned the names of the brother and father we had jointly lost, and whom I needed badly to talk about. In my worst moments I tried simply to write off my brother. *Totally disconnected*, I would grimly pronounce to myself.

Yet even I could see that such a label didn't fit. During our father's long hospitalization, Phil had visited him every single day—far more often than I had. Meanwhile, my youngest brother had always been close to our mother, and since our father had died they seemed more connected than ever. When my mother commented to me once, in passing, "You know, Phil and I can talk forever," I remember feeling stung—and bewildered. *You can?*

Meanwhile, Donna and I were firming up our bond. Even before our family losses, my sister and I had begun to grow closer, and now our long-distance calls were becoming more frequent, our subject matter closer to the bone. We shared and compared feelings about Bob and Dad, traded memories and at some point embarked on an extended exploration of the family dynamics that had helped to shape the people we now were. These talks, alternately mind-expanding and simply comforting, helped to solidify my growing conviction that Donna was the sibling who was "like me"—that is, the one who cared about relationships, the one who talked about what really mattered. It didn't occur to me that I had never tried to initiate similar conversations with my brother. It only seemed that Phil and I were on different planets, and that he had no interest in making contact with mine.

Then, one muggy June afternoon, I drove over to Phil's house to return a cooler he had lent me for a party. He lived only fifteen minutes away from me, just two towns over, but as I turned onto his street, I realized that I wasn't sure which house was his. I knew it was on the left, but was it the white clapboard with red trim or the one with black shutters two doors down? I became conscious of a faintly tight, sick feeling in my stomach; without warning, tears came to my eyes. *I don't know where my brother lives.* How can it be, what must it mean, that my own brother lives only minutes away from me but I don't know where?

I parked in front of his house—I finally found it because I recognized his van in the driveway—and sat in my car for several minutes to collect myself. It had been, I realized, a good six years since I had last been to Phil's house. I started to feel angry: *So why hadn't he invited me in all that time?* But another, more disturbing thought then settled over me: In six years, neither had I found any reason to go there. What kind of effort, really, had *I* made since we had left our childhood home to get to know my brother? The truth was that Phil and I had both been raised to be highly independent, boundary-conscious people, individuals first, members of the tribe second. Love was the underlying reality in our family, but distance was the habit. I sat in the car a few minutes longer, stunned and deeply sad. I had lost one of my brothers not so long ago. Had I been losing the other all along, without even knowing it?

The house-search incident came on the heels of the birthday visit I described in an earlier chapter, and together they jolted me into an awareness of the depths of longing that had lain hidden beneath my chronic blame-slinging irritation toward Phil. We had been a family of six; now, much too suddenly, we were a family of four. When we were six, I could much more easily tolerate the emotional distance that stretched between Phil and me, not just because there were more Sandmaiers to ally with (however loosely), but also because I was wrapped in the cozy illusion that where family relationships were concerned, I had all the time in the world. If my little brother and I weren't close now, well, someday we probably *would* be. No rush; in fact, no need even to let the matter flutter near my conscious awareness. But even more than my father's death, Bob's sudden disappearance from the world slammed into my brain and soul the sheer precariousness of life. Nobody is supposed to die at thirty-three, and certainly, most especially, no brother of mine. But one of my brothers was already gone.

Not long after I searched for Phil's house, I called my mother to arrange a time for the three of us to meet for dinner. After we had agreed on a date I said to her, automatically, "Why don't you give Phil a call to see if that's okay with him?" She agreed, as she always did, and as I hung up the phone I realized that I had just done what I had done my entire adult life—cut off any possibility of getting to know my brother by using our mother as message-runner. I called her back to cancel my request, then called Phil myself. He sounded glad, if a little surprised, to hear from me, and we chatted amiably about bike racing and Mom and magazine writing and how I could buy a new car without being totally swindled. Nothing special, except that I noticed we chatted for half an hour instead of our usual ten minutes.

It was the beginning of something—though for some time it would have been hard to define exactly what. I began to make a conscious effort to get in touch with my brother more often, with no special agenda in mind. After some months, I noticed that he was calling me more often, too. Not a lot more, but *more.* Encouraged, I began to invite him to our house for dinner now and then; he, at various points over the next year, began to offer his time and help at what seemed to me a new level—giving me an electric heater for my frigid home office, fixing my recalcitrant car and, during one particularly lean season of book writing, offering to loan me "whatever you can use—just let me know." I tried to reciprocate and, over time, we developed a pleasant, amicable mutual aid relationship. I would have liked to know a bit more about what my brother was thinking, but I was frankly grateful for the level of solidarity we had already managed to achieve.

Then at one family gathering, Phil and I drifted into the kitchen while everyone else was in the living room, and we began to talk, for the first time, about our father. "There were times when I hated him," I whispered. "I know," my brother said, and he made no move to leave the kitchen. Shortly afterward, we went out to dinner together—alone. For the first time, I told him some of my feelings about Bob's death, and that they had, in turn, made me aware of a whole lot of buried feelings toward *him*. Phil listened very carefully, then began to talk a bit about what our family losses had been like for him. How he had always felt much closer to Dad than to Bob, so that our father's death had affected him much more deeply than our brother's had.

"But you never *talk* about it," I told him, and he said that anytime I wanted to, he would be glad to talk about Dad or Bob or pretty much anything else, but that he just didn't feel the need to verbalize his feelings to the same extent that I did. "We're a little different that way," he said simply, as though he had figured that out long ago, and it didn't much matter. And we talked on for three more hours, long after our plates had been cleared and the tab paid, so maybe my brother was right; maybe it didn't matter. If it did, I was no longer sure I could explain how.

I made another discovery that evening. As Phil and I traded thoughts back and forth, first about our family and later about parenting and taking risks in one's life and other things we had been thinking about lately, I remember noticing—with some surprise—how intently my brother lis-

tened whenever I spoke. It wasn't just a matter of not inter-
rupting; Phil was right *there*, obviously and genuinely interested, asking me questions, making perceptive comments,
seeming by his responses to understand fully and sympathize
with whatever I was trying to communicate. While I was happily flabbergasted that night by this "new" side of my brother,
I have since realized that I had rarely witnessed Phil's capacity
for empathy and supportiveness before because I had rarely
let him show it. Partly out of habit and partly because it made
me feel so competent, I had a lot invested in maintaining the
role of self-sufficient big sister, perpetually ready to give my
little brother advice, but rarely able to seek it; available to con-
sole, but never to be consoled. But our family losses had made
the maintenance of my invincible posture both absurd and impossible; I badly needed to feel the support of people who
mattered to me. Once I allowed Phil into my life—the unre-
touched version—I saw little trace of the "little brother" who,
until then, I had insisted he be.

None of this, of course, means that my brother and I have
sailed into the sibling version of the sunset, never again to feel
exasperation, flip back into old roles or disappear into silence.
We still do all of those things, though less often than before,
and we now face an entirely new challenge—maintaining the
closeness we've developed from a distance of six hundred
miles. Last summer Phil moved to South Carolina, and it was
a sign of our progress that before he left, we actually talked
about what this new turning point would likely mean for our
relationship. We joked about being card-carrying Sandmaiers
for whom the phone is an optional household appliance, yet
before he took off we also managed to agree that we would
try to fight our "island mentality" and keep on calling each
other frequently. Just to talk.

So far we're doing that, as best we can, and just two
months ago, when I flew down to visit Phil at his new home
for the first time, he made a big point of telling me how glad
he was that I had come. I started to make some joky, keep-
your-distance rejoinder when something stopped me, mid-
word, and instead I told Phil that I was very glad, too, and
also that I loved him. And my brother told me, without the

slightest hesitation, that he loved me, too. We hugged then, and continued our conversation.

It was a small moment, but one that still warms me. For there was a time—not all that long ago—when I simply could not have imagined it.

# 9

# The Long Goodbye

Everyone can master a grief but he that has it.

William Shakespeare, *Much Ado About Nothing*

Shortly after my brother Bob died, I heard that an acquaintance of mine had recently lost her brother. We knew each other only slightly; in fact, neither of us had even known that the other *had* a brother. One morning as I rode the trolley to work, I saw her step on; our eyes met and she sat down beside me. "I heard about your brother," Cindy said simply, and I told her that I had heard about hers. Without further preamble we began to talk about those brothers of ours: how they died, how they lived, who they were to us, what it felt like to be a grown-up person who had just lost a sibling. There was an intensity about our conversation, a level of concentration that made us not care that people were staring at us, some even leaning in to hear a bit better. When I rose to get off at my stop, Cindy stood, too, and followed me to the door so that we could prolong our conversation for a few extra moments. When I stepped down off the trolley and the doors closed between us, we were still talking.

That scenario repeated itself several times in the weeks that followed, and I came to look forward to those early-morning "trolley talks," as public and truncated as they were. Partly, Cindy and I were so eager to talk with each other because the synchrony of our horrible losses had given each of us someone who uniquely, deeply understood our grief. But each of us also was aware—because we compared notes on this, too— that we talked simply because the other was willing to listen. Each of us had a large network of friends, relatives, neighbors and colleagues who, we knew, cared for us. But the fact was that I was to Cindy, and she was to me, one of the few people who could hear the other talk of her brother without flinching, changing the subject or promising that we would feel much better soon.

The public discomfort, silence and discounting of our losses that both of us repeatedly confronted in the face of our brothers' deaths were encountered by nearly every one of the eighteen people I spoke with who had lost a sister or brother in adulthood. Such responses, of course, are experienced not only by survivors of siblings. Our culture's pervasive anxiety about death, as well as its equation of rigid self-control with "strength," severely limits our freedom to grieve openly for any loved one. While some variation exists among ethnic groups, by and large our society stipulates that mourning is to be brief, after which we are to briskly "get on with our lives," and that it is to be private, so as to shield others from its unseemly excesses—and frightening reminders. In the introduction to his landmark study, *Death, Grief, and Mourning,* anthropologist Geoffrey Gorer describes how friends responded when, in the months after the death of his younger brother, he refused invitations to cocktail parties, explaining straightforwardly that he was in mourning:

> The people who invited me responded to this statement with shocked embarrassment, as if I had voiced some appalling obscenity. . . . Educated and sophisticated though they were, [they] mumbled and hurried away. They clearly no longer had any guidance from ritual as to the way to treat a self-confessed mourner; and, I suspect, they were frightened lest I give way to my grief, and involve them in a distasteful upsurge of emotion.[1]

Amid this widespread fear and denial of death, however, our culture offers some limited recognition of the impact of losing certain family members, especially a spouse or a child. Several organizations are entirely devoted to providing emotional support to widows and widowers, to parents of children who have died and to those who have suffered miscarriage. Moreover, a large body of psychological research exists to help mental health professionals steer people through such losses, and scores of self-help books are available. Encouragingly, in recent years researchers also have begun to pay some attention to sibling loss in childhood, and some support services are now available for children who have suffered the death of a brother or sister.[2]

Yet sibling loss in adulthood remains an almost wholly unacknowledged reality—even though most sisters and brothers will face such a loss during those years. Support groups and other grief-recovery services are almost nonexistent, and I located only one published research study on the entire subject of adult sibling loss.[3] In the few self-help books I found on the topic of grieving that included sibling death at all, the loss of an adult brother or sister was either never mentioned or dismissed as insignificant. In one such book, *Letting Go with Love*, which carries a cover endorsement by Elisabeth Kübler-Ross, psychologist Nancy O'Connor writes:

> When adult siblings die, the emotional impact is usually reduced. Often their lives have taken them in different directions and the intensity of early childhood connections begins to fade. . . . The main effect of a sibling death is to remind you of your own vulnerability or aging and what a fragile gift your own life is.[4]

Such dismissiveness both illustrates and reinforces our society's persistent assumption that adult siblings are mere background figures in our grown-up lives, people to whom we may still feel loyalty and residual affection, but rarely a strong, meaningful, continuing connection. So when we lose an adult sister or brother, by the logic of this assumption, we should not expect to feel great pain.

How to explain, then, what I witnessed at a recent annual

conference of a national grief-support organization? On the second of three packed days of meetings in Philadelphia sponsored by The Compassionate Friends, a self-help organization for grieving families and particularly bereaved parents, was an afternoon workshop listed in the conference program simply as "Adult Siblings Speak Out." Of sixty-two workshops, it was the only one on that topic, and I was glad I arrived early. By the time the session began, at least sixty people jammed the small meeting room, and those who couldn't find seats lined the walls. When, after a short introduction, the two workshop leaders asked participants to talk about any aspect of their loss they wished, a dozen hands shot up, and for the next ninety minutes participants never stopped talking of their brothers and sisters who had died, and of what their lives were now like without them.

Many cried as they spoke. One thirtyish woman whose sister had died two years earlier told of feeling shattered by "losing a part of me," then quickly entering a bad marriage "just to try to feel close to somebody again." Another woman, who looked to be in her mid-twenties, talked of responding to her older brother's death in a car accident by diving into alcohol and drugs and frenetic activity, "anything to stuff up this hole I feel inside." A woman in her eighties stood up to say that her sister had been her best friend, her traveling companion, the sharer of a lifetime of joys and sadnesses, and that ever since that sister had died last year, she hadn't been sure she wanted to live anymore. Some described desperate attempts to "be" their lost sibling for their bereft parents, and told of efforts to swallow their own grief in order to support a mother or father. Other talked of still-painful guilt, of the terror of loss that now touched all of their relationships, and of great rushes of grief that still overtook them three, five, a dozen years after a sister or brother had died.

Nearly everyone spoke of how little permission they had to mourn. One woman seemed to speak for the group when she said, "A lot of the time I feel like a freak. I had this brother who died and I'm supposed to feel fine. Being here today— this is the first time I haven't felt like a freak." Around the room, people were nodding.

\* \* \*

Later, when I interviewed individuals in depth about their experience of sibling death and they felt unconstrained by the usual need to "put a good face on it," many revealed similar depths of pain and difficulty in coming to terms with their loss. I spoke at length with Suzanne, a thirty-four-year-old woman whose brother Paul, two years older, had died of AIDS the previous year. An Episcopalian minister who presents herself as cheerful and purposeful and who spends much of her professional life "trying to give hope to others," she admitted that privately, each day is still a struggle:

> I'm always conscious of darkness. It's a very dark time for me. Dark is the best word. At first, it felt like it was just closing in on me all the time, but even to this day, I wake up in the morning and I think, Oh, this is going to be a great day. And then, all of a sudden: *But your brother's dead*.
>
> I wake up pretty much every morning that way. And it clouds—it's pretty much always at the edge of my thoughts. I hope the joy in life will come back for me. You know, my brother lived in San Francisco and when I would visit him, it would often be foggy and dull-looking in the morning and Paul would always say, "Not to worry, not to worry, the fog'll burn off by noon." I think of that sometimes. 'Cause the fog really hasn't burned off since he died.

For some, the struggle continues for many years. I spoke with Jonathan, a forty-four-year-old self-employed carpenter whose younger sister had died nearly seventeen years earlier, when he was twenty-seven and she was twenty-six. There were times, he admitted, when he felt he would "never get over having her disappear":

> I can still remember the night. I remember when I was told. [Silence.] The phone call came and the sky fell. My sister had inoperable ovarian cancer and had maybe three months to live.
>
> And I just—I just went berserk, you know. Not yelling. Just the pain, the pain. I remember walking up and down

my living room, no, no. It can't, it's ridic—no, my God, *no*. I just remember the desperation I felt. The powerlessness. I couldn't tolerate the thought that my sister was dying. I just could not accept it.

After she died, for a lot of years I really didn't function. I quit school and went to work in my father's furniture store. I was very depressed. At one point I tried to go back to school, and I failed. I was in the middle of nowhere. I felt I had nothing.

Finally I did go into therapy, and it helped somewhat. But it was only last year that I was able to read some of the poems and songs Lizzie had written just before she died. You know, I had this notebook full of the stuff she had written, and I carried it around with me for sixteen years. I couldn't open it till last year.

Not everyone is devastated by the death of an adult sister or brother. Some I spoke with felt only a transient sadness, while a few even admitted a sense of relief. In a major review of the literature on mourning titled "The Myths of Coping with Loss," psychologists Camille Wortman and Roxane Silver conclude that contrary to professional and popular assumptions that people mourn according to prescribed stages and timetables, individuals in fact exhibit enormous variations in the nature, intensity and length of grieving. For example, while conventional wisdom dictates that one should be "over" a death in a year, Wortman and Silver have found that a sizable minority of individuals still struggle with depression, anxiety and problems in functioning two to four years after a significant death. Similarly, they found that while some people do pass through well-defined stages of grief—denial, anger, bargaining, depression, acceptance—others may skip one or more phases entirely, get stuck in another or confront feelings that fit no established phase at all. The bottom line, Wortman and Silver conclude, is that there is simply no single or "right" way to grieve, for each of us is subject to a unique combination of influences on the grieving process and its resolution.[5]

Critical among these influences is the stage of adult development at which one suffers a significant loss. If a sister or brother dies while one is still a young adult—before the age of twenty-five—in many cases "the dance of distance and close-ness is aborted, and mourning takes a strange twist,"[6] psychologists Stephen Bank and Michael Kahn observe in *The Sibling Bond*. At this stage, some individuals may have only recently embarked on a life separate from childhood family members, so that a sibling's death may evoke tremendous guilt and regret—"I should've stuck around"—especially if unfinished business lingers.

Many young adults also feel driven to try to fill the hole in their grieving parents' lives, either by attempting to behave more like the sibling who has died, or by being constantly available to assuage parental loneliness. A twenty-six-year-old married woman whose twenty-year-old brother died in a car accident four years ago observes, "Even now, I feel so responsible. I know my parents' needs are great—especially Mom's—and if I haven't gone over there in a week, she'll say, 'We haven't seen you in such a *long* time,' as if I lived in California. And it's hard to draw a line in my mind, you know, to say, 'Look, I have my own life now, I'll give this much but *no more*'—without feeling real selfish."

Other young adults may still identify extremely closely with a sibling who has died, and some younger siblings in particular may be highly dependent on an older, idealized brother or sister for a sense of fundamental worthiness. One young woman whose older brother and "absolute hero" died last year, when she was twenty-two and he was twenty-four, acknowledges how profoundly empty and paralyzed she now feels:

> Growing up with Kenny, I was always trying to win his approval. I'd show him my grades, and if I ever *won* anything [laughs] he'd be the first to know it. I think my self-esteem has always been connected with how my brother saw me. I would say that it was of paramount importance; I worshiped the ground he walked on.
>
> And so now, the thought of—I don't want to say suicide, but it's like, how can I go on now that I don't have Kenny to perform for? [Silence.] It's occurred to me more than once. Like, how can I have a baby now? Kenny won't be around to say, "That is the most *beautiful* baby in the

world," which is exactly what he would say. And the thought of finishing college has occurred to me, but how could I do it now? When Kenny wouldn't be there at the graduation? So that I could say to myself [whispers] ah, stamp of approval.

Those of us who lose a sibling in middle adulthood or old age, by contrast, are less apt to be still emotionally "glued" to a sister or brother, and therefore somewhat more able to confront the irrevocable separation of death. Maturity, however, does not necessarily protect us from profound grief. In the only study to date on adult sibling loss, which focuses on elderly individuals, half of the subjects reported that it was "not so hard" to face the death of a brother or sister—yet nearly all of the others rated it as "very hard" or "extremely hard."[7] One might speculate that for individuals whose sibling's death represents the end of their childhood family—and the end, as well, of probably the longest-lasting relationship of their lives—the loss might be particularly difficult to face. The study's authors, Sidney Moss and Miriam Moss, also point out that each of us has a "personal pool of grief" that begins from the time of our first significant loss. As we age we tend to collect more losses, and "each added loss tends to deepen or intensify that pool with painful memories of earlier losses."[8]

Moreover, other research indicates that sisters and brothers tend to grow closer and more accepting of each other as they age, so that for many older adults, a sibling's death may mean not only the loss of a loved person, but also a safe and treasured place to be oneself. A sixty-one-year-old man who recently lost his sixty-four-year-old sister observes that "it's a cliché, but our relationship was like a good bottle of wine. We had finally gotten beyond the point of 'maybe you're okay or maybe you're not okay' and we just appreciated each other for what we were. There were no more tests. That felt very good. And there really aren't too many places where you can go to feel that. Especially in this society, which is nothing but tests."

The circumstances surrounding a sibling's death also help to shape the grieving process. Not surprisingly, research indicates that a sudden death, such as from a car accident or drug overdose, may be more difficult to recover from than a death that is anticipated.[9] There is the sheer shock of a loved one's abrupt and irreversible departure from the world; worse, one is cheated forever of the chance to say goodbye.

Among sudden deaths, none is more painful or more difficult to adapt to than suicide. When a brother or sister commits suicide, an individual must confront the terrible reality that his or her sibling did not *choose* to live, and the intense rage, guilt and sense of abandonment that commonly follow this recognition can contaminate the lives of surviving siblings for years afterward.[10] There is also the stigma of suicide to cope with, which research indicates is very real: People tend both to blame and to avoid suicide survivors more than those bereaved by other circumstances, thereby exacerbating guilt and loneliness that are already apt to be acute.[11] As a young woman attending the adult sibling "speak-out" bitterly told the group, "When Luke died, nobody came over with a cake."

While a loved one's death is shattering under any circumstances, those who are able to anticipate a sibling's death may at least have some opportunity to complete whatever may have remained unfinished in their relationship with a brother or sister. Those I spoke with who seized that opportunity—by expressing previously unspoken feelings of love or appreciation, by trying to heal still-painful divisions, or simply by spending more time with that sibling—felt that they thereby gained some measure of peace about the relationship itself. Suzanne, the woman whose brother died of AIDS, lived across the country from him but called and wrote often, acutely conscious that there would soon be no more chances. She gave me permission to quote from one of the letters she wrote him just three months before his death:

Paul,

Hi! I've been thinking a lot about you. . . . The thought has crossed my mind more than once lately, that not only are you my best friend, but you've always been able to fill me with inspiration for life. Have I ever told you that? What a profound impression you've had? You are spontaneous and so enthusiastic about life, and that has positively influenced me—who thinks she has to have everything so planned out and ordered in her life. And you have always given me great advice. It's so selfish of me—but lately I've been afraid of life without you. . . .

I love you so much, Paul. How lucky I am to have you as a brother! I wish to hell I could take your pain away. I've enclosed a tape—I was thinking you could listen to it when you couldn't sleep, or when you're just hanging out.

I'll call soon.

Love,
Suze

Still another influence on the grieving process is, quite simply, our felt freedom to *do* that grieving. John Bowlby and others who have studied loss observe that the capacity fully to feel and express all of the feelings about the person who has died is critical to an eventual acceptance of the loss. Denying, stifling or editing emotions, by contrast, is apt only to keep us mired in suppressed grief.[12] Critical to this unimpeded grieving is the support of others who will not flinch from our pain—individuals who can listen to us talk about the sibling we have lost, who will not disappear when we cry, who won't judge, label or try to tamp down the unruly, often contradictory tangle of emotions we are apt to feel. Yet this is exactly the kind of support most bereaved siblings find so lacking.

One's immediate family is a potentially powerful source of such support, for the loss is apt to be a deeply shared one. Yet many individuals I spoke with found the rule of silence most rigidly enforced within their own families. In some, a stoic, pull-yourself-together ethic was made explicit: A week after her sister's death, one woman was told by her mother, "We're *through* crying." Others palpably sensed their parents' overwhelming yet unspoken grief, and dared not broach what was clearly a taboo topic. Jonathan, whose sister died when he was twenty-seven, says:

I don't ever remember being asked by my parents how I felt about her death. In fact, I'm sure they never did. I don't suppose that's uncommon, but it's something that I now understand is a serious loss for me. Not to have had that.

It's not that my parents were not open. In many ways, they were. You could talk about somebody's sex life at the dinner table. There was no problem with that, whether you were five years old or twenty-five. But Lizzie's death—it was untouchable. If it happened now, maybe I'd be able to say, "Mom, Dad, stop, I need to talk to you about Lizzie." Maybe I would. But then, I didn't even know what to ask for. It was not a possibility in my family. If you don't know something exists, you're not going to ask for it.

Several individuals I spoke with remembered that others seemed unable to appreciate the depth of their bond with "just" a sibling, and so made light of their loss—often by comparing it to some other death that was deemed "worse." Invariably, this kind of response stopped cold any further expression of sadness. When one woman told an older acquaintance of the recent loss of her brother, the woman she confided in immediately responded, "Oh, you're lucky—imagine if it had been your *husband!*" And she then began to talk at length of her own husband's death three years before. It is still painful for me to remember that, about a week after Bob's death, my father found me in my parents' den looking at some framed photos of my brother. "I'm sure it's no fun to lose a brother," I heard him say to me, "but you certainly can't compare it to losing a son." I was too stunned to ask him how he knew.

It took me a long time to understand, though, that not everyone who shies away from another's grief is lacking in empathy. In many cases, just the opposite may be true. One close friend of mine, usually quick to explore the emotional underpinnings of any subject at hand, was strangely quiet about my brother's death. "I'm sorry," she said once; then the subject was clearly closed. Much later, she apologized to me for her avoidance of the topic, and tried to explain her silence. My loss of Bob, she said, had brought up past losses of her own, losses still so painful that she hadn't been sure she could bear to face them again, and feel them anew, through a close-up exposure to my grieving.

There was something else, too, that had made her afraid. Both she and I were thirty-seven when Bob died, and his death, an accidental one, was utterly unexpected, a mortal blow from nowhere. "If you could lose a brother," she told me quietly, "then so could I."

Because so many people find it difficult to take the initiative to support a grieving person, a bereaved sibling may have to ask for support directly to get it. Men, by and large, find this harder to do than women. When I arrived at the adult sibling workshop at The Compassionate Friends conference, I did expect to see more women than men in attendance, but I was stunned to find that among the sixty people who crowded into that meeting room, there was *not a single man* who had lost a sibling. Later, when I called the coordinator of a recently formed sibling loss support group in Philadelphia to find out whether there were any male participants I might interview for this book, she told me, "Men don't stay. They come to one or two meetings, and usually they are very quiet. Then we never see them again."

The greater tendency of bereaved men to grieve alone[13] is not surprising, given male gender-role taboos on asking for help and on losing control. But keeping such a "stiff upper lip" in the face of loss may make one's passage through grief especially painful. In one study of older adults who had recently lost family members—primarily siblings—the bereaved men were much more depressed than the women, and the most depressed men were those who had the fewest social and emotional ties.[14]

Among the many factors that shape one's response to a brother's or sister's death, one is so obvious that its critical influence often goes unacknowledged: the particular meaning of one's bond with that sibling. While those who confront a sister's or brother's death face certain losses in common—the loss of a lifelong blood bond, the loss of an irreplaceable link to one's history—each bereaved sibling also faces the loss of a unique relationship, shaped by its own complex set of childhood and adult influences.

Some who experience a sibling's death lose what British social scientist Peter Marris calls a "keystone" relationship, one that consciously or unconsciously provides structure, meaning and a vital sense of connectedness in one's life.[15] Adult sisters and brothers who identify closely with each other, or who rely on each other for regular companionship and emotional support, may be such "keystones" to each other, and the irrevocable separation of death is apt to leave the surviving sibling bereft. Suzanne remembers:

Lots of times I would call Paul but the line would be busy because he was calling *me*. That happened all the time. Our phone bills were astronomical. And I remember one time he said to me, "You know, we are as close as any two human beings can get. Hopefully, you'll find the man of your dreams, and hopefully *I'll* find the man of my dreams, but that won't change what we have." And he was right. So now, the loneliness is horrible.

This sounds nuts, but I'd give anything to have him around so I could talk to him about my grieving. He and I always traded insights and advice and there's nobody else I can do that with, in just that way. I want to tell him what I've learned about myself so far and he'd love all that. He'd say, "God, Suze, that's *great!*" And then we'd analyze it for hours.

For others, the pain issues from a sense of missed chances, of cut-off potential. One fifty-year-old woman who lost her younger sister in a car accident three years ago talked of how competitive and conflict-ridden their childhood had been, but then how, in their mid-forties, the two had finally begun to heal their divisions and get to know and enjoy each other. Now, she says, it is hard to overcome her sense of injustice and longing:

I lost a friend at the beginning of a friendship. At first I hated God, I hated everybody who had a sister, I hated *her* for leaving, and I thought, If this is what this life business is all about, count me out. I don't want to be part of it. And to be honest, I'm still in a lot of pain. I feel like I

was robbed. She was my only sister. We were finally getting to the good part and then she skips out.

By contrast, those who never felt emotionally close to a
sibling may feel little sense of loss at his or her death. Some
individuals I spoke with attributed their lack of intense or pro-
longed grieving to a large age gap that had prevented them
from ever really knowing the brother or sister who had died.
For a few people whose sibling ties had been extremely rivalrous and hostile, meanwhile, there was a sense of liberation
from a lifetime of conflict, and in one case a feeling of uneasy
triumph over a now permanently vanquished opponent. Finally, some individuals who had been caregivers to chronically ill or emotionally troubled siblings reported feeling a
measure of relief at a sibling's death. When such feelings were
mixed with guilt—which was frequent—passage through the
grieving process was often protracted and very painful.

Of course, no one can neatly categorize his or her response
to a sibling's death as merely a "guilt reaction" or a "separation crisis" or a "sudden loss effect." One's response is apt to
involve many intersecting factors that mutually influence each
other and can be enormously difficult to name and untangle—
particularly in a culture that offers minimal support for understanding death *or* the nature of the sibling bond. Yet grief
researchers concur that only through understanding the facets
of our loss experience can we acquire the kinds of new perspectives that ultimately allow us to move through mourning.[16] "Time heals all wounds," we are told, but time is rarely
enough. Particularly critical, those who study loss believe, is
our ability to understand the often complex meaning of our
bond with the person now gone, for until we clearly perceive
what we *had* with a loved one, we cannot come to terms with
what it is we have lost. I know this from experience.

It was seven years ago on a cool, sunlit October afternoon
when I came home from work to find my husband, Dan, waiting for me in the front hall, strangely grim. When he told me
that he needed to talk to me right away, no, no, not after I
checked my mail but right *now*, some clenched note in his
voice made me walk straight past him to my eight-month-old

daughter crawling on the living room rug and pick her up in my arms. There, I thought, I'm holding my beautiful, laughing, squirming baby, how bad can any bad news be? But now Dan was telling me to sit down, and I felt an ache rising in my throat.

"Your brother Bob is dead."

I heard Dan's words; he spoke them clearly enough, but I could not make them fit together. *Bob* and *dead*. They didn't match up. The Bob I knew, *my* Bob, was thirty-three years old and six-foot-four and perpetually in motion, utterly incapable of stillness. This brother of mine, karate black belt, Zen enthusiast, maker and loser of fortunes on the Pacific Options Exchange, this brother of the charming, loopy grin and the don't-mess-with-me walk, had just called me last Sunday, and he was *fine,* as funny and fast-talking and wired as ever, and before we got off the phone, he actually invited me to come out to San Francisco to visit him. Why was Dan saying something so stupid, why was he saying *dead?*

"Because he is," my husband said gently. "John just called." John was Bob's best friend. He had never called us before. I began to weep.

My brother had been found that morning on his living room couch, John had said, the TV still chattering in front of him, surrounded by books and magazines and a half-empty medicine bottle. He had left work early four days before, complaining of a bad back, taking with him a bottle of prescription codeine lent by a sympathetic colleague. Later, some people would say that Bob should have known better, should have known he couldn't stop at the prescribed two teaspoons. Only months before, after all, he had entered a treatment program to defeat dual addictions to cocaine and alcohol, and had emerged with a written recovery plan that plainly stated: *No mind-altering substances.*

But the people who spoke of knowing better didn't know my brother. No warning label, reasoned argument, set of rules, prior disaster or appeal to common sense ever had or could contain Bob. I had watched my little brother walk the edge since he was five years old, and I had chosen to believe, against all logic and odds, that he would never fall off.

But now he had. There were weeks of stunned, desperate

protest—Bob, Bob, where'd you *go?*—and then, when I understood that it did not matter where my brother had gone, for he would not be coming back, I was seized by the most ferocious loneliness I had ever known. Each time I was reminded of my brother—by some guy on the street with Bob's graceful, loose-limbed stride; by a newspaper report of a young man's sudden death; by an innocent question about how many siblings I had; by any song about a missed connection—I felt nearly disabled by longing. Yet even as I silently raged at my brother, *Why did you leave? How could you disappear on me?* I was bewildered by the violence of my own feelings. Being this undone, feeling so robbed—none of it made sense. For in my memory, Bob and I had never been close.

"Never been close" was an understatement. From the time Bob was a scrappy six-year-old and I was a scrappier ten, we had faced each other down, wrangling constantly and often ruthlessly for supremacy in the realms we had come to believe mattered most—brains, talent and worldly achievement. There was nothing friendly about our competition. Every game we played was a fierce, focused effort to win; every conversation a new opportunity to establish the other as a being of inferior intelligence. No offense was forgotten. Once, after committing some crime against Bob, I opened the door of my bedroom to find every piece of clothing I owned, every treasured book, every fragile knicknack, flung violently about the room. I spent my childhood with my back to the wall.

After we left our family home, it was true, the hard edges of our rivalry softened, and by his late twenties, my early thirties, Bob and I each had made a few genuine, tentative efforts to connect. But these didn't go very well, for we had never lost a fundamental wariness around each other, an instinct in the other's presence to keep our dukes up. So we would approach, then nervously retreat, usually glad for the three thousand miles that stretched between us. Why, then, was I so flattened, so full of protest, at Bob's sudden exit from the world? I settled on the idea that one simply loves one's brother no matter what, so that the loss of him is inherently, inevitably a terrible thing. There was nothing to do, then, certainly nothing I *knew* to do, except quietly wait out the misery, endure it, trust that it would slowly ebb and finally disappear.

Others had told me much the same thing—that these things just take time.

But more than two years after Bob's death, I still could not say his name without a heaviness settling over me. I still wanted him *back*, with a desperation and a ferocity that had softened not one iota, and I didn't know how not to feel that way. I was constantly fighting some infirmity or other—a cold, a migraine, a bout of neck pain—and my sleep was full of dreams of Bob. In one, I had been told he was still alive and I stood at a pay phone, trying to call him but unable to remember his number; in another, I could see only the back of my brother's head because he refused to turn around; in the worst dream, I found out that Bob had faked his own death in order to escape from me.

Then one evening I called Donna, ostensibly just to talk, and at some point in our conversation I asked her, tentatively, how she was feeling these days about Bob. We hadn't spoken about our brother in a long time, because after the one-year mark had passed I had felt too ashamed to expose my still-acute grief. But now I was desperate; I needed to know: Was my sister as miserable as me? And Donna told me that she was not, that Bob's death had been very painful at first, but that she had recovered fairly quickly. "But then," she pointed out, "he and I were never close."

Right, I answered, but Bob and I weren't either, didn't she remember the way we battled, undermined, humiliated each other? How most of the time, I didn't *like* our brother? She did recall it, very well, but surely I remembered, didn't I, all the other stuff that went on? "Remember at the dinner table, when you and Bob would conspire and giggle and make Dad mad?" she asked me. "There was something between you guys. I always felt it."

Well, sure, I told her, I remembered those moments of dinner-table solidarity, too, but come on, compared to our devoted warfare, the sheer quantities of blood spilled between us, they were hardly significant. After we hung up, though, her words stuck in my mind: *There was something between you guys.* I dismissed it again as an outsider's misperception, but the thought kept creeping back until, at some point, I gave up trying to block it. The idea was sticking with me for a reason,

I figured; if I knew what it was, maybe it would help me find my way out of the muddle I was in. Writing, I knew, often helped me make connections. It occurred to me that if I wrote down everything I could remember about growing up with Bob—big events, small moments, and all the feelings that went with them—then maybe I could begin to make something of it all. Time and patience hadn't worked. But maybe memory would.

And, very slowly, it did. For what began to emerge, as I filled the pages of a notebook with incidents and images and conversations I thought I had forgotten, was a picture of my brother and me that was much more complicated than the one I had been insisting on. Bob and I *had* clashed like crazy, no question about it. But beneath that relentless rivalry—and surely connected to it—were all the ways in which my brother and I deeply, irrefutably resembled each other. Looking down through our past, I began to perceive clearly, for the first time, that elusive core of kinship: the independence of spirit that resisted anybody's efforts to control us; the convincing tough-guy act that hid, in each of us, a sometimes desperate self-doubt; our joint weakness for the absurd and the romantic; and, perhaps above all else, the boiling rage at our father and the simultaneous yearning for his blessing that had defined us, that had dogged us, and that we had struggled to get free of for the better part of our lives.

I saw that even as we determinedly competed, Bob and I had, in fact, silently established a tiny cell of dissent within our family, founded on an unspoken pact of resistance to our father's authority, without which I would have felt utterly and hopelessly alone. I relived those dinner-table scenarios in which we children were silenced, again and again and again, and the way Donna and Phil would respond with stoic compliance and Bob and I with an outraged *No way, Dad.* I remembered, too, another scene I had managed not to think about for more than twenty years: the terrible afternoon when I heard my father and my teenage brother arguing loudly about something I couldn't quite make out, and ran upstairs to see them standing face to face in my father's office, Bob's face contorted with pain and rage, and heard my now six-foot, black-belted brother warning my father that if he ever, *ever* said what he had just said again, he would knock my father to the floor. I stood in the hallway, shaking, thinking two thoughts: one, Let them stop! and two, *Whatever this is about, Bob, I'm on your side.*

As this memory washed over me, I cried for a long time. But finally, I was beginning to understand the roots of my deep sadness, then and for most of the preceding three years. All of our relentless dueling notwithstanding, in some vital, binding way I *had* been on Bob's side, and he'd been on mine. We had never been soul mates in any conventional sense, yet the two of us had grown up viewing and feeling the world around us in much the same way, and had done so in a family in which no one else seemed to share our particular, sometimes precarious vantage point. Sitting across from Bob at the dinner table as we systematically sabotaged talk of billing procedures with our diversionary jokes and songs, my brother had helped me believe that I wasn't crazy or bad, but deeply angry—and that I had a right to be.

Yet, during the thirty-three years of my brother's life, I had never acknowledged this underground affinity of spirit between us. Partly it was because our noisy, relentless clashing had simply drowned it out, but that was not all that had gotten in the way. All my life, I only now began to see, I had resisted any conscious identification with my brother because what he represented simply scared me to the core. As a child, he was the designated "problem" in our family, thrower of thrashing tantrums, destroyer of family vacations, provoker of my father's wrath and my mother's tears, and I was just enough of a troublemaker myself to fear being lumped with him—and to go to great lengths to establish that I was *not like Bob.*

Then we grew up and I watched my brother become a gentler person to others, and more and more dangerous to himself. I saw his life explode like fireworks, over and over and over again, as he gambled untold thousands of dollars, totaled his cars, confronted guns in his face, dove into alcohol and cocaine, walked into and away from recovery programs, always ready for the next risk, the next thin edge. I watched that self-immolating spark in my little brother and I ran from it and from him, as far as I possibly could. For I, struggling with my own vulnerabilities, didn't want to imagine, not for one moment, that that spark could possibly ignite in me.

And now he was gone, and I could change nothing. But now, at least, I had finally connected my sadness about Bob to its source. Now that I finally understood the truth of my bond with my brother, I could mourn, finally, what I had truly lost when he died. And I did. I grieved now for Bob, my brother, who was not only a member of my family but someone who knew me, who understood me, who felt with me, in a way no one else on this planet ever did or would. Someone who, more than I had ever dared know, *was* me. My brother-double.

And I grieved, too, still more deeply, for all that now would never be. For except in brief, nervous flashes, my brother and I had never been able to truly convey to each other the emotional kinship between us. We had never really been able to express it, enjoy it, sustain each other through it, make anything *of* it in our lives. We may have wanted to—and I think, as we grew older, that both of us truly did—but we just couldn't manage it. There had been too much history between us, too many cruel gibes and long silences, too much fear. And that was why, whenever we said hello, we were already edging away, already saying goodbye.

And when I finally understood all of this, fully and deeply, I was able to forgive both of us the chance we had missed with each other and would never have again. Given who we were, and given the world in which we found ourselves, Bob and I had done the absolute best we could. And as that recognition deepened within me over the next weeks and months, I felt my grief lifting. A measure of peace and energy returned to me. And unexpectedly, as the pain receded, I began to feel Bob's presence more vividly. While before I had been able to think of my brother only with sadness and longing, I now was beginning to remember him also with amused affection, to be able to enjoy memories of his con-man charm, his absurdist humor, his breathtaking, unstoppable energy.

I did not stop missing my brother then. I still miss him, greatly, and I expect that I always will. But sensing Bob's spirit nearby—chortling, manic, ready for the next high-stakes game—helps me fill the space where he once was.

* * *

"I am no longer the same person." I knew this to be true of myself after Bob's death, but as I spoke with others who had lost siblings, I was struck by how many people expressed some version of the same conviction. They spoke of values shaken up, beliefs turned inside out, goals reordered, relationships reconsidered, their view of the world and very sense of self irrevocably altered. It was as though, said one woman who had lost her sister,

> someone had dropped a bomb on all of the things I valued in my life, all of my priorities, all of my assumptions. I just picture all of the things I believed up in the air, tumbling around and you're wondering how are they going to come down and settle and when they do, what order are they going to be in. You're almost starting all over again.

Most individuals experienced at least some of these shifts as additional losses. Nearly everyone I spoke to said that he or she had lost a kind of fundamental innocence about life, some measure of trust in its essential benevolence and orderly unfolding. Especially when a sibling died in early or middle adulthood—what psychologists call an "off-time" death—surviving brothers and sisters were apt to feel deeply this loss of faith in a predictable world, replaced by the permanently wary sense that, as one man put it, "anything can happen, anytime, anywhere, to anybody."

Often, this loss of faith was accompanied by new and abiding fears—especially fear of more loss. A forty-seven-year-old man who lost both of his sisters told me he struggles daily not to overprotect his two young daughters, and believes that "in the context, I think I'm doing a hell of a good job letting them take chances. Because every day, I am terrified of losing them." Others I spoke with were less able to contain their anxieties about the possible death of loved ones, and this chronic fear—what one woman called her "disaster mentality"—seemed particularly acute among those who had lost a sibling suddenly. A thirty-two-year-old woman whose brother died in a motorcycle accident when she was twenty-two says:

If someone is supposed to be at a certain place at a certain time and is more than reasonably late and has not called, I go crazy. I know it's over. I have a real hard time with my husband around this, because, if he's on the road with his job and he says he'll be home around seven, well, being home by nine is the same thing to him. But to me it's not. And when he finally shows up my anger is extreme. I'll scream, "Why did you put me *through* this?" He doesn't understand that for me, an hour ago, he was already dead.

The shocked recognition of the precariousness of life that a sibling's death often spurs, however, frequently leads to a heightened appreciation of other significant relationships. Many people I spoke with felt a new urgency about these bonds, conscious now as they looked upon a loved one: *If my brother/sister died, so could you.* Many spoke of taking the initiative to try to heal damaged ties, of working to bridge emotional distances, or of articulating affection that had long been deeply felt but had remained, until then, unspoken.

Other siblings, not surprisingly, were often the targets of this new urgency, and many reported the forging of stronger connections with surviving sisters and brothers. Yet this process was by no means effortless or automatic. New bids for sibling intimacy were sometimes met with resistance, and some individuals recognized, in retrospect, that they had erred by trying to replicate the kind of relationship with a surviving sibling that they had had with the deceased one, or that they had simply pushed too hard, too fast, for intimacy with an unprepared sister or brother. Others, especially those who had no surviving siblings, talked of similar unsuccessful attempts to instantly "adopt" a friend, a cousin, or even a mate as a surrogate sibling. At some point, however, many individuals recognized the impossibility of truly replacing a sister or brother and were able, at a later point, to renew their bonds with other siblings, friends and others on their own terms.

The greater connectedness with others felt by many bereaved siblings nearly always encompassed a deeper empathy with others' losses. Some became aware, for the first time, of the sheer pervasiveness of loss in the human condition, not only through death but also through divorce, children who leave to find their own lives, friendships that fail, careers that shatter, hopes that never come to fruition. And many, remembering the pain of feeling unsupported in their own grief, now felt strongly about breaking the silence when someone they knew suffered a loss. One woman observed:

I'll say things that I would have never known I could say. I'll say, "Please talk about him or her if you want. If you know a funny story and want to tell me, do. And if you cry, it's okay with me." I'm still uncomfortable sometimes, but I'm much less afraid to be around grieving people. I always used to worry about saying the right thing. Now I know that you can't say anything that would be *right*. All you can say is, "I am sorry." And then try to listen.

While for some, a readiness to comfort others was a direct consequence of their own remembered loneliness while grieving, others connected their deepened empathy to more profound inner shifts. Jonathan, the man who lost his sister to ovarian cancer, remembers:

When I was young, I thought I was in control of my emotions. Especially that I was in control of pain. Or of loss. I guess that's what it was. [Deep breath.] I guess you feel, as a young person, and maybe especially as a male, that you can control it all, that you are omnipotent, but now I have been shown otherwise. Lizzie died and I found out all about my frailty and my weaknesses and my humanness. I no longer have any need to put on a show.

So I think it's easier now for me to talk about my own emotions and to hear other people talk about their pain. Not to always try to keep everything under control. I see this as positive, even though social norms see it as negative. But social norms are not my priority anymore. There's no time.

*There's no time.* Nearly all those I spoke with mentioned, at some point during our interview, that losing a sister or brother had made them more keenly aware of their own mortality. Unlike a parent's death, the death of a sibling is the loss of a peer, and, as Jessamyn West wrote when she contemplated the death of her younger sister, "The bell that tolls for them will toll for you. . . . Its knell doesn't stop reverberating, and it says, 'You next. You next.' "[17] While for a number of individuals I spoke with, that knowledge was initially depressing and frightening, it ultimately energized many to reconsider fundamental life goals and priorities. The question is made conscious: Is what I am doing in my life worthy of my time and passion? What *is* important to do—and to be? Suzanne, the minister who lost her brother to AIDS, said with quiet conviction toward the end of our interview:

> This is the big thing. This is the big thing. I would put this in front of everything. Losing my brother taught me that the best things in life are not *things*. He taught me that it doesn't matter that he sold multimillion-dollar homes in Marin County, which he did. It didn't matter that he was a rising star at his computer company, because he was. It didn't really matter that he had a gorgeous apartment on the Bay and owned a red MGB. None of that mattered. At the end, he was stripped of all that shit.
>
> The only thing that mattered were the people who loved my brother. And at his memorial service, you know, it never came up that he was a software marketing genius. People just kept coming up to me and saying, "You don't know me, but I want to tell you what your brother meant to me in his life. How much he inspired me. How kind he was to me, all the times when I was ready to pack it in."
>
> So I think about that, about what's really important in life. Helping, encouraging, loving people—just all of that. And boy, God, do we get bogged down.

No one should have to lose a sibling to gain such a perspective, I thought as Suzanne spoke those words. There must be other, better, gentler ways to learn it, and I knew, for myself, that I would trade every worthwhile insight I had ever gleaned from Bob's death to have him back. But loss, of course, offers no such deals. We can only work with the choices and chances we have.

Yet it seems to me that many of these unasked-for chances—especially those to do with enriching our connections to the living and making choices that more truly reflect our deepest convictions and enthusiasms—are the very opportunities many of us determinedly flee from, even as we long to admit them into our lives. They require reflection and risk; we are often busy and scared. Loss, despite the suffering it dispenses, and because of it, may push us to discover what we want most from the rest of our lives—and spur us to try to make those visions real.

# 10

# Choosing Connection

Look, walking on water wasn't built in a day.

Jack Kerouac

Throughout this book, women and men have talked of what it means to them to have a sibling—and to be a sibling—as they move through their adult lives. Yet whenever we learn of other people's experience in relationships, few of us can resist making connections with our own. If you have a brother or a sister, some of these stories may have resonated with your own experience, prompting you to think a bit more about the current state of your own sibling bond—its satisfactions, its frustrations, its untested possibilities.

Perhaps you would like to put more energy into this relationship, to try to make it a more central and meaningful part of your life. Maybe you have already begun this reconnection process. Or perhaps you're simply curious to know what might be involved in trying to move your bond with a brother or sister in a different direction, given so much habit and history between you.

This chapter is about the way the change process works in adult sibling relationships, and about the way you might use an understanding of that process to begin—or continue—to work effectively on your own bonds with sisters and brothers.

I do not mean to suggest, however, that anyone "should" change his or her relationship with a sibling. Some people, through luck or effort or both, already enjoy a bond of such intimacy that they can't imagine improving on it. Others who feel they have little in common with a sibling may be content with a relationship of cordial distance, and are not necessarily denying an unconscious need for a deeper tie. For still others, their history with a brother or sister has been so fraught with abuse, humiliation or betrayal that there is simply no desire to reconnect, or any realistic hope of doing so. As a sixty-one-year-old woman said of her older brother, by whom she has felt belittled all her life, "To this day I don't feel safe around him. The less I see of him, the better."

If, on the other hand, you are conscious of wanting a different kind of bond with your sibling, and sense some potential for a more satisfying tie, then working to move the relationship forward may be well worth the effort. Perhaps you feel some genuine attachment to a sister or brother, yet serious unresolved issues—old jealousies, disappointments or rejections—make current encounters tense and painful. Or you may still be bound by ancient, automatic patterns of interacting with a sibling that leave you chronically irritated or overwhelmed. Maybe your sibling tie has never been especially troubled *or* especially intimate, but at this particular point in your life, you've become conscious of wanting a more sustaining, supportive connection with a sister or brother. Or perhaps you and your sibling were close in childhood or adolescence but have become increasingly distant over the years—and you now miss that early solidarity. As a thirty-year-old woman who had grown apart from her older sister observed, "There's a part of me that's sort of suffering because of it. That's my signal that I've got to find some way back to her, even though I'm not sure yet what it is."

Beyond the most obvious benefits of efforts to reconnect—warmer, more enjoyable ties with our brothers and sisters—working to repair or deepen sibling bonds also may help us to finish old business that may be distorting other key relationships in our lives. Psychologist Harriet Goldhor Lerner observes that because "we know our greatest anger, as well as our deepest love" in our ties with family members, we are more apt to get stuck in positions of extreme dependence or distance in these bonds, which in turn influence the way we manage other emotionally significant relationships. Therefore, Lerner points out, if we can learn to use our energy "to get unstuck in our closest and stickiest relationships, we will begin to move with greater charity, control and calm in every relationship we are in."[1]

Still, we may hesitate. Much as we may want to push a sibling relationship in a different direction, we may feel an equally powerful urge to keep things exactly as they are. Change is stressful and difficult in any relationship, not merely because old patterns are hard to break, but because when we begin the process, the outcome is unknown. We are taking a risk, and when family ties are involved—bonds we can't easily walk away from—the stakes can feel frighteningly high. We may wonder: If I behave differently toward my sister, will my relationship with her really work better—or will she stop speaking to me? How will I deal with the anxiety that begins to rise when I even *think* about becoming clearer and more direct in my interactions with my brother? In short, will disturbing the peace in my sibling relationship make me happier in the end, or considerably more miserable?

No one, of course, can guarantee the result of an effort to renegotiate a sibling bond. We can't control every aspect of the process—especially not our sibling's response—and we need to ready ourselves for all possible outcomes. Yet those who study and work with families have identified a number of perspectives and strategies that can substantially improve our chances of making positive change in significant relationships. What follows is by no means a step-by-step guide to change, for every sibling relationship is uniquely shaped and driven by its own mixture of childhood and adult influences; there is no standard-issue "sibling bond" to be led from one predictable stage to the next. Instead, this chapter will point out some of the underlying processes that permit people to move forward (as well as stay stuck) in key relationships of all kinds. Then we will look at some specific approaches—different ways of thinking about sisters and brothers as well as some concrete "new moves"—that have worked for others in renegotiating and revitalizing their sibling bonds.

While not every single perspective here is apt to fit your own relationship, do consider, at least, that it *may*. As one woman said of her long-standing troubles communicating with her older sister, "When the door wouldn't open, I would just sort of rattle the doorknob harder. It's only recently entered my mind—maybe I need a new key."

## How Relationships Do—and Don't—Change

When we first recognize that we want a different kind of relationship with someone, many of us tend to focus on what the *other* person is doing to keep it from materializing, and therefore on what he or she should be doing differently. "If only my sister would stop criticizing me!" "Why won't my brother get a real job and stop borrowing money from me all the time?" "How can she (or he) be so selfish/cold/nosy/crazy/irresponsible/competitive?" Many of us then direct our efforts toward getting our sibling to change his or her behavior, which, as many of us have found to our frustration, almost never works.

Whether we angrily demand or patiently counsel a sibling to change, he or she is apt only to feel blamed, judged and pressured, and to respond with either counterattack or withdrawal. We may then try a new tactic, such as silently waiting for a wayward brother or sister to "shape up" or enlisting other family members in our renovation efforts. Still, nothing is apt to change—except our own escalating resentment and frustration. And then we say to ourselves, "See? It's all *hopeless*."

### Looking to Ourselves

And it is hopeless to try to "fix" somebody else, no matter how creative our tactics or how long we persevere. The only way to change any relationship effectively, those who study family dynamics observe, is to exercise the considerable power we do have—over our own behavior. Family theorists liken a relationship to a circular, mutually reinforcing dance, in which each "dancer" continually prompts, encourages and reinforces the other's steps. We can't force somebody else to move differently, but if we try out new moves ourselves, the dance itself cannot possibly remain the same.[2]

Shifting the focus to ourselves involves figuring out what we really want from our sibling relationship, then acting on our new priorities regardless of what our brother or sister may be doing—or not doing—at the moment. Fifty-eight-year-old Lee, for example, was chronically irritated at her younger sister for "never having time for me unless she *wants* something." When she finally recognized that beneath her anger was a longing for closeness with her only sibling, she began to consider ways she might try to make that happen. "So I told Carol that I planned on calling her once a month, just because I missed her and wanted to find out how things were going," she recalls. After several months of Lee's making such "just checking in" calls, Carol began to call *her* from time to time—to talk of nothing special. "It's probably too simple to say that reaching out breeds more of the same," says Lee, "but something is definitely shifting here. Nothing real revolutionary—but *something*."

With our siblings, often we don't realize the degree of choice we have in our relationship transactions. We may have moved in a fixed, unexamined pattern for so long that the steps we do with them seem inevitable, even necessary—and change therefore all but unthinkable. One man who chronically extricated his older brother from late-night drinking crises felt, "I *had* to keep it together for him," until, with a therapist's support, he finally told his brother he would no longer be available to make two a.m. pickups at bars, emergency rooms or the county jail. He remained in regular touch with his brother, but each night at eleven p.m., he took his phone off the hook. After taking these steps, he reflected:

I felt liberated, and also like a class-A jerk. Here I was, thirty-eight years old, and I never realized I had alternatives in how I did things with my brother. And by God, I *did*.

## Preparing for Backlash

Even though our motive may be a sincere desire for a more balanced, satisfying sibling bond, there is no guarantee that a sister or brother will greet our change agenda with enthusiasm or gratitude. For whether the sibling status quo involves excessive dependence, distance or conflict, it is nonetheless predictable and secure. Confronted by our new behavior, a sibling may try any number of countermoves—accusations of disloyalty, hurt withdrawal, threats of rejection—to get us to return to the "old way."

Moreover, he or she may recruit others to the cause. Because the adult sibling bond remains embedded in the family system, any significant change in behavior toward a brother or sister is apt to challenge deeply entrenched beliefs and rules of behavior, as well as cause reverberations in other family relationships. According to pioneering family systems theorist Murray Bowen, all families offer some degree of resistance to a member's declaration of independence from the "family way," and will try to persuade the prodigal sister or brother to return to the monolithic fold.[3] Preparing for such backlash, as well as for our own anxiety in the face of family resistance, can help us stand our ground as we take a new position in a sibling relationship—as one woman I spoke with discovered through painful experience.

For as long as she could remember, Toni, thirty, had been ensconced in a student-mentor relationship with her thirty-six-year-old sister, Kay. While she still valued and even enjoyed some aspects of her "little sisterhood," in recent years she had begun to feel uncomfortable with the degree to which she allowed Kay to step in and try to manage her life problems, especially those involving her marriage. Once she clarified for herself what she wanted—more privacy to run her own life—she told Kay of her new priorities, making an effort to focus on her own needs and plans rather than on her sister's behavior:

I started by saying something about the "little sister" thing. About how I wanted my family's approval so much, but when I kept running to them I was never trusting myself. And I told her how glad I was that I was finally seeing this, and how I was going to work on it by not feeling that my sister—or anyone else—had to know everything about me. That my husband and I could have our own private issues, and the two of us would now start working on them ourselves.

Because Toni knew her strong-willed sister so well, she was not surprised by the instant backlash that followed her small declaration of independence in their relationship:

> Right away she began to lecture me. Kay is very good at this; she begins to sound like some kind of psychoanalyst. She said to me, "Secrets aren't good. You really shouldn't keep any. We're your *family* . . ." and pretty soon you can't even hang onto what she's saying, but she's *good* at it. You can feel how much she wants you to do whatever it is she wants. No matter where you're making your stand. And my stand was privacy, and she was going to ignore all that and get what she wanted.
>
> But I called her on it. I said, "No, this is what I really believe. This is as far as I'm going. I'm sure about this." And she kept trying for a while, and then she changed the subject and talked about other things.

Toni felt terrific after that conversation: She felt she had firmly held her ground and had "won" her right to privacy. But she seriously underestimated her sister's need to pull her back into their old pattern—as well as the resistance of other family members to her new separateness. Three days later their middle sister, Ruth, called Toni to report that Kay was very upset that Toni was "shutting out the family." When Ruth then rebuked her for hurting Kay's feelings and encouraged her to apologize, Toni felt suddenly anxious and doubtful. *Had* she in fact rejected her oldest sister, who had always taken such an intensely protective interest in her? And if she didn't apologize to Kay, would the whole family now think she was ungrateful?

But before she could fully sort out her feelings, Kay called *her,* now accusing Toni of blaming her and the entire family for all of her personal problems. "I tried to tell her I was doing what was best for me," recalls Toni, but her sister talked over her, declaring that Toni now seemed to think she was too smart to need her own family. The conversation ended in an angry, accusatory argument. For two months, the sisters didn't speak.

Then one evening, without fanfare or explanation, Kay called Toni, "just to chat." As they talked, at first stiffly and cautiously, then finally relaxing enough to begin trading "what's up?" stories, Toni immediately noticed a difference in the way her sister pursued the conversation. "I could tell she still wanted the facts, but she didn't push quite so hard," Toni recalls. "I felt her kind of struggling not to pry." Toni responded by describing her feelings about her new job and her volunteer work at a local women's center, but didn't bring up her marital situation. "And that's pretty much still my mission with Kay," says Toni. "I want to stay close, but not to feel I owe her the story of my life."

## Our Own Stake in the Status Quo

While it is easy to spot other people's resistance to change, we often don't recognize our *own* reluctance to alter established patterns, even when we are deeply dissatisfied with a relationship. Woody Allen indicated his understanding of this dynamic in the last words of the film *Annie Hall,* which is heard as a voice-over:

> This guy goes to a psychiatrist and says, "Doc, my brother's crazy. He thinks he's a chicken." And the doctor says, "Well, why don't you turn him in?" And the guy says, "I would, but I need the eggs."[4]

For an individual who has long been overly dependent on a sibling, the "eggs" might be a safe, secure feeling of being taken care of, even as he or she resents feeling patronized or controlled. For a caretaking sibling, the "eggs" might be a powerful sense of competence that is hard to relinquish, even in the face of anger and frustration at a perpetually needy brother or sister. Only when we recognize our own stake in our sibling status quo can we begin effectively to interrupt the circular pattern we're caught up in. Nonetheless, making such a shift is rarely easy. Rob, a forty-seven-year-old trial lawyer whose older sister has long depended on him to help her out of jams, recalls:

> Just last Friday, Jean called me to tell me that her son got arrested again. And right away, I felt I had to do something about it. God, I'm a lawyer. I'm very, very competent and superorganized and I take charge and I get it *done*. And I think coming from the kind of dysfunctional family unit I did, I always relied on that "taking charge" to give me admiration. I need people to keep saying, "Isn't he wonderful?" Which is love all screwed up. So it's very hard for me to give that up. I want her to need me less— and I also don't.

## Going Slow

Lao-tzu, the Chinese philosopher, said, "Trying to make things easy results in great difficulties." Intellectually, we may recognize that reconnecting with a sibling is a complex undertaking, yet our desire for a better bond and our anxiety about the change process often make us try for instant results, to get the whole thing over and *done* with. There is the urge, observes family therapist Michael Kerr, to burst in on a family member with the goal of getting everybody's feelings expressed, or enthusiastic plans for a new kind of relationship, or simply a pledge to spend more time together, without understanding that "there is more to the task than having some kind of 'roots' experience."[5] The hazard of such "hit-and-run" approaches is that when they don't work—and they rarely do—many of us simply give up, concluding, "I tried, I got burned, it's no use."

Instead, because resistance to change is so powerful—in our siblings, in other family members, and in ourselves—our efforts demand enormous staying power. We need to be tolerant of both ourselves and our sister or brother as we try something new and "blow it," as old habits reassert themselves, as entrenched family rules ("Keep the peace," "family first," "don't interfere") get in our way, as we get derailed again and again by fear or frustration or guilt. From his experience working with adult siblings in therapy, psychologist Stephen Bank observes:

> Siblings rarely act as if a light has suddenly been turned on illuminating wondrous possibilities. What happens is that they realize a relationship may be possible in small ways; they are willing to experiment more, to take little risks which sometimes can lead to an expanded relationship.[6]

Keeping goals manageable and expectations realistic—as well as savoring small victories—can help us stay optimistic as we confront the slow, challenging work of renegotiating a lifelong bond.

## Changing Our Minds: Thinking Differently About Our Siblings

Because our underlying assumptions about people so critically influence how we feel and behave toward them, it may be useful to consider some of the habitual ways we may *think* about our sisters and brothers. A small but critical shift in perspective can sometimes free us to move differently in a sibling relationship that has seemed irredeemably stuck in conflict or distance.

### Reframing the Family Portrait

Many of us find it hard even to begin working for positive change in our sibling relationships because we are so *angry*. We may be angry about old injuries or about current disappointments—or some of both. Anger can initially be helpful, for it can signal that something is fundamentally unbalanced or hurtful in a relationship with a brother or sister. But when we cannot work our way through rage and the blaming that fuels it, it is extremely difficult to move toward reconnection.

To move beyond anger at a sister or brother—and unproductive guilt as well—it may help to recognize how little control we and our siblings actually had over the development of our early relationship. Parents wield enormous and lasting influence over the shape of sibling bonds, both because parents make the family rules and because children so need their love. If parents clearly favored one child over another, assigned one child to be another's caretaker, tolerated sibling abuse, modeled extreme distance or overinvolvement, or left siblings to fend for themselves, the children involved had little power to stop it. Stephen Bank, who has studied the sibling bond for two decades, observes that when such parental actions produce severe and lasting sibling conflict, it amounts to a "stolen birthright"—the loss of a fundamental right to a warm, caring relationship with a sister or brother. He notes further that we tend to resist recognizing the source of this loss because it is less threatening, ultimately, to feel rage toward a sibling than toward a parent.[7]

This is not to suggest that we should now heap blame on our parents for their child-rearing inadequacies. In their own early, vulnerable years, our parents' relationship capacities, behaviors, beliefs and rules were shaped by those of *their* parents, and so on back through the generations. Developing such an "intergenerational" perspective, in fact, can be very helpful in understanding our sibling bonds more fully and objectively, since attitudes and expectations toward sibling relationships themselves are frequently passed down through many generations.[8] Many individuals I interviewed could link characteristics of their parents' (and sometimes even their grandparents') sibling bonds—expectations of closeness or distance, tendencies toward overinvolvement or estrangement, habits of rescuing or rivalry—to the current tenor of their own sibling ties.

Such a broadened perspective, of course, doesn't mean that we and our siblings bear no responsibility for our current relationships. Yet by recognizing that our bond is truly "bigger than both of us," we may be able to approach a brother or sister with a bit more empathy and understanding, and also work more effectively for the kind of relationship we truly want—not one predetermined by the "family way."

## Resisting Categories

More than we do with friends, colleagues or even most other relatives, we tend to stereotype our siblings. Because families are so prone to labeling children, most of us learned early on that a brother or sister was a particular sort of person—"the wild one," "the baby," "the dreamer," "the saint." If we never consciously questioned a sibling's ancient family label, it may have hardened into what Stephen Bank and Michael Kahn call a "frozen image," whereby we keep a sister or brother "bound to an old identity—an indelible, ir-revocable, unchanged and unchanging characterization of the self."[9] Consequently, we are apt to continue expecting and even encouraging the behavior advertised by a sibling's im-prisoning label—even when it gets in the way of a satisfying relationship. For example, if we automatically view the youn-gest in our family as selfish, we are unlikely to give him or her opportunities to be generous toward us—or to notice when he or she behaves that way—because we already "know" that such behavior is beyond that sibling's capacities.

In her landmark book about the way thinking processes shape experience, *Mindfulness,* Harvard University psycholo-gist Ellen Langer suggests that we combat such tyrannical mind-sets by cultivating "creative uncertainty" about signifi-cant people in our lives.[10] An attitude of having much to learn can free us to notice the complexity of a sister's or brother's self in the present moment, rather than simply seeking hypothesis-confirming data. Such a limber state of mind can also help us escape from our limiting notions of who *we* are vis-à-vis our siblings—and free us to try out new roles and re-sponses.

## Accepting Difference

Perhaps more often than we'd like to admit, our conflicts with siblings may arise from wanting them to be more like *us.*

We may want them to share our values, our aims, our style of living, our vision of a "good" relationship—and then we feel disappointed and angry when they do not. This frustration in the face of difference is apt to emerge in any close relationship, but we may feel it particularly acutely with our sisters and brothers. For one thing, the actual differences between us and our siblings—especially those who are of the same sex and close in age—may in fact be dauntingly large, in part because of our earlier, collaborative efforts to carve out identities distinct from each other. Moreover, because we are of the same blood and roots, we may feel deeply that our siblings "should" think and live more as we do, and their insistent individuality may feel akin to betrayal. Our brothers and sisters, in turn, may feel similarly about our perverse refusal to be more like *them*.

The root of this dilemma may lie in our definition of closeness. In *The Dance of Intimacy*, Harriet Goldhor Lerner writes, "We commonly confuse closeness with sameness and view intimacy as the merging of two separate 'I's' into one worldview."[11] Granted, we are unlikely to feel close to someone—sibling or otherwise—with whom we constantly conflict on issues that are extremely important to us, or whose personality harshly clashes with ours. But as Lerner observes, all of us view the world through our own perceptual filters, uniquely shaped by our own particular biological equipment and life experience. So even though we and our siblings share both of our parents and roughly half of our genes, our numerous different filters—those of temperament, gender, age, sibling position, experience of love and conflict in the family, interaction with the larger world—mean that even the sibling we feel most connected to will inevitably approach life from a somewhat different vantage point than our own.

Genuine sibling intimacy, it would seem, is about deeply respecting each other's fundamental separateness even as we enjoy the ways we mirror and second each other; it is about the continuous, vigilant effort to maintain the balance between the "we" and the "I." One forty-nine-year-old woman describes what has finally allowed her to strike this critical balance with her "wild man" younger brother:

The thing I want most in the world—other than hitting the lottery—is I just want to *be*. Just to become more comfortable with me, the person. And I'm finding that the more I'm able to do that, the more I'm able to allow other people to do the same thing. I'm not sure I ever learned how to do that. Certainly not well.

But my brother is entitled to be himself. What he does with his girlfriends and his carrying on and et cetera, that's his business. I have no right to be judgmental. You know, sometimes I look back on our childhood and I think, There but for the grace of God go me in his shoes. I really feel that. We all need to cut each other a break.

# New Moves: Changing Our Steps in the Sibling Dance

For some people, altering an entrenched perspective about a sibling may be enough to shift the relationship into a more positive gear. Others, however, may feel locked in automatic patterns of behavior with a sibling that seem to promote conflict or distance or both—and that may require acting differently as well as thinking differently in the relationship. Below are some specific ways we might alter our behavior to try to encourage more equality, understanding and intimacy in our ties with brothers and sisters. The more we can keep in mind the general guidelines on relationship change considered earlier—looking to ourselves for change, preparing for resistance (our sibling's and our own) and going slow—the more effective these "new moves" are likely to be.

## Unhooking from Roles

For some of us, conflict with adult siblings tends to be chronic, stemming from the repeated enactment of old, complementary roles that we may hate—yet can't quite seem to shed. No sooner does your brother, "the problem child," call you with a crisis than you, "the organizer," begin to renovate his life for him. Or no sooner do you, "the rebel," express a mildly offbeat opinion at a family gathering than your sister, "the straight arrow," reprimands you for upsetting the parents with your subversive ideas—which spurs you to offer a few more. As a thirty-two-year-old woman with three older siblings observes in frustration:

> It's like an outfit you wear. As soon as you get together, you put on your outfits again. You try to see past it, but it's always there. It's something I'm always working at— the trying to get past it. But it's bizarre. The uniform. I think we all do it to one another.

When such complementary role-playing is rigid, it tends to cause trouble between siblings because one or both individuals are apt to feel badly treated and unable to be fully themselves in the relationship. If you are the designated "child" in a "child-parent" sibling bond, for example, you may feel patronized and prevented from demonstrating your own competence. If you are the "parent" sibling, you may feel exploited and unable to acknowledge your own needs for support in the relationship.

Because such roles are mutually reinforcing—that is, each behavior invites the other—many family experts suggest the strategy of *reversing* roles to begin to alter this entrenched dynamic.[12] Toni, for example, the woman who no longer wanted her older sister Kay to solve her life problems, eventually recognized that the long-standing student-teacher bond between the sisters was unlikely to change as long as she remained passively in the "pupil" position:

> After things had calmed down some between us, I said to her, "You know, it's always *my* problems we're working out, *my* life we're discussing, and I don't know a whole lot about yours." And I told her I'd like to know more. Like I knew she was a partner in her company, and that a lot of stress went with that, but I didn't really know what her issues were, what she went through day by day. So I started to ask her about that.

When Kay responded by telling her sister something about the complex problems she was currently facing with hiring and firing, Toni felt immediately overwhelmed and inadequate. "I just wasn't *there* yet in my job—I didn't know anything about that end of it," she recalls. "And I thought, What made me think I could help her?" Gradually, however, she realized that her sister didn't need her advice as much as her active, sympathetic listening, and she was gratified when Kay told her one evening that talking with her had been enormously helpful because it had allowed her to clarify her feelings about a conflict she was facing with another partner in her firm. While the bond between the sisters is still far from perfectly balanced—"We still talk 'me' more than we talk 'her' "—Toni now feels a growing measure of respect from Kay, as well as an increasingly solid sense of her own capacity to support a formerly "omnipotent" older sister.

## Ending Rescue Missions: Guilt and the Bottom Line

Of all the roles that siblings adopt vis-à-vis their siblings, perhaps the most painful—and the most difficult to shed—is that of rescuer. Millions of us have siblings who are alcoholic or drug-addicted or mentally ill, or who simply can't seem to get their lives "together" in one way or another. For years, many of us have bailed these brothers and sisters out of crises, have repeatedly provided financial aid or other new starts, and have otherwise tried to fix their lives. Then we've watched our money go down the drain, our advice ignored, the stable situations we've created for them abandoned. We feel furious and overwhelmed—and then we rescue some more.

It's not that we don't know what we "should" do. For the past two decades, the addiction recovery movement has widely publicized the necessity to halt such rescue missions so that a troubled individual is forced to confront the consequences of his or her behavior, thereby providing a real incentive to change. But most such advice, which centers on rescuing behavior within marriage, fails to consider the particular legacy of guilt that adult siblings often face when they try to extricate themselves from a savior role. For many, sacrificing for a brother or sister has been their "job" since childhood. One woman whose sister is schizophrenic recalled that "at least since grade school, I was always supposed to halve whatever I had—friends, fun, *everything*—and give it to my sister."

Layered atop this source of guilt is often additional guilt for having been the parents' favored "well" or "strong" child, and for having thereby derived, in the words of Stephen Bank and Michael Kahn, "a distinct and satisfying subidentity from having a deviant brother or sister."[13] Still more guilt may issue from feeling ashamed of or even disgusted by a "weak" sibling, or from fearing that we may have somehow contributed to whatever misery he or she now faces. Further fueling our rescue missions may be genuine caring for a disturbed sibling, as well as the terror that if we stop doing what we're doing, our brother or sister may disintegrate utterly—or die.

Dropping an entrenched savior role depends on coming to grips with our guilt and our fears; on understanding that this brand of "help," in fact, inevitably maintains our sibling's illness rather than heals it; on recognizing that ceasing our fix-it missions in no way means abandoning a sister or brother. We can define a clear bottom line—what we will no longer do or tolerate in the relationship—while still remaining connected and supportive in constructive ways. As one man said he told his cocaine-addicted brother, "I'll shell out any amount of money you need for a recovery program. I'll support your health, but I won't support your addiction."

Yet because the guilt and sense of responsibility can be so deeply lodged, and because backlash by an "abandoned" sibling is apt to be so powerful ("If you don't help me out of this jam, I'll kill myself"), reworking a bond with a troubled sister or brother can be a very difficult challenge. You may want to consider getting outside support for this effort, through either professional counseling or a self-help group for family members of addicted or chronically ill individuals.[14]

## Stepping Out of Triangles

The maxim "three's a crowd" may embody more wisdom than we realize. Family systems theorists observe that the more tension that exists between any two individuals, the more likely they are to pull in a third person and form a relationship triangle. The third person serves the original pair by detouring and diluting the tension between them.[15]

Siblings commonly draw in such third-party players. The third "point" on the triangle may be another sibling, to whom we regularly complain about a brother or sister with whom we are angry—rather than talk directly with him or her about our irritation. Or a third party may be a sibling's spouse, on whom a brother and sister blame their growing distance from each other, rather than directly confronting the difficulties between them that may be fueling their alienation. Using a third person to pad the problems between ourselves and siblings usually does a good job of easing our anxiety, but at the price of never resolving the problems themselves. When we don't talk directly to a brother or sister about the sources of conflict or distance in our relationship, we are apt simply to go on feeling angry or hurt—and to cheat ourselves of the chance to develop a genuine, person-to-person connection with that sibling.

Triangles that involve parents can be especially hard to step out of. Typically, one sibling will ally with a parent to worry about a second sibling, who is the designated "problem child" or "fragile one" in the family. When we continually huddle with a parent to analyze or fret over a sister or brother, we may honestly believe we are helping. But as Harriet Goldhor Lerner observes, through such alliances "we consolidate our relationship with one party at the expense of a third. . . . Gossip has nothing to do with intentions. Our conscious intentions may be only the best."[16]

Beneath those conscious intentions may be our wish to fortify our bond with a parent by continuing to be the "solid" child who can be counted on to help the parent deal with the other, far more "difficult" child. In the process, however, we forfeit all possibility of mutual respect and trust between ourselves and that sibling. To extricate ourselves from such a triangle, we must be prepared to drop our insider role with parents vis-à-vis a sister or brother—and to gird for backlash. Because a parent may have pulled us into the triangle in the first place to keep from directly facing his or her own conflicts with another child, the parent may strenuously resist our efforts to stop commiserating, trading advice, acting as messenger or otherwise continuing to be the sibling-in-the-middle. It makes sense to go slowly here, and to try to stay connected both to parents and to sibling as we chart a more independent course.

## Comparing Notes: The Way It Was

Each of us believes that he or she has a "fix" on the way it was in our childhood families—who terrorized whom, who was favored by Mom and by Dad, who had the hardest and the easiest time of it. But do we really know? Writer Laurie Lee muses:

> Seven brothers and sisters shared my early years, and we lived on top of each other. If they all had written of those days, each account would have been different, and each one true. We saw the same events at different heights, at different levels of mood and hunger—one suppressing an incident as too much to bear, another building it large around him, each reflecting one world according to the temper of his day, his age, and the chance heat of his blood. Recalling it differently, as we were bound to do, what was it, in fact, we saw? . . . The truth is, of course, that there is no pure truth, only the moody accounts of witnesses.[17]

Listening to "the truth" as a sister or brother felt it, way back when, can go a long way toward melting frozen misunderstandings, healing old injuries, and deepening a sense of empathy with a sibling. These are not always easy conversations, for we may find out that a brother or sister is still hurt or angry about something that happened between us long ago. In fact, when there is still significant conflict or distrust between siblings, such explorations of the past may be better done with a therapist present. Approached in a spirit of learning and sharing, however, listening to each other's childhood memories and perceptions can help us to feel powerfully the connectedness between ourselves and our siblings.

This began to happen for Donna and me in our mid-thirties, when for the first time we started talking about "the way it was" in our early years. In the course of one of those conversations, I tentatively told my sister how hard it had been for me to grow up alongside her. Because she had been the undisputed "good girl," I told her, I had always felt that our parents had approved of her more, and that her straight-arrow ways had made me look even worse—more defiant and less lovable—than I actually was. Also, I told her, I had always felt tremendous pressure to achieve from our father, while it seemed to me that Donna had been accepted for herself.

To say that my sister was astounded by my version of our past is an understatement. From Donna's perspective, *I* had been the favored child in the family, the nonstop center of attention who was praised for her school grades and achievements while she withdrew, feeling massively eclipsed. "Think about it," she said. "You were the achiever, Bob was the troublemaker and Phil was the baby. My personality was quiet; I didn't make *any* kind of waves. So I was just sort of—well, I just couldn't compete for attention."

I listened, surprised and saddened by the depth of my sister's childhood pain. In the days and months that followed, we talked more about our contrasting realities, memories that had meant one thing to me, another to my sister. And paradoxically, the more our versions differed, the more we began to sense the deep strains of commonality beneath our obvious contrasts, and the lingering resentments held over from our contentious childhood began to lose their reason to be—and their power to divide us. For we now understood: It hadn't been easy for either of us.

## Saying the Words

For some siblings, direct expressions of caring come easily and naturally. The rest of us may feel much, yet say very little. We may rarely tell our siblings the ways in which we value them or what we enjoy most about them. We may never, ever tell them that we love them.

Maybe it feels too corny, or melodramatic, or even frightening, to convey directly to a sibling that we care about him or her. And in fact, for those of us who grew up in families that discouraged open expressions of warmth or appreciation,

doing so now—particularly with a member of that family—
may constitute a real act of courage. Yet we know from our
own experience what it feels like to hear, in no uncertain
terms, that someone thinks well of us: Rarely can we hear it
*enough*. We feel validated, appreciated, known—and, in turn,
more open and trusting with the person who has risked saying the words.

Often we don't bother to express positive feelings toward a
sibling because we feel it's belaboring the obvious. We assume
that our brother or sister "must know" how deeply we appreciate what he or she did for us when we were small, or the
ways in which he or she currently validates or supports us.
But we can't read each other's minds, and particularly in relationships that have had their share of conflict or ambivalence,
a sibling may be little aware of his or her positive impact.

I remember my own amazement—and deep gratification—
when Phil told me recently that in his early teenage years, I
was the only person in the family he could talk with about
girls, sex and feelings. "I mean, at that age, you don't have
any *idea* what to do," he told me. "And I'd ask you, and I'd
come away with a sense of how to think about something."
He told me that we'd had many, many such talks, and that he
had always known that I would never laugh at him. And because of that history of trust, Phil told me, he felt that even
now, "I don't do it that much, but I always know you're the
one I *can* go to."

Phil was surprised that *I* was surprised to hear this: How
could I not have known how important those conversations
had been to him? But I hadn't. My memories had been mainly
of the guilt-ridden variety, centering on the many times I had
been inattentive or outright unkind toward my little brother,
which I believed had caused him to harbor a deep, unspoken
resentment toward me. To discover instead how much Phil
appreciated me, both then and now, washed away much of
that long-standing remorse, which had always made me feel
vaguely unworthy of friendship with my grown-up brother—
and also very fearful of rejection. I came to understand, instead, that the safe distance I had been keeping from him
might no longer be necessary.

Conveying caring toward a sibling, of course, doesn't have

to involve detailed statements of gratitude or solidarity. Small gestures can make a powerful impact. When I asked the women and men I interviewed, "What has a sister or brother done recently that you have most appreciated?" many mentioned getting a supportive phone call or note when they were starting—or ending—something important in their lives. Others spoke of receiving offers of specific help—I'll fix your car, I'll edit your résumé, I'll take your kids ice-skating—when they were in a crunch. Several mentioned a sibling's willingness simply to listen to them when they were feeling particularly discouraged or scared or confused.

What such seemingly small acts appeared to convey to their recipients was thoughtfulness—in the true sense of that word. People were deeply gratified to know that they were on a sibling's mind, and that amid the busyness and distractions of daily living, a brother or sister had made a genuine effort to demonstrate that "mindfulness."

## When Nothing Works

Some individuals work hard to resolve long-standing conflict with a brother or sister, or to bridge the gap from distance to connectedness, and come up against a brick wall of resistance. No matter what they try, or how long they persevere, a sibling doesn't respond. Sometimes this happens because a sister or brother is simply too deeply invested in the current relationship pattern. A relentlessly "superior" sister, for example, may feel profoundly inadequate if she cannot continue one-upping her sibling; an emotionally guarded brother may be too fearful of intimacy to move closer to a sibling who has made overtures. In other cases, a brother or sister may resist connection because he or she chooses not to give up old, deeply rooted resentments. Still other siblings who suffer serious emotional illnesses, or who are addicted to alcohol or other drugs, may simply lack the resources to participate in an equal, mutually supportive relationship. Whatever the reasons, when sibling connection fails, the individual who has tried to move closer is apt to feel deeply rejected and saddened by the loss. As one man whose sustained efforts to connect with his older brother were met with cool disinterest told me, "I have friends who have sisters and brothers who they're best buddies with and all. And I'm jealous. It hurts me that I don't have it. That at this point, you know, I really don't have a brother."

For those I talked with whose gestures of connection were repeatedly rebuffed or ignored, coming to terms with their loss involved giving up their long-held expectations of a brother or sister, and also mourning the sibling they had wished for, but did not have. Many ultimately looked beyond the family for a siblinglike bond, finding a "good brother" or a "good sister" in a special friendship that sustained them. One young woman, aware of the limitations of her relationship with her schizophrenic sister, views her closest female friend as a kind of surrogate sibling:

> I think I sought out a real sisterly, familial kind of relationship with Pat. There are real sisterly aspects to it—we're very close and we also fight, and then we always make up. [Laughs.] The bottom line is, we can never quite give each other up. And I think she feels that way too. At my wedding, she gave the bridal toast and her last words were, "You're my sister." And I was really touched by that.

## Choosing Connection

Even when we make encouraging progress in reworking and renewing ties with siblings, we may persistently feel that "not enough" has happened. We may feel that after all the effort we have expended, we should be closer to a brother or sister than we now are, or that the bond should be more evenly balanced than it is. And in part, this sense of incompleteness merely reflects the reality that the sibling bond is a perpetually unfinished one. As we continue to develop through adulthood and confront new turning points and internal priorities, new needs and challenges in our sibling relationships will almost inevitably emerge. In this sense, there always will be more to do.

But a nagging sense of "not-enoughness" may also issue from the deep, unspoken hopes that many of us harbor about this bond. We may hope—especially at the outset of a reconnection effort—to transform a sibling into a best friend, or, because of our ties of blood and history, something even finer and more sacred than that. We may hope that once we resolutely "confront," "work on" and finally "resolve" our problems with a brother or sister, we will be rewarded with a relationship of surpassing mutuality and solidarity. We may know better, yet some piece of us still longs for the perfect harmony of the March sisters in *Little Women*, the perfect loyalty of Hansel and Gretel, the perfect forgiveness of Joseph for his brothers. And so we may still hold our real siblings at arm's length, waiting for more progress to happen before we can truly welcome them into our lives.

Perhaps the greatest challenge we face in this relationship, after all, is not to root out its every surviving flaw and frailty, but rather to begin to accept that we never will. That no matter how diligently we pursue a sibling change agenda, our brothers and sisters may not always be "there" for us, that they will persist in understanding us imperfectly, that they will forever be other than who *we* are. That some ancient habits may be stronger than our will to bury them; that ambivalence may persist. And that in spite of these implacable limitations, our relationships with our brothers and sisters may still be worth what it takes to pursue and nurture them as we move through our adult lives.

For if we're able to find in this bond, as one woman put it, "enough straight-up-goodness to want to hold on to," our lingering frustrations may be less important than what our sisters and brothers uniquely have to give us, and we to them. To say that *they were there,* back in the days when we were so young and it all mattered so much, only begins to suggest the unduplicable brand of validation, self-knowledge, humor and healing perspective that we now may be able to offer each other. None of us does this flawlessly, or at all the "right" moments. Yet when we're lucky enough to encounter the pleasures of this bond, when those ineffable signals of shared history and sympathy and understanding flash back and forth between us and our siblings, we find out something vital about ourselves. We discover that we are known, and that we belong, and in experiencing this connectedness, we may find out how deeply we need it.

# Notes

**INTRODUCTION**

1. Bedford, 1989a; Dunn and Kendrick, 1982; Gold, 1989b; Lempers and Clark-Lempers, 1992.
2. Lerner, 1987.

**CHAPTER I**

1. Cicirelli, 1982; Gallup Poll, 1989; Ross and Milgram, 1982.
2. Bedford, 1989b.
3. Avioli, 1989; White and Riedmann, 1992.
4. Barrera, Chassin and Rogosch, 1993.
5. Wideman, 1984, p. 98.
6. Shaw, quoted in Colonna and Newman, 1983, p. 287.
7. Freud, 1900, p. 250.
8. Freud, 1916–17, p. 153.
9. Gay, 1988, p. 507.
10. Radcliffe-Brown and Forde, 1950, p. 275.
11. Weisner and Gallimore, 1977.
12. Williams, quoted in Weisner and Gallimore, 1977, p. 177.
13. Weisner, 1982.
14. Marshall, 1983.

15. Forrest, 1982.
16. Kipp, 1986.
17. Bureau of the Census, 1991.
18. National Center for Health Statistics, 1991.
19. Bureau of the Census, 1992b.
20. Bureau of the Census, 1992a.
21. Connidis, 1989.
22. Blake, 1989.
23. Blake, 1989.
24. Bureau of the Census, 1992b.
25. Cicirelli, 1988, p. 441.
26. Bowlby, 1973, p. 359.

## CHAPTER 2

1. Woolf (10 August 1909) *Letters*, vol. I.
2. Joyce, quoted in Kimball, 1983, p. 74.
3. Bank and Kahn, 1982; Ross and Milgram, 1982.
4. Hartman and Laird, 1983.
5. Wideman, 1984, pp. 78–80.
6. McGoldrick, 1989a, p. 69.
7. Woehrer, 1982.
8. Johnson, 1982, p. 157.
9. Johnson, 1982.
10. Gold, 1990a.
11. Woehrer, 1982.
12. Welts, 1988.
13. Mott, 1965, p. 49. Mott arrived at these figures by calculating the sum of all possible subgroups (pairs, threesomes, etc.) for each family size. Each total is increased by one to account for the possibility of a simultaneous interaction among all members.
14. Ross and Milgram, 1982.
15. Stocker, Dunn and Plomin, 1989. But fathers matter, too. For the impact of paternal favoritism on sibling relationships, see Brody, Stoneman and McCoy, 1992.
16. Dunn and Plomin, 1990.
17. Eileen Joyce, quoted in Kimball, 1983, p. 89. For research documenting the tendency of favored children to have distant or hostile sibling bonds, see McHale and Pawletko, 1992.

18. Milgram and Ross, 1982.
19. Bank and Kahn, 1982, pp. 112–13.
20. Rhodes, 1990, p. 153–54.
21. Woolf (31 May 1928), *Diary*, vol. III.
22. Woolf (20 June 1928), *Diary*, vol. III.
23. Woolf (2 October 1937), *Letters*, vol. VI.
24. Woolf (10 August 1922), *Letters*, vol. II.
25. Cicirelli, 1980.
26. Bank and Kahn, 1982; Pulakos, 1987.
27. Atwood, 1988, p. 3.

**CHAPTER 3**

1. Abramovitch, Pepler and Corter, 1982. For other discussions of the intensity and range of interactions among young siblings, see also Brown and Dunn, 1992, and Lempers and Clark-Lempers, 1992.
2. Bowlby, 1969.
3. Ernst and Angst, 1983.
4. Minuchin, 1974, p. 47.
5. Bank and Kahn, 1982, p. 99.
6. Brook, Whiteman, Brook and Gordon, 1991; Gforerer, 1987; Jensen and Overgaard, 1993; Needle, McCubbin, Wilson, Reineck et al., 1986.
7. Canin, 1991, pp. 69–70.
8. Caro, 1982.
9. Azmitia and Hesser, 1993.
10. de Beauvoir, 1963, p. 45.
11. Dunn and Plomin, 1990.
12. For evidence of a link between sibling support and psychological adjustment among socially isolated children, see East and Rook, 1992.
13. Gilligan, quoted in Aylmer, 1989.
14. Schachter, 1982.
15. Bank and Kahn, 1982, p. 24.
16. Cornell, 1983, p. 325.
17. Conroy, 1986, p. 53.
18. Raffaelli, 1992.
19. Schachter, 1982, pp. 129–30.

## CHAPTER 4

1. For a notable exception, see Downing, 1988. For studies that pay close attention to gender differences, see especially the work of Victor Cicirelli, Judy Dunn, Deborah Gold and Monica McGoldrick.

2. Keniston, 1988, p. 12.

3. Adams, 1968; Cicirelli, 1989; Cumming and Schneider, 1961; Gold, 1989b; Gold, 1990a; Suggs, 1985; White and Riedmann, 1992.

4. Tannen, 1990, p. 81.

5. Fischer and Narus, 1981; Reisman, 1990; Wright and Scanlon, 1991.

6. Rubin, 1985, p. 61.

7. Osborne, 1991.

8. Epstein, 1988; Lips, 1988.

9. Stoller, quoted in Kaschak, 1992, p. 38.

10. Brannon, 1976.

11. Zern, 1984.

12. Miller, 1986, p. 50.

13. Chodorow, 1978. For analyses and extensions of Chodorow's theory, see also Apter, 1990, and Rubin, 1985.

14. Rubin, 1985, pp. 95–96.

15. For example, a number of studies indicate that parents respond even more negatively toward sons who choose "girl" interests or toys than toward daughters who gravitate to "boy" activities. See Basow, 1986, for a discussion of this research.

16. Blakemore, 1990; Furman and Buhrmester, 1992.

17. Pulakos, 1989.

18. Gallup Organization, 1989.

19. Borland, 1987.

20. Cicirelli, 1979; Gold, 1989a; Hoyt and Babchuk, 1983; Troll and Smith, 1976; White and Riedmann, 1992.

21. Cicirelli, 1989.

22. Cicirelli, 1980.

23. Hartmann, 1991.

24. Vaillant and Vaillant, 1990.

25. Ross and Milgram, 1982.

26. Pulakos, 1989; Ross and Milgram, 1982.
27. Gilligan, 1982, p. 62.
28. Gold, 1989a.
29. Adams, 1968.
30. Wright, 1982.
31. Miller, 1986, p. 83.

## CHAPTER 5

1. Bernikow, 1980, pp. 74–75.
2. Woolf (2 June 1926) *Diary*, vol. III.
3. "Gender intensification" refers to the increased pressure on both girls and boys in early adolescence to conform to sex-typed roles and behaviors. See Apter, 1990; Hill and Lynch, 1983.

## CHAPTER 6

1. Cicirelli, 1982.
2. Cicirelli, 1982.
3. Basow, 1986.
4. Basow, 1986; Tognoli, 1980.
5. Mangold and Koski, 1990; Straus, Gelles and Steinmetz, 1980.
6. Bennett, 1990.
7. Gully, Dengerink, Pepping and Bergstrom, 1981.
8. Keen, 1991, pp. 174–75.
9. Tannen, 1990, p. 282.

## CHAPTER 7

1. Lindenbaum, 1979.
2. Cicirelli, 1989; Cicirelli, 1982; Cicirelli, 1977; Troll and Smith, 1976.
3. Bernays, 1940, p. 337.
4. Basow, 1986; Ho, 1987; McGoldrick, Garcia-Preto, Hines and Lee, 1989.
5. Ho, 1987.
6. Jacobs and Moss, 1976; Marjoribanks, 1989; Taubman and Behrman, 1986.
7. Thomas, 1983.

8. Hennig and Jardim, 1977.
9. Rosenberg, 1982.
10. DuHamel, 1988.
11. Stewart, 1983; Stoneman, Brody and MacKinnon, 1986.
12. Finkelhor, 1980; Greenwald and Leitenberg, 1989.
13. Finkelhor, 1980. For a thorough analysis of the long-term impact of sibling incest on women, as well as a discussion of identification and treatment issues, see Canavan, Meyer and Higgs, 1992.

## CHAPTER 8

1. Ross and Milgram, 1982.
2. Gold, 1989a.
3. Epstein, 1988; Levinson, 1986.
4. Baltes, Reese and Lipsett, 1980, p. 94.
5. Fintushel and Hillard, 1991.
6. Boszormenyi-Nagy and Spark, 1973, pp. 217–18.
7. Ross and Milgram, 1982.
8. Didion, 1968, p. 165.
9. Johnson, 1982.
10. Bedford, 1989a; Johnson, 1982.
11. Brody, Hoffman, Kleban and Schoonover, 1989; Coward and Dwyer, 1990; Finley, 1989; Lee, Dwyer and Coward, 1993; Matthew and Rosner, 1988.
12. Brody, Hoffman, Kleban and Schoonover, 1989.

## CHAPTER 9

1. Gorer, 1965, p. 14.
2. For a comprehensive review of the literature on childhood sibling loss, see Paulson, 1990. Key services for young bereaved siblings include a nationwide network of support groups sponsored by The Compassionate Friends, P.O. Box 3696, Oak Brook, IL 60522; and counseling and recovery groups offered by the Center for Grief Recovery and Sibling Loss, 4513 N. Ashland, Chicago, IL 60640.
3. Moss and Moss, 1989. See also Moss and Moss, 1986, for a groundbreaking essay on adult sibling loss.
4. O'Connor, 1984, pp. 108–9.
5. Wortman and Silver, 1989.

6. Bank and Kahn, 1982, p. 283.
7. Moss and Moss, 1989.
8. Moss and Moss, 1989, p. 102.
9. Neeld, 1990; Wortman and Silver, 1989.
10. McIntosh and Wrobleski, 1988.
11. Ness and Pfeffer, 1990.
12. Bowlby, 1980; Neeld, 1990.
13. Neeld, 1990.
14. Siegal and Kuykendall, 1990.
15. Marris, 1974.
16. Neeld, 1990; Pincus, 1974.
17. West, 1976, p. 95.

**CHAPTER 10**

1. Lerner, 1985, p. 11.
2. Hartman and Laird, 1983; Lerner, 1989.
3. Bowen, 1978.
4. Allen, 1982.
5. Kerr, 1984, p. 25.
6. Bank, 1988, p. 348.
7. Bank, 1988.
8. Kerr, 1984.
9. Bank and Kahn, 1982, p. 73.
10. Langer, 1989.
11. Lerner, 1989, p. 70.
12. Harris, 1988; Hartman and Laird, 1983.
13. Bank and Kahn, 1982, p. 232.
14. Organizations that offer support groups and informational materials include:

For siblings and other family members of alcoholics:
  Al-Anon Family Group Headquarters
  P.O. Box 862
  Midtown Station, New York, NY 10018
  (212) 302-7240

For siblings of the mentally ill:
    Siblings and Adult Children's Network
    National Alliance for the Mentally Ill
    2101 Wilson Blvd., Suite 302
    Arlington, VA 22201
    (703) 524-7600

15. Bowen, 1978.
16. Lerner, 1989, p. 153.
17. Lee, 1975.

# References

Abramovitch, R., Pepler, D., and Corter, C. 1982. Patterns of sibling interaction among preschool-age children. In M. E. Lamb and B. Sutton-Smith (eds.), *Sibling relationships: Their nature and significance across the lifespan* (pp. 61–86). Hillsdale, N.J.: Lawrence Erlbaum.

Adams, B. 1968. *Kinship in an urban setting.* Chicago: Markham.

Allen, W. 1982. *Four films of Woody Allen.* New York: Random House.

Apter, T. 1990. *Altered loves: Mothers and daughters during adolescence.* New York: St. Martin's Press.

Atwood, M. 1988. *Cat's Eye.* New York: Doubleday.

Avioli, P. 1989. The social support functions of siblings in later life. *American Behavioral Scientist 33*, 45–57.

Aylmer, R. 1989. The launching of the single young adult. In B. Carter and M. McGoldrick (eds.), *The changing family life cycle: A framework for family therapy*. Boston: Allyn and Bacon.

Azmitia, M. and Hesser, J. 1993. Why siblings are important agents of cognitive development: A comparison of siblings and peers. *Child Development 64*, 430–44.

Baltes, P. B., Reese, H. W., and Lipsett, L. P. 1980. Life-span developmental psychology. *Annual Review of Psychology 31*, 65–110.

Bank, S. P. 1988. The stolen birthright: The adult sibling in individual therapy. In M. D. Kahn and K. G. Lewis (eds.), *Siblings in therapy: Life span and clinical issues* (pp. 341–55). New York: W. W. Norton.

Bank, S. P. and Kahn, M. D. 1982. *The sibling bond*. New York: Basic Books.

Barrera, M., Chassin, L., and Rogosch, F. 1993. Effects of social support and conflict on adolescent children of alcoholic and nonalcoholic fathers. *Journal of Personality and Social Psychology 64*, 602–12.

Basow, S. 1986. *Gender stereotypes: Traditions and alternatives*. Monterey, Calif.: Brooks/Cole.

Bedford, V. 1989a. Ambivalence in adult sibling relationships. *Journal of Family Issues 10*, 211–24.

Bedford, V. 1989b. Sibling research in historical perspective. *American Behavioral Scientist 33*, 6–18.

Bedford, V. 1989c. Understanding the value of siblings in old age. *American Behavioral Scientist 33*, 33–43.

Bennett, J. C. 1990. Nonintervention into siblings' fighting as a catalyst for learned helplessness. *Psychological Reports 66*, 139–45.

Bernays, A. F. November 1940. My brother, Sigmund Freud. *American Mercury*, 335–42.

Bernikow, L. 1980. *Among women*. New York: Harper & Row.

Blake, J. 1989. Number of siblings and educational attainment. *Science 245*, 32–36.

Blakemore, J. 1990. Children's nurturant interactions with their infant siblings: An exploration of gender differences and maternal socialization. *Sex Roles 22*, 43–57.

Borland, D. C. 1987. The sibling relationship as a housing alternative to institutionalization in later life. *Lifestyles 8*, 55–69.

Boszormenyi-Nagy, I. and Spark, G. 1973. *Invisible loyalties: Reciprocity in intergenerational family therapy*. New York: Harper & Row.

Bowen, M. 1978. *Family therapy in clinical practice*. New York: Jason Aronson.

Bowlby, J. 1969. *Attachment*. Vol. I in *Attachment and loss*. New York: Basic Books.

Bowlby, J. 1973. *Separation: Anxiety and anger*. Vol. II in *Attachment and loss*. New York: Basic Books.

Bowlby, J. 1980. *Loss: Sadness and depression*. Vol. III in *Attachment and loss*. New York: Basic Books.

Brannon, R. 1976. The male sex role. In D. David and R. Brannon (eds.), *The forty-nine percent majority: The male sex role* (pp. 1–45). Reading, Mass.: Addison-Wesley.

Brody, E., Hoffman, C., Kleban, M. and Schoonover, C. 1989. Caregiving daughters and their local siblings: Perceptions, strains and interactions. *Gerontologist 29*, 529–38.

Brody, G. H., Stoneman, Z., and McCoy, J. K. 1992. Associations of maternal and paternal direct and differential behavior with sibling relationships: Contemporaneous and longitudinal analyses. *Child Development 63*, 82–92.

Brook, J., Whiteman, M., Brook, D., and Gordon, A. 1991. Sibling influence on adolescent drug use: Older brothers on younger brothers. *Journal of the American Academy of Child and Adolescent Psychiatry 30*, 958–66.

Brown, J. R. and Dunn, J. 1992. Talk with your mother or your sibling? Developmental changes in early family conversations about feelings. *Child Development 63*, 336–49.

Bureau of the Census. 1991. *Recent movers*. Washington, D.C.: U.S. Department of Commerce.

Bureau of the Census. 1992a. *Home alone*. Washington, D.C.: U.S. Department of Commerce.

Bureau of the Census. 1992b. Marital status and living arrangements: March 1992. *Current Population Reports, Series P-20, No. 468*. Washington, D.C.: U.S. Government Printing Office.

Canavan, M. M., Meyer, W. J., and Higgs, D. C. 1992. The female experience of sibling incest. *Journal of Marital and Family Therapy 18*, 129–42.

Canin, E. 1991. *Blue river*. New York: Houghton Mifflin.

Caro, R. 1982. *The years of Lyndon Johnson: The path to power* (Vol. I). New York: Knopf.

Chodorow, N. 1978. *The reproduction of mothering*. Berkeley: University of California Press.

Cicirelli, V. G. 1977. Relationships of siblings to the elderly person's feelings and concerns. *Journal of Gerontology 32*, 317–22.

Cicirelli, V. G. May 1979. *Social services for the elderly in relation to the kin network* (Report). Washington, D.C.: NRTA-AARP Andrus Foundation.

Cicirelli, V. G. 1980. A comparison of college women's feelings toward their siblings and parents. *Journal of Marriage and the Family 42*, 95–102.

Cicirelli, V. G. 1982. Sibling influence throughout the lifespan. In M. E. Lamb and B. Sutton-Smith (eds.), *Sibling relationships: Their nature and significance across the lifespan* (pp. 267–84). Hillsdale, N.J.: Lawrence Erlbaum.

Cicirelli, V. G. 1988. Interpersonal relationships among elderly siblings. In M. D. Kahn and K. G. Lewis (eds.), *Siblings in therapy: Life span and clinical issues* (pp. 435–53). New York: W. W. Norton.

Cicirelli, V. G. 1989. Feelings of attachment to siblings and well-being in later life. *Psychology of Aging 4*, 211–16.

Colonna, A. B. and Newman, L. M. 1983. The psychoanalytic literature on siblings. *Psychoanalytic Study of the Child 38*, 285–309.

Connidis, I. 1989. Siblings as friends in later life. *American Behavioral Scientist 33*, 81–93.

Conroy, P. 1986. *The prince of tides*. Boston: Houghton Mifflin.

Cornell, D. 1983. Gifted children: The impact of positive labeling on the family system. *American Journal of Orthopsychiatry 53*, 322–35.

Coward, R. and Dwyer, J. 1990. The association of gender, sibling network composition, and patterns of parent care by adult children. *Research on Aging 12*, 158–81.

Cumming, E. and Schneider, D. 1961. Sibling solidarity: A property of American kinship. *American Anthropologist 63*, 498–507.

de Beauvoir, S. 1963. *Memoirs of a dutiful daughter*. Translated by J. Kirkup. Middlesex, England: Penguin Books Ltd.

de Beauvoir, S. 1977. *All said and done*. Translated by P. O'Brien. Harmondsworth, England: Penguin Books.

Didion, J. 1968. *Slouching toward Bethlehem*. New York: Dell.

Downing, C. 1988. *Psyche's sisters*. San Francisco: Harper & Row.

DuHamel, M. 1988. Aspects and effects of the younger sister/older brother relationship as perceived retrospectively by the sister. Unpublished master's thesis. Northampton, Mass.: Smith College School for Social Work.

Dunn, J. 1990. *A very close conspiracy: Vanessa Bell and Virginia Woolf*. Boston: Little, Brown.

Dunn, J. and Kendrick, C. 1982. Siblings and their mothers: Developing relationships within the family. In M. E. Lamb and B. Sutton-Smith (eds.), *Sibling relationships: Their nature and significance across the lifespan* (pp. 39–60). Hillsdale, N.J.: Lawrence Erlbaum.

Dunn, J. and Plomin, R. 1990. *Separate lives: Why siblings are so different*. New York: Basic Books.

East, P. L. and Rook, K. S. 1992. Compensatory patterns of support among children's peer relationships: A test using school friends, nonschool friends, and siblings. *Developmental Psychology 28*, 163–72.

Epstein, C. F. 1988. *Deceptive distinctions: Sex, gender and the social order*. New Haven, Conn.: Yale University Press.

Ernst, C. and Angst, J. 1983. *Birth order: Its influence on personality*. New York: Springer-Verlag.

Finkelhor, D. 1980. Sex among siblings: A survey on prevalence, variety, and effects. *Archives of Sexual Behavior 9*, 171–94.

Finley, N. 1989. Theories of family labor as applied to gender differences in caregiving for elderly parents. *Journal of Marriage and the Family 51*, 9–86.

Fintushel, N. and Hillard, N. 1991. *A grief out of season: When your parents divorce in your adult years*. Boston: Little, Brown.

Fischer, J. L. and Narus, L. R. 1981. Sex roles and intimacy in same sex and other sex relationships. *Psychology of Women Quarterly 5*, 444–55.

Forrest, D. 1982. The eye in the heart: Psychoanalytic keys to Vietnam. *Journal of Psychoanalytic Anthropology 5*, 259–98.

Freud, S. 1900. The interpretation of dreams. *Standard Edition of the Complete Psychological Works of Sigmund Freud*, Vols. 4 & 5. London: Hogarth.

Freud, S. 1916–17. Introductory lectures on psycho-analysis. *Standard Edition of the Complete Psychological Works of Sigmund Freud*, Vols. 15 & 16. London: Hogarth.

Furman, W. and Buhrmester, D. 1985. Children's perception of the qualities of sibling relationships. *Child Development 56*, 448–61.

Furman, W. and Buhrmester, D. 1992. Age and sex differences in perceptions of networks of personal relationships. *Child Development 63*, 103–15.

Gallup Organization. July 1989. *Gallup poll no. 286*. Princeton, N.J.: Gallup.

Gay, P. 1988. *Freud: A life for our time*. New York: W. W. Norton.

Gforerer, J. 1987. Correlation between drug use by teenagers and drug use by older family members. *American Journal of Drug and Alcohol Abuse 13*, 95–108.

Gilligan, C. 1982. *In a different voice: Psychological theory and women's development.* Cambridge, Mass.: Harvard University Press.

Gold, D. 1989a. Generational solidarity. *American Behavioral Scientist 33*, 19–33.

Gold, D. 1989b. Sibling relationships in old age: A typology. *International Journal of Aging and Human Development 28*, 37–51.

Gold, D. 1990a. Late-life sibling relationships: Does race affect typological distribution? *Gerontologist 30*, 741–48.

Gold, D. 1990b. Relationship classification using grade of membership analysis: A typology of sibling relationships in later life. *Journal of Gerontology 45*, 543–51.

Gorer, G. 1965. *Death, grief, and mourning.* London: Cresset Press.

Greenwald, E. and Leitenberg, H. 1989. Long-term effects of sexual experiences with siblings and nonsiblings during childhood. *Archives of Sexual Behavior 18*, 389–99.

Gully, K., Dengerink, H., Pepping, M. and Bergstrom, D. 1981. Research note: Sibling contribution to violent behavior. *Journal of Marriage and the Family 43*, 333–37.

Hampl, P. 1991. The need to say it. In J. Sternburg (ed.), *The writer on her work: New essays in new territory.* New York: W. W. Norton.

Harris, E. G. 1988. My brother's keeper. In M. D. Kahn and K. G. Lewis (eds.), *Siblings in therapy: Life span and clinical issues* (pp. 314–37). New York: W. W. Norton.

Hartman, A. and Laird, J. 1983. *Family-centered social work practice*. New York: Free Press.

Hartmann, E. 1991. *Boundaries in the mind: A new psychology of personality*. New York: Basic Books.

Hennig, M. and Jardim, A. 1977. *The managerial woman*. Garden City, N.Y.: Anchor/Doubleday.

Hill, J. P. and Lynch, M. E. 1983. The intensification of gender-related role expectations during early adolescence. In J. Brooks-Gunn and A. C. Petersen (eds.), *Girls at puberty: Biological and psychological perspectives*. New York: Plenum.

Ho, M. K. 1987. *Family therapy with ethnic minorities*. Newbury Park, Calif.: Sage Publications.

Hoyt, D. R. and Babchuk, N. 1983. Adult kinship networks: The selective formation of intimate ties with kin. *Social Forces* 62, 84–101.

Jacobs, B. S. and Moss, H. A. 1976. Birth order and sex of sibling as determiners of mother-infant interaction. *Child Development 47*, 315–22.

Jensen, E. J. and Overgaard, E. 1993. Investigation of smoking habits among 14- to 17-year-old boarding school pupils: Factors which influence smoking status. *Public Health 107*, 117–23.

Johnson, C. L. 1982. Sibling solidarity: Its origin and functioning in Italian-American families. *Journal of Marriage and the Family 44*, 155–67.

Kaschak, E. 1992. *Engendered lives: A new psychology of women's experience*. New York: Basic Books.

Keen, S. 1991. *Fire in the belly*. New York: Bantam.

Keniston, K. May 8, 1988. Wife beating and the rule of thumb. *New York Times Book Review*, p. 12.

Kerr, M. E. 1984. Theoretical base for differentiation of self in one's family of origin. In C. E. Munson (ed.), *Family of origin applications in clinical supervision* (pp. 3–36). New York: Haworth Press.

Kimball, J. 1983. James and Stanislaus Joyce: A Jungian speculation. In N. Keill (ed.), *Blood brothers: Siblings as writers* (pp. 73–113). New York: International Universities Press.

Kipp, R. S. 1986. Terms of endearment: Karo Batak lovers as siblings. *American Ethnologist 13*, 632–45.

Langer, E. J. 1989. *Mindfulness*. New York: Addison-Wesley.

Lee, G. R., Dwyer, J. W., and Coward, R. T. 1993. Gender differences in parent care: Demographic factors and same-gender preferences. *Journal of Gerontology 48*, 9–16.

Lee, L. 1975. *I can't stay long*. London: Andre Deutsch Ltd.

Lempers, J. D. and Clark-Lempers, D. S. 1992. Young adolescents' comparisons of the functional importance of five significant relationships. *Journal of Youth and Adolescence 21*, 53–97.

Lerner, G. 1987. *The creation of patriarchy*. New York: Oxford University Press.

Lerner, H. G. 1985. *The dance of anger*. New York: Harper & Row.

Lerner, H. G. 1989. *The dance of intimacy*. New York: Harper & Row.

Levinson, D. J. 1986. A conception of adult development. *American Psychologist 41*, 3–13.

Lindenbaum, S. 1979. *Kuru sorcery*. Palo Alto, Calif.: Mayfield.

Lips, H. M. 1988. *Sex and gender*. Mountain View, Calif.: Mayfield.

Lively, P. 1987. *Moon tiger*. New York: Harper & Row.

McGoldrick, M. 1989a. Ethnicity and the family life cycle. In B. Carter and M. McGoldrick (eds.), *The changing family life cycle: A framework for family therapy* (pp. 69–91). Boston: Allyn and Bacon.

McGoldrick, M. 1989b. Sisters. *Journal of Feminist Family Therapy 1*, 25–56.

McGoldrick, M., Garcia-Preto, N., Hines, P., and Lee, E. 1989. Ethnicity and women. In M. McGoldrick and F. Walsh (eds.), *Women in families: A framework for family therapy* (pp. 169–99). New York: W. W. Norton.

McHale, S. M. and Pawletko, T. M. 1992. Differential treatment of siblings in two family contexts. *Child Development 63*, 68–81.

McIntosh, J. L. and Wrobleski, A. 1988. Grief reactions among suicide survivors: An exploratory comparison of relationships. *Death Studies 12*, 21–39.

McNaron, T. (ed.) 1985. *The sister bond: A feminist view of a timeless connection*. New York: Pergamon Press.

Mangold, W. and Koski, P. 1990. Gender comparisons in the relationship between parental and sibling violence and nonfamily violence. *Journal of Family Violence 5*, 225–35.

Marjoribanks, K. 1989. Perceptions of family learning environments: The influence of sibling background. *Perceptual and Motor Skills 69*, 955–61.

Marris, P. 1974. *Loss and change*. New York: Pantheon Books.

Marshall, M. (ed.) 1983. *Siblingship in Oceania: Studies in the meaning of kin relations*. Lanham, Md.: University Press of America.

Matthew, S. and Rosner, T. 1988. Shared filial responsibility:

The family as the primary caregiver. *Journal of Marriage and the Family 50*, 185–95.

Milgram, J. and Ross, H. 1982. Effects of fame in adult sibling relationships. *Journal of Individual Psychology 38*, 72–79.

Miller, J. B. 1986. *Toward a new psychology of women* (2nd ed). Boston: Beacon Press.

Minuchin, S. 1974. *Families and family therapy*. Cambridge, Mass.: Harvard University Press.

Moss, M. S. and Moss, S. Z. 1986. Death of an adult sibling. *International Journal of Family Psychiatry 7*, 397–418.

Moss, S. Z. and Moss, M. S. 1989. The impact of the death of an elderly sibling. *American Behavioral Scientist 33*, 94–106.

Mott, P. E. 1965. *The organization of society*. Englewood Cliffs, N.J.: Prentice Hall.

National Center for Health Statistics. 1991. *Cohabitation, marriage, marital dissolution, and remarriage: United States, 1988.* Hyattsville, Md.: NCHS, U.S. Department of Health and Human Services.

Needle, R., McCubbin, H., Wilson, M., Reineck, R. et al. 1986. Interpersonal influences on adolescent drug use: The role of older siblings, parents and peers. *International Journal of the Addictions 21*, 739–66.

Neeld, E. H. 1990. *Seven choices: Taking the steps to new life after losing someone you love.* New York: Clarkson Potter.

Ness, D. E. and Pfeffer, C. R. 1990. Sequelae of bereavement resulting from suicide. *American Journal of Psychiatry 147*, 279–85.

O'Connor, N. 1984. *Letting go with love*. Apache Junction, Ariz.: La Mariposa Press.

Osborne, R. W. August 16, 1991. *Men and intimacy: An empirical review*. Paper presented at the Symposium on Men, Emotions and Intimacy, American Psychological Association.

Paulson, M. 1990. *Children's reactions to the death of a sibling*. Paper presented at the Great Lakes Regional Conference, Division 17, American Psychological Association, Akron, Ohio.

Pincus, L. 1974. *Death and the family: The importance of mourning*. New York: Schocken Books.

Pulakos, J. 1987. Brothers and sisters: Nature and importance of the adult bond. *Journal of Psychology 121*, 521–22.

Pulakos, J. 1989. Young adult relationships: Siblings and friends. *Journal of Psychology 123*, 237–44.

Radcliffe-Brown, A. R. and Forde, D. 1950. *African systems of kinship and marriage*. London: Oxford University Press.

Raffaelli, M. 1992. Sibling conflict in early adolescence. *Journal of Marriage and the Family*, 652–63.

Reisman, J. M. 1990. Intimacy in same-sex friendships. *Sex Roles 23*, 65–82.

Rhodes, R. 1990. *A hole in the world: An American boyhood*. New York: Simon & Schuster.

Rosenberg, B. G. 1982. Life span personality stability in sibling status. In M. E. Lamb and B. Sutton-Smith (eds.), *Sibling relationships: Their nature and significance across the lifespan* (pp. 167–224). Hillsdale, N.J.: Lawrence Erlbaum.

Ross, H. G. and Milgram, J. I. 1982. Important variables in adult sibling relationships: A qualitative study. In M. E. Lamb and B. Sutton-Smith (eds.), *Sibling relationships: Their nature and significance across the lifespan* (pp. 225–49). Hillsdale, N.J.: Lawrence Erlbaum.

Rubin, L. B. 1985. *Just friends: The role of friendship in our lives*. New York: Harper & Row.

Schachter, F. 1982. Sibling deidentification and split-parent identification: A family tetrad. In M. E. Lamb and B. Sutton-Smith (eds.), *Sibling relationships: Their nature and significance across the lifespan* (pp. 123–52). Hillsdale, N.J.: Lawrence Erlbaum.

Siegal, J. M. and Kuykendall, D. H. 1990. Loss, widowhood and psychological distress among the elderly. *Journal of Consulting and Clinical Psychology 58*, 519–24.

Stewart, R. 1983. Sibling attachment relationships: Child-infant interaction in the strange situation. *Developmental Psychology 19*, 192–99.

Stocker, C., Dunn, J. and Plomin, R. 1989. Sibling relationships: Links with child temperament, maternal behavior and family structure. *Child Development 60*, 715–27.

Stoneman, Z., Brody, G. and MacKinnon, C. 1986. Same-sex and cross-sex siblings: Activity choices, roles, behavior and gender stereotypes. *Sex Roles 15*, 495–511.

Straus, M., Gelles, R. and Steinmetz, S. 1980. *Behind closed doors: Violence in the American family.* New York: Anchor Press/Doubleday.

Suggs, P. K. 1985. *The application of a theoretical model of intergenerational helping to the older adult sibling dyad.* Unpublished doctoral dissertation, University of North Carolina, Greensboro.

Tannen, D. 1990. *You just don't understand: Women and men in conversation.* New York: William Morrow.

Taubman, P. and Behrman, J. 1986. Effect of number and position of siblings on child and adult outcomes. *Social Biology 33*, 22–34.

Thomas, J. 1983. The influence of sex, birth order, and sex of sibling on parent-adolescent interaction. *Child Study Journal 13*, 107–14.

Tognoli, J. 1980. Male friendship and intimacy across the life span. *Family Relations 29*, 273–79.

Troll, L. and Smith, J. 1976. Attachment through the life span: Some questions about dyadic bonds among adults. *Human Development 19*, 156–70.

Vaillant, G. E. and Vaillant, C. O. 1990. Natural history of male psychological health, XII: A 45-year study of predictors of successful aging at age 65. *American Journal of Psychiatry 147*, 31–37.

Walker, A. 1983. *In search of our mothers' gardens*. New York: Harcourt Brace Jovanovich.

Weisner, T. S. 1982. Sibling interdependence and child caretaking: A cross-cultural view. In M. Lamb and B. Sutton-Smith (eds.), *Sibling relationships: Their nature and significance across the lifespan* (pp. 305–23). Hillsdale, N.J.: Lawrence Erlbaum.

Weisner, T. S. and Gallimore, R. 1977. My brother's keeper: Child and sibling caretaking. *Current Anthropology 18*, 169–90.

Welts, E. P. H. 1988. Ethnic patterns and sibling relationships. In M. Kahn and K. Lewis (eds.), *Siblings in therapy: Life span and clinical issues* (pp. 66–87). New York: W. W. Norton.

Welty, E. 1984. *One writer's beginnings*. Cambridge, Mass.: Harvard University Press.

West, J. 1976. *The woman said yes: Encounters with life and death*. New York: Harcourt Brace Jovanovich.

White, L. K. and Riedmann, A. 1992. Ties among adult siblings. *Social Forces 71*, 85–102.

Wideman, J. E. 1984. *Brothers and keepers*. New York: Holt, Rinehart and Winston.

Woehrer, C. 1982. The influence of ethnic families on intergenerational relationships and later life transitions. *Annals of the American Academy of Political and Social Science 464*, 65–78.

Woolf, V. 1975. *The letters, vol. I: The flight of the mind 1888–1912*. N. Nicholson and J. Trautmann (eds.). New York: Harcourt Brace Jovanovich.

Woolf, V. 1976. *The letters, vol. II: The question of things happening 1912–1922*. N. Nicholson and J. Trautmann (eds.). New York: Harcourt Brace Jovanovich.

Woolf, V. 1980. *The diary, vol. III: 1925–1930*. A. O. Bell (ed.). New York: Harcourt Brace Jovanovich.

Woolf, V. 1980. *The letters, vol. VI: Leave the letters 'till we're dead 1936–1941*. N. Nicholson and J. Trautmann (eds.). New York: Harcourt Brace Jovanovich.

Wortman, C. and Silver, R. 1989. The myths of coping with loss. *Journal of Consulting and Clinical Psychology 57*, 349–57.

Wright, P. 1982. Men's friendships, women's friendships and the alleged inferiority of the latter. *Sex Roles 8*, 1–20.

Wright, P. and Scanlon, M. B. 1991. Gender role orientations and friendship: Some attenuation, but gender differences abound. *Sex Roles 24*, 551–66.

Zern, D. S. 1984. Relationships among selected child-rearing variables in a cross-cultural sample of 110 societies. *Developmental Psychology 20*, 683–90.

# Index

## About the Author

Marian Sandmaier is a freelance journalist specializing in psychological issues. She is the author of *The Invisible Alcoholics*, a study of women's alcohol problems from a gender perspective, and *When Love Is Not Enough*, an exploration of the family dynamics of adoption. She lives in Merion, Pennsylvania, with her husband and daughter.